HEAVENLY DECEPTOR

by

NATHAN LANDAU

New links between the Kennedy, King, and Jonestown murders are revealed through an examination of historical files hidden from the public for fourteen years.

An examination of the lawyer that represented: Jim Jones, James Earl Ray, Marguerite Oswald, John Hinckley and The Liberty Lobby.

Mark Lane's conspiracy theories blaming the C.I.A. for the Kennedy, King and Jonestown murders are refuted, based upon the new confessions of Lane's secret mistress, Teresa Buford, Jim Jones' second in command.

Published by Sound of Music Publishing Inc.
Suite 24F, 140 Cadman Plaza, Brooklyn, New York 11201
Copyright ©1992 By Nathan Landau

ISBN 0-9620285-1-7

Library of Congress No. 93-144008

TABLE OF CONTENTS

PART TWO   AXIS

PART THREE   THE LAST STAND

PART FOUR ODYSSEY

PRINCIPALS
(alphabetical order)

Charles Buford	Naval Commander and super spy operative in Vietnam war; Terri Buford's father.
Terri Buford	Temple's Second in Command; financial manager; public relations advisor; main courier; lover to Jim Jones, Mike Prokes, and Mark Lane. Mother of Lane's daughter.
Forbes Burnham	Prime Minister of Guyana.
Charles Garry	Jim Jones' first lawyer.
Jim Jones	Leader of the cult: The Peoples Temple.
Mark Lane	Lawyer who promotes the theory that the C.I.A. is behind King, Kennedy and Jonestown murders. Lawyer to both Jim Jones and Terri Bufford. Terri Buford's lover; father of Terri Bufford's child.
Larry Layton	Alleged murderer of Congressman Leo Ryan.
Harvey Milk	Murdered San Francisco politician.
Mayor Moscone	Murdered Mayor of San Francisco. He hired Jim Jones as Housing Commisioner.
Michael Prokes	Bodyguard to Jones.
John Stoen	Child held hostage by Jim Jones.
Congressman Ryan	Murder victim of Jonestown.
Tim Stoen	Temple defector, former assistant District Attorney of San Francisco, father of John Stoen.
Dan White	Killer of Mayor Moscone and Harvey Milk.

PREFACE

This narrative contains new evidence about double dealings surrounding key groups involved in the Kennedy/Martin Luther King assassinations and Jonestown. A tapestry of new facts is still emerging. Vital information has been recently released.

In 1988, *The New York Times* (1) reported that eight boxes were found containing dozens of notes describing personal correspondence and other pertinent memoranda from Jonestown. Letters were exchanged from Jonestown leaders to political allies in the U.S.

These boxes of newly unsealed records were turned over to the California Historical Society (2) to benefit historians eager to learn the truth.

Through the efforts of various politicians in the San Francisco area, I was granted the opportunity to review the previously locked files regarding the Peoples Temple within the Historical Society Archives. The Court appointed receiver, Mr. Robert Fabian, lifted the restrictions for me in the interests of historical review.

I presented my case for seeing these closed files on the basis that I had a personal source for this study at my disposal: Jonestown's second in command, Terri Buford, whom Mr. Fabian interviewed fourteen years ago. As Jim Jones' personal mistress and chief financial manager, her historical recollections provided me with new insights. I have had private interviews with her over a three year period. Her allegations matched the materials locked in those files and added to them.

In addition, sealed correspondence between San Francisco politicians, including Mayor Moscone and Harvey Milk, with top Jonestown officials which has been kept closed from the general public under a court order for fourteen years, has now been opened for this investigation.

Buford's subsequent professional and romantic involvement with famed, radical attorney, Mark Lane, sheds new light upon the major historical events of our time.

Besides representing Jim Jones, Lane has played a major part in the Martin King murder investigation. He represents James Earl Ray, the P.L.O. and the anti-semitic Liberty Lobby. He was also hired by Marguerite Oswald, Lee Harvey's mother, to represent her son's interests before the Warren Commission.

Lane's book blaming the C.I.A. for the Kennedy assassination, *Rush to Judgment,* was the number one best selling book in the U.S. soon after the murder. In addition, Mark Lane once ran for Vice-President under the Peace and Freedom Party during the turbulent Vietnam era. Since then, Lane's role on the fringes of American politics has been extensive. He is the original architect of the many conspiracy theories that blame the C.I.A. for most major assassinations of our time.

Currently, he has even added John Hinckley as a client. Hinckley attempted to assassinate President Reagan.

Mark Lane has released *Plausible Denial,* a new book that explores his newly revised thesis concerning Kennedy's assassination. It scored high on the best seller list. In the conclusion, Lane suggests that George Bush played a major role in the Bay of Pigs operation and links Bush with George de Mohrenschildt, whom, Lane asserts, directed Oswald's actions.

Recently other related books have surfaced such as Robert J. Grodin and Edward Livingstone Harrison's *High Treason* (Berkley Books, 1990). A movie was released about Jack Ruby. Oliver Stone had a new blockbuster movie, *JFK,* about the Kennedy assassination as well. Mark Lane worked together with *JFK's* Jim Garrison on the case suggesting that Clay Shaw was connected to a group involved in the Kennedy assassination.

The source for the newest Lane book, the Stone movie, and the Grodin-Livingstone book is ex-C.I.A. agent, Fletcher Prouty. He is the mysterious Colonel in *JFK*. According to Peter Earnest (3) of the C.I.A., Prouty was never an agent at all. Prouty is a key member of the Liberty Lobby, a fascist group which Lane represents. Prouty wrote the introduction to Lane's book. More than mere coincidence, Garrison is quoted on the back cover extolling its virtues.

If *Plausible Denial* is Lane's follow up to *Rush to Judgment*, than Lane's book about Martin Luther King, *Code Name Zorro* has spawned a sequel as well.

Jesse Jackson provides the foreword to yet another new book about the Martin Luther King assassination. Its author is supposedly James Earl Ray, himself, with Ray's lawyer and best man at his wedding, Mark Lane, masterminding the project deflecting blame to the American government for his client once again.

Who Killed Martin Luther King?: The True Story by the Alleged Assassin, (4) has an unlikely ally in Jesse Jackson. Jackson now believes there was a conspiracy.

Ray is being prepared for interviews on television. The royalties from the new book, according to *New York Magazine* (5), will go to Ray's legal fees.

Jackson, a Democrat, hints at U.S. Government's involvement in the King murder through the F. B. I. (under Republican administration's jurisdiction) This was the idea originally concocted by Lane in *Code Name Zorro*.

All of the above mentioned works point the finger at the C.I.A. Even Norman Mailer wrote a new, fictional account of the C.I.A., *Harlot*, and mentions E. Howard Hunt as well. Yet no American official directly involved in what must have been an extensive plot has ever come forward and blown a whistle. Furthermore, the conspiracy theorists are spared strenuous cross-examination.

Until now!

These works chip away at the public's larger perception of American history. The current conspiracy thesis regarding Kennedy that Lane suggests is based

The current conspiracy thesis regarding Kennedy that Lane suggests is based upon Fidel Castro's mistress, Marita Lorenz. She is also the mother of Castro's child. Together, Lane and Lorenz implicate E. Howard Hunt of Watergate fame as having a role in Kennedy's assassination.

Lane's book ends with an epilogue suggesting that President George Bush, who was associated with the C.I.A. at the time of Kennedy's assassination, had something to do with the crime.

The conspiracy theorist vaguely suggests that the Republicans achieved their power through the murder of Liberal Democrats by the C.I.A. and the F.B.I. in some kind of an American Coup D'Etat even though Kennedy was murdered long before George Bush ran the C.I.A.

In November, 1991, there was a three-day Assassination Symposium (ASK) on John F. Kennedy spurred on by the Stone movie. In this gala event, the *Woodstock* for conspiracy theorists, Mark Lane chaired a 22 member panel. The public was charged $125 per person. Yet no one defended the Warren Commission and asked questions of the panelists as to their own possible agendas.

Heavenly Deceptor is an in-depth examination of these conspiracy experts' allegations and specifically a study of crusader, Mark Lane, the foremost anti-C.I.A. conspiracy theorist in the world. Lane invented this idea and was the main subject for Walter Cronkite's T.V. show regarding the Warren Commission. No one has ever scrutinized his private life and career.

Lane's new book, *Plausible Denial*, will certainly create a new era of mistrust by Americans toward their own government by cleverly presenting the case that the C.I.A.'s Frank Sturgis and E. Howard Hunt were involved in the Kennedy assassination even though Lane's scant information allegedly comes from Fidel Castro's mistress!

Turnabout is fair play. Lane's work is based upon Castro's mistress. *Deceptor* is based upon information from Lane's mistress, Terri Buford. She is also the **mother of his child,** Vita. The work explores Lane's work with various clients including Jim Jones, James Earl Ray, Oswald, and the Liberty Lobby.

This approach is original and has never been attempted by a researcher. In effect, it is a look beyond merely blaming the C.I.A. Real blame is placed upon real people and a variety of groups linked by their attorney, Mark Lane. Upon full examination, these groups and Lane's motives become frightfully clear.

Deceptor explores these many, many murders. It is a tale of deception, cunning, violence, sex, torture, and profit. People were blamed and murdered. Others escaped, survived and flourish. Our lives were transformed by these events.

This work utilizes Terri Buford, whom Mark Lane shared sexually with Jim Jones, as its primary source. She was estranged from Lane and was free to divulge his innermost secrets when this book was being researched. Videotapes and pictures along with other supporting documents are available for review. School records proving Lane had a daughter with Terri are available. Within her personal confessions, she exposes pertinent hitherto unknown details about Jonestown as well.

Besides functioning as Jim Jones' lover, Terri Buford was his trusted, top financial manager! Then she escaped from Jonestown and lived intimately with Lane for four years. Mark Lane had also been Jim Jones' attorney. She worked with him on many important cases after Jonestown and now finally exposes his strategy of blaming the C.I.A. for all the mysterious political murders that occur in the U.S.

During the time Buford worked with Lane, she observed how he operated, met with forces that ally themselves against America and infiltrated their secrets. She met James Earl Ray and worked on his defense case with Lane.

Through her own fascinating story, the common links between groups connected to all of these murders through Lane take new and frightening shapes. To comprehend the full picture, even Jonestown must be reexamined in the context of Buford's new information. Since Lane and Terri were so involved in Jonestown, their relationship must be closely reexamined to comprehend its connection to the King and Kennedy murders.

There are political forces lined up against America that have yet to be fully examined due to a lack of information. During the Gulf War, the Liberty Lobby adopted a strong antiwar stance. Surprisingly, their allies included long time left-wing leaders like Ramsey Clark who journeyed to Iraq to meet with Saddam

Hussein as well as black civil rights activist Dick Gregory who was a key speaker at the 1990 Liberty Lobby convention. The Liberty Lobby contributed to David Duke's campaign.

The unholy alliance between fascism and communism also occurred at the time of the Hitler-Stalin pact in 1939. It is a natural alliance since it unites the enemies of opposing groups with a common hatred, of both Israel and America, Jews and Americans.

Dick Gregory, the keynote speaker, once ran for President of the U.S. under the banner of the *Peace and Freedom Party* in 1968 at the height of the Vietnam War. His running mate was...Mark Lane.

Dick Gregory, through his association with Lane, was invited to speak as an honored guest at the Liberty Lobby convention.

Heavenly Deceptor is an inside look at these very violent forces. This document will explain precisely how the coverup operation began with respect to the assassinations of Kennedy and King. A focus will be placed upon Lane's role as Jim Jones' attorney and his relationship with his mistress, Terri Buford.

Furthermore, armed with this greater understanding, people can defend against recurrences of this nature. It will portray, expose, and analyze the hidden mechanisms which have not only shaped the Jonestown saga, but molded the decades beyond it.

PROLOGUE

Dear Anne,
"Please help me: I have to die tomorrow the voices have
told me to cut out my heart. Please tell them to go away, Anne.
Tomorrow at 9 a.m. I'm going to have to cut my heart out".

Terri Buford

(California Historical Society letter from the Peoples Temple Collection,
Terri Buford folder file #MS380 BB-7-AA40)Appendix -B-

Terri Buford was described by Charles Garry, Jim Jones' attorney, as being the Second in Command of the Peoples Temple. Garry has issued a signed statement to that effect. (Appendix, Exhibit A) During our personal interview, he stated that he hasn't seen or heard a word from her in over twelve years.

Replacing Charles Garry as Jones' attorney, Mark Lane, reiterates the same charge in his own book about Jonestown (1) in which Terri Buford, Lane's new mistress, served as the central character. Tim Stoen (2), a top Temple leader, reiterated the charge that Terri Buford had really been Jones' powerful second in command.

Like Garry, Stoen has also neither seen nor heard from Terri Buford in all the years since Jonestown. She has been well hidden from the public. Her recent disclosures focus upon the heretofore undisclosed political basis of the Peoples Temple and its relationship to other political events, such as the Kennedy and Martin Luther King assassinations.

Buford fled the Jonestown commune in Guyana only three weeks before the massacre in a prearranged escape plot that Jones had formulated. Most of the other upper echelon members had no knowledge of the plan.

Yet even Jim Jones was caught unaware that his closest accomplices had actually planned to double-cross him. The actions of other top aides to Jones will also be examined, as will the identity of a suspect in Jones' assassination.

After Jones' death, Terri Buford was left in charge of the entire operation. Nine days later there were mortal repercussions. A rash of suspicious murders in the San Francisco area followed Jonestown's wake. These included Mayor George Moscone, who had strong Jonestown ties and the popular Commissioner Harvey Milk, who was also a friend and associate of Jim Jones.

Just before Buford fled the Temple, she had cleverly deposited millions of dollars into secret bank accounts in her own name. Since her escape, she has been hiding under various identities. Her trail has been traced from Norway and Japan through San Francisco, Guyana, Memphis and to New York.

Michael Prokes, Terri's lover before she joined the Temple, served Jones as another of his top aides, functioning as Jones' media expert and bodyguard. Prokes was the Stockton Bureau Chief of KXTV-TV before he entered Jonestown.

Two months after Jonestown died, Prokes shot himself on national T.V. as he pleaded for further investigations of the massacre. In his suicide note he called for a *Deep Throat* to come forth and tell the world the truth about Jonestown. His former girlfriend, Terri Buford, finally answered his plea.

Tim Reiterman, one of the reporters who was shot and wounded during the murders, won the Pulitzer Prize for *The Raven* (3), thus far the definitive account of Jonestown. He concludes his study with an unanswered question about Jones' escape plans, of which he knew absolutely nothing.

Reiterman also ponders the possibility of a Jonestown murder plot and seeks further documented information from any source available. He speculates about who might have actually killed Jim Jones and what those circumstances could have been. Terri Buford, whom he never met, has the answers to all these questions and much more.

The plan was called *The Last Stand*, an extremely complicated and premeditated murder plot.

Digging as deeply as he could, Reiterman focuses his study squarely upon Jonestown's leader, Jim Jones, who had been already assassinated by the time he began the investigation. Other conspirators were too afraid to talk. The congressional investigations were still in progress and Jonestown's lawyers were advising their clients to remain silent.

Furthermore, the feared Jonestown hit squads were still in operation. The real answers can only come from direct information culled from those ex-leaders who have managed to stay alive. Buford must be recognized as a central player and her role examined in detail.

Terri's father, Charles Buford, was a Naval Commander during the Vietnam War. His top secret involvement in that war triggered her political rebellion. Cmdr. Buford coordinated the secret bombings of Laos and Cambodia.

During that war, a new type of nerve gas was developed by Larry Layton, Sr. of the Defense Department. Another of Jones' key aides was Layton's son, Larry Layton, Jr., a close friend of Terri's. Layton, Jr. is currently serving a lifetime sentence, convicted of murdering Representative Leo Ryan, the only instance of an assassination of a Congressman in the entire history of The United States.

Layton, a Jew, has been the only person ever convicted for any crime relating to the deaths at Jonestown. The reasons why he was specifically picked to be the scapegoat will be analyzed. Most of the members that perished in Jonestown were either blacks or Jews; many were children.

Every so often there are events that are inexplicable, both because of their enormity and the lack of immediate facts. However difficult it becomes to digest, no emotional denial of the material is permissible.

For the last ten years, no one has cared to probe the escaped leaders and risk their fearsome, lethal wrath.

No one has probed Mark Lane and his secret role in deflecting blame onto agencies of the U. S. Government to defend his clients from murder charges, until now. The facts about the deaths of Martin Luther King and John F. Kennedy have been slanted to suit the groups that Lane represents. They are dangerous.

Every cowardly nerve in my body cried out to not write this book, but I found that I could not...not write it.

I would defeat my own ends if I were suspected of having a few private grievances against the leaders of Jonestown and the murderers of the greatest political leaders of our times.

But I certainly do.

Besides our leaders, they have even murdered children in Jonestown; cold, deliberate murder, at that. Our leaders have been killed in cold blood right before our eyes; presidents, mayors (Moscone), religious leaders and even a congressman (Ryan), elected to serve our country. Whenever someone comes forward to expose their plots for power, they are assassinated.

Vast funds from every American taxpayer have been stolen and this process has never been fully questioned! As a historian, it is necessary to detach oneself and put the creatures under the microscope of common sense.

One central myth must finally die.

The almost one thousand Americans that died in Jonestown, Guyana, in 1978, were all actually considered by the press and the U.S. Government to be part of a fantastic mass suicide, even though many people were later found to have been shot and forcibly injected with a deadly poison. This is what the leaders of Jonestown wanted the public to believe so they could get away with the money.

It worked so far.

"Foul Murders", declared Magistrate Bacchus of Guyana as he examined the details of the largest mass murder of American civilians in history. This was the realization of the citizens of all other countries.

Yet, soon after that the official story presented to and accepted by most Americans was one of an amazing, mass *suicide*.

Second in command, Teresa Jean Buford, was the **last person** to successfully escape from Jonestown before the massacre. One year before the incident even occurred, on October 9, 1977, Terri Buford wrote a threatening letter (4) to the government. It stated that the people have the right to choose the circumstance of their own death. The children and adults that died in Jonestown never had the right to choose life. In her letter, Buford cryptically refers to a *Last Stand,* the actual name for the preconceived, contingency plan devised only for Jones and his top leaders' safety.

Before her escape, why didn't she try to stop the largest mass murder in United States history? What were the underlying reasons for the catastrophe? What happened to Jim Jones' fortune? In her work with Mark Lane, what has she learned that sheds light upon other murders: Martin King's, John Kennedy's? What were the Nazi influences in Jonestown? What is Mark Lane's real strategy in pointing the murder finger constantly at the C.I.A.?

Let us start at the beginning, the moment Terri decided to escape from Jonestown and team up with Lane.

PART ONE
QUADRILATERAL

CHAPTER 1
DEFECTION

Jim Jones kept his small Cessna
airplane hidden deep in the jungle
....Alert....Alert....Alert.....Alert.....

In their heart of darkness, the remote South American jungle outpost of Jonestown, Guyana, a thousand souls waited anxiously, dependent upon carefully edited information that arrived in the control room, their only access to the outside world. The short wave radio was kept there, along with the computer records of every man, woman, and child in the compound.

All computerized information had private access codes that the second-in-command, Terri Buford, carefully created for secrecy. Only she could interpret the incoming data. Her obsequious manner belied her true position and concealed her activities.

The terrifying news that arrived from the central base in San Francisco had panicked the more than twenty thousand followers that still remained back in the U. S. The plot might have succeeded if only the government hadn't interfered.

Buford wondered if this was just another drill, another false alarm to test everyone's loyalty to Jim Jones. These drills were to serve as a cover for the escape plan's successful execution. Clutching her gut in sharp pain, Buford had to appear calm. Jones could no longer deal with the reporters' probing questions. She couldn't protect him any longer. For Jones, there would be no way out.

She would certainly be exposed, along with him and the other key leaders, as the architects of a conspiracy. There were too many witnesses to avoid prosecution. She was determined to survive.

Thinking back to when she was a little girl in Japan, she longed for her loving *mama-san*. Now, more than ever, a calculated plan of action was needed.

It was obvious there would be violence. Many innocent people would die in their jungle trap. While they were suffocating from their lack of information, Terri knew that Jones' preconceived escape plan, *The Last Stand*, included her. Other top aides also knew about the plan. Jones had always spoken to them about getting away in case of a government probe and promised to take his favorites along with him.

According to one of those top leaders, Al Mills (1), Jim would say that someday the leaders would leave Guyana and start a commune again in another country. In spite of the fact that he was a white man, Mills, whose real name had been Mertle, had been very active in the civil rights movement.

Mills had been close to Martin Luther King, walking side by side with King in the freedom march at Selma, Alabama. Mills now considered Jones an opportunistic racist who betrayed the movement. Circumstances in Jonestown made Al certain that obviously Jones did not plan to die with his followers.

He observed that a man who is planning to die doesn't give his bodyguard a suitcase filled with money and two passports. Obviously, Jones planned to leave Jonestown with his trusted bodyguard.

Furthermore, the coincidence that Jim Jones' sons were in Georgetown, the capital of Guyana, during the massacre and that so many of his key staff people survived, convinced Al Mills that Jones was planning to actually continue his hell bent ministry. A man planning to die doesn't deposit **hundreds of millions** of dollars into foreign bank accounts.

For disclosing this type of secret information about Jim Jones and other aides, both Al Mills and his wife were declared to be *fair game*. In fear, they had changed their names to Mills from their original ones, Elmer and Deanna Mertle. It didn't save them from reprisal. They were cruelly killed in their home in Berkeley after leaving the Temple. Their daughter Daphne was also shot.

Jones was afraid that people like the Mills would lead The United States Government into an investigation that would uncover the true nature of the Temple's operation. Certainly, funding would have then been immediately cut and a violent revolution against both Jones and all of his remaining accomplices would have ensued. Assassinations had to be planned to silence all the talkative defectors.

Besides the Mills, another of Jones' top aides, a financial courier, Debby Blakey, bravely risked her life to escape the Temple and defect to Congressman Leo Ryan with vital Temple information. Only 25 years old, Debby knew that Jim Jones held her family hostage when she left the Temple.

"S.O.S...S.O.S." Jim Jones screamed over his loudspeakers. He was positive that Debby Blakey would open up Jonestown to the government investigators.

Min S. Yee studied and wrote specifically about the Blakey-Layton family. He states (2) that Blakey's best friend in the Temple was her superior, financial manager Terri Buford. Buford was Jones' lover as well as a top press aide. Not only did this financial wizard know all of the Temple's secrets; she had direct access to every penny in the Swiss bank accounts.

Since the numbers of these accounts were too valuable to be disclosed to anyone else, Buford had them all memorized in her photographic mind. Furthermore, as Jones' top courier, she was indispensable to the escape plan.

But after Blakey's betrayal, Jones lost his trust in Buford. He began to suspect her of plotting against him. His leadership undermined, he had begun to unravel. After the Blakey defection in May, 1978 Jones seemed emotionally out of control. This was intolerable to Buford. She had finally lost her respect for the leader who had once claimed both her love and devotion.

Jones began to realize that the woman who had once been a rose in his garden had now become a thorn in his side. He ordered an armed guard to follow her around twenty-four hours a day. She couldn't even go to the bathroom without a rifle being leveled at her by an escort. It was physically impossible for her to leave the compound, since Jones confiscated all the members' passports and money.

Fifty trained armed killers, Jim Jones' personal guards, patrolled the perimeter of the encampment. Beyond that lurked dangerous jungle animals. Buford deduced that she had to gain back Jones' complete trust to successfully defect.

She also knew that Jim Jones had a viciously vindictive personality combined with a volcanic temper. She learned that as a little boy, he tortured and killed small kittens and helpless puppies for fun. He had violent ways of dealing with traitors. Reiterman describes an incident in high school involving Jones' best friend, Don Foreman. Jones tested out his powers by commanding Don to stop dead in his tracks, warning him that he would shoot him if he did not obey.

Don was stunned. As he left to go home, Jim took aim at him and fired a bullet that took off a chunk of a tree branch right above his head. Don fled, as Jim Jones experienced his first betrayal from a loyal friend.

Jones had always worn dark sunglasses so no one could ever see his eyes. It created a *Macho* image of power. The sun bothered this shady character, especially that of the intense, equatorial Guyanese sky. He preferred the night.

Angry at Terri Buford's rebellious attitude, Jim Jones summoned her for some private interrogation. Pulling out a gun, he aimed it directly at her face SCREAMING...

"Do you love me? Would you ever think of betraying the cause?"

Terri answered him, trembling, "of course not, 'Father'. I could never betray you." She describes how Jim Jones then took aim at her head, pulling the trigger and firing a shot that barely missed her face by only a few feet.

Then he erupted, screaming, "if you do I will find you wherever you run and you will beg on your knees for a quick death. Remember, I OWN YOU."

Then, taking a sobbing, terrified Terri Buford in his arms to console her, the two embraced for hours reaffirming their passionate love and loyalty for each other. He never took off his sunglasses.

Afterwards, fully satisfied, Jones took his seat upon his favorite green throne and sat back with his beloved pet monkey, Mr. Muggs, draped around his arm. Jones scanned his flock for any further signs of rebellion.

In the jungle sky, a flock of ravens drifted overhead in silent observation above the fearful citizenry of Jonestown.

Secretly, Buford realized that she had to follow her friend, Debby Blakey, out of Jonestown. She held her stomach in painful fear. Even if her defection was successful, she knew she needed a more complicated plan, not only just to escape, but to neutralize Jones as well. He would come after her. She was too valuable to him.

Though her adopted son, Dietrich, might have to be abandoned in the jungle to face his own fate, she was determined to survive. To totally regain Jones' trust, she pleaded her case.

"Debby was the traitor, not me", she cried to him. "I love you, Jim", she whispered as she massaged his back.

"You can always trust me", she said, as she threw him the sweetest smile he ever saw. Applying intense lip service to Jones' monster ego, he renewed his faith in her submissive loyalty. Expecting government trouble, Jones sent Buford overseas on a sensitive financial mission: to rearrange the millions in the bank accounts in case of any problems. They had chosen Panama for their banking center, both because of its proximity to Guyana and its flexible banking laws. By using coded numbers, no one would ever know where the money came from. The U.S. Government would never get it back. Jones' plan was to escape and then rejoin Buford with all that money.

However, Terri Buford had her own plans for Jones and his money. She had a secret plan involving Jones' trusted attorney. First, she had to get the money into her name.

In tracing her banking activities, Reiterman states that after a couple of days of running financial errands in Panama City, she headed for the airport. Then she flew to London. She spent days at a local library analyzing economic books concerning possible countries such as Cuba, Russia, Costa Rica and Panama...for the planned escape.

Dressing in an inconspicuous manner, she then flew to Paris and on to Zurich. Her suitcase was loaded with cash. She entered a Swiss bank and was brought from one elegant sitting room to another. After the bank official checked her identification, she deposited $2 million in the main account.

According to Reiterman about twenty-six million dollars of the Temple's money was eventually admitted by the leaders to have been deposited in foreign bank accounts. However, Reiterman's guess was to prove a very low estimate after the income was eventually totalled.

Yee discloses that Terri travelled to Rumania and spent an entire month in Eastern Europe, in her search to find the very best financial havens that the world had to offer for the wealthy Temple.

Seizing the moment, Buford then deposited the Temple's money, which was in cash, in her own name.

Jones slowly lost control of his wealth. She returned to Jonestown with her mission successfully accomplished. She had thrown Jones off by returning since to successfully escape she had to plan his demise as well to prevent his revenge. The task of transferring the money was completed only six months prior to the November 18, 1978 bloodbath.

Terri Buford was no hippie. She looked like a college preppie, a perfect natural disguise for the courier position. In fact, she had joined the Temple in the early seventies while she was still a University of California student.

Now, after six years of serving Jones, she was twenty-six years of age. At only 110 pounds, she had waist-length light brown hair that covered an excruciatingly thin frame. She combined her complete loyalty with unlimited energy. Quickly, she had risen in the Temple to become the chief strategist, showing superior ability in quickly plotting complicated schemes. Like many other top executives of Jones' staff, she was very secretive, conspiratorial and usually spoke in a gentle whisper.

Her unobtrusive persona was carefully cultivated since total anonymity was essential for the proper handling of Temple finances. First of all, Jones feared government investigations and private lawsuits. No one but he and Terri knew how much wealth the Temple actually possessed. They wanted to preserve the image of a needy organization in order to keep the generous donations flowing.

Jones needed Buford to make the financial drops since he was too visible and would certainly be recognized upon leaving the compound. But no one would suspect timid Terri Buford during her secretive financial runs.

Slowly, Buford had amassed such power that Charles Garry, Jones' original attorney (3) considered her to be the second in command of the entire operation. According to Mark Lane, Charles Garry also made that announcement to a large public press conference as early as 1979. Before that time, no one ever suspected Terri Buford's immense power.

Buford had once functioned in San Francisco as Garry's premier liaison to Jones. She spied upon Charles Garry for Jones while she worked with him. If anyone was in a position to understand the Temple's inner structure, certainly, Jones' lawyers and their close aides had the best perspective. Jonestown expert, author Yee, felt that as Jones' most trusted aide, Buford's information could have the power to destroy the entire Jonestown empire.

While her former financial assistant, Debby Blakey, was working with Congressman Ryan, trying desperately to warn the American public that a terrible mass murder of Americans was being formulated in the Guyanese jungle, Terri Buford began shifting funds into her own name for her smooth getaway. Her father had taught her an old axiom: If you want out...git!

Terri J. Buford made her last financial run out of Jonestown soon after Debbie Blakey went to the government...and then Terri vanished. She went into complete hiding under an assumed identity and finally proved to be the last member to escape from Jonestown just three weeks before the massacre.

Her ticket out was bought in bloodshed.

CHAPTER 2

REVENGE

The easiest thing of all is to deceive one's self;
for what a man wishes he generally believes to be true.
Demosthenes, Olynthiaca

For her escape, Buford needed help from someone she could trust: an adviser to protect her both from the wrath of Jim Jones and the inquiries of the U.S. Government. Mark Lane had been targeted by her to become a key ally.

Lane was hired by Lee Harvey Oswald's mother to defend her son before the Warren Commission. Lane developed the strategy of defending his client by attacking the U.S. Government, especially the C.I.A. to deflect blame. He also had James Earl Ray as a client in the Martin Luther King murder case. He blamed the F.B.I. for that murder.

Jim Jones and his top advisors needed to deflect from their project as well.

Terri Buford had first been introduced to radical lawyer, Lane in 1974 during a secretive mission at which time she was sent by Jones to donate Jonestown funds to Dennis Banks, the American Indian militant under siege at Wounded Knee.

The money was given to Bank's lawyers, Mark Lane and William Kunstler, who defended both Banks and Russell Means, another Indian activist.

Lane ran for Vice President of the United States on the Peace and Freedom Party in 1976 behind presidential candidate, Dick Gregory. Their platform was anti-Vietnam war and their official platform amassed considerable support from various radical groups who hated America. They hated the C.I.A. and co-authored books blaming them for assassinations.

According to Charles Garry, Buford, who had been assigned as liaison to Garry for Jim Jones, began to use her leverage to spy upon Garry. According to Lane (1) in *The Strongest Poison*, Buford tattled to Jim Jones that Garry had stolen Temple funds. Her plan was to replace Garry with Mark Lane as attorney for the Temple. After replacing Garry, Lane could then successfully blame the C.I.A. for any future trouble in Jonestown.

Garry was the Black Panther attorney as well as Jim Jones'. Allegedly, the sum of five thousand dollars was donated by Jones, through Terri, to Black Panther leader, Huey Newton, who was hiding out in Havana. Newton claimed, however, that he never received the money. Reiterman (2) states that Garry freely admits that he withheld this donation but claimed his reason for holding the money was that Newton was strung out on drugs at the time. He felt that it was unethical to give Newton the money to merely waste on purchasing drugs.

Buford claimed that Charles Garry kept the money without giving it to Newton or returning it to Jones. Jones angrily replaced Garry with Mark Lane. Garry was set-up. He never realized Buford's true motive until years later. At the time, he never knew that Buford was involved with Lane on a deeper level. They had their own plans. Buford's replacement of Garry with Lane had actually been a complicated, preplanned maneuver to protect herself in the event of trouble.

In order to gain Jones' permission for her proposed departure from Jonestown, Buford then crafted a four-page confidential letter to Jim Jones. Her alibi was that she intended to spy on Jones' enemies by infiltrating Tim Stoen's anti-Jonestown group.

Stoen had been another important defector and was responsible for the forthcoming U.S. Government investigation. Terri concluded her letter by warning Jones that even if he attempted to interfere, she would commit hari-kari.

Stunned, Jones realized that if Buford was serious about her suicide threat, he would lose access to his own money which was all deposited in her name. Forced to put his faith in her loyalty, he granted his permission for her to leave the Temple to carry out her spying mission. Buford made airline reservations under her cousin's name, Kim Agee. She mailed her personal belongings to her older sister, Caroline.

Terri then called Mark Lane and they agreed to meet secretly in New York. She used some money her parents were sending her to buy a one-way airline ticket. She swore to Jim Jones that she would call him with a private coded message and let him know that everything was going according to his instructions.

She kissed Jones goodbye. Terri didn't have to crawl through a hostile jungle to leave Jonestown. She left first class; her brilliant plan had worked perfectly. She and Lane had planned every detail in advance.

Jones never heard from his beloved, Terri Buford, again. She vanished only three weeks before the massacre. Jones' escape plan was effectively thwarted. It was at this stage of his life that something in Jones cracked. Jones sent one of his agents, Tim Carter, to look for her among Stoen's group. Carter couldn't find her and confirmed her betrayal.

Jim Jones was furious. He went into a jealous fit. Terri Buford's defection was the ultimate betrayal. On October 27, 1978, at a time when he was already dealing with more than he could handle from the U. S. Government, Jim Jones totally gave up.

Buford, whom Reiterman labels, *The Strategist*, knew more about the complex Temple's bank accounts and finances than any other member. Even Jones had become unaware of the total whereabouts and extent of his vast holdings. She was his financial wizard and indispensable to the Temple's operation.

Furthermore, it wasn't merely losing her knowledge of the Temple's finances that tilted Jones' equilibrium. Buford had made off with his fortune...in her own name. The master con artist was himself, conned. He had no credit cards, no wallet, no job and not much hope. He had cash in suitcases and other hiding places and his only hope was to escape with whatever liquid assets he could carry.

In fear of a rebellion, other high level Jonestown leaders were experiencing a loss of confidence. All those years of hard work to amass their fortune was now in jeopardy. Jones called his personal *Doctor*, Larry Schacht, for special medication. With his brain exploding from too many medications, Jones had become addicted to a variety of drugs.

Jones desperately wanted Buford back. Furthermore, he had become addicted to her sexually. Jones sent Temple member Sandy Bradshaw to murder Terri. Because Terri had previously tried to poison Sandy on the order of Jim Jones, Sandy hated her and gladly volunteered for the murderous assignment.

Now Terri Buford was considered fair game.

Reiterman states that Bradshaw checked every feminist bar in Berkeley since Jones knew that Terri Buford was bisexual and actually preferred women to men.

Jones conjectured that Buford was planning to betray him and join forces with Debby Blakey and Congressman Leo Ryan, the key investigator for the Government inquiries. When he discovered that Buford wasn't there, he realized that she might intend to keep the Jonestown money all to herself.

Jim Jones had been cleverly outsmarted. The man who had fooled everyone, the politicians, the churches and even the government, was craftily played like a Stradivarius, by his ex-mistress, Terri Buford.

He had believed that she was fully trained to follow all orders without question. Now, there was no escape. Jones had said in a one of his sermons: "He who rides the tiger dare not dismount". Jones did not mention that the only safe alternative would be to slaughter the tiger.

Thrown by his tigress, Jones never suspected that Terri was actually hiding in Memphis, Tennessee with his own trusted lawyer and loyal friend, Mark Lane. That was the last place he'd search; a key reason why Terri decided to make Lane's home the place of her refuge. She knew how much Jones had foolishly trusted Lane. As her loyalties shifted, she disclosed everything about Jones and his business to Lane.

At the time Lane entered Terri Buford's web, he was fifty one years of age. He welcomed a young Terri Buford with open arms, eager to learn all her innermost secrets. As his reward, they became passionate lovers almost immediately. According to Buford, as she was now a fugitive, she had little choice but to ardently accept his advances.

In great terror of Jones' death squads, she slept with a watchdog and a loaded rifle next to her bed at all times. That precaution was justified since Jean Brown, Peoples Temple secretary, told him that Jim Jones would probably be willing to pay a ransom of a million dollars in cold cash for her head.

She told Lane that only she knew where all Jones' money was kept, how to withdraw it, and plus other critical secrets. Lane's eyes bulged wide as he began to realize just what a treasure he now had within his grasp. She was worth more to him than a mere million dollars.

Lane knew that it was the end for Jones. Buford's defection had spoken for itself. Lane promised to protect her from Jones reach, as well as from the imminent government probes. She was worth the risk. He had his alibi prepared. Even if Jones were to survive and discover that he had Buford, he would explain that he was temporarily safeguarding her and the money.

In that event, Jones might even reward him with his gratitude for turning Buford in, after keeping her *safe*. Appealing to Jones' enormous ego, Lane had Jones convinced that he would also defend him from the final judgment of history by writing a book exonerating him of crimes through his time worn tactic of blaming the C.I.A. for everything.

When he was questioned by Jones about the location of Buford's whereabouts, Lane kept his new client's hideout his secret. According to reporter John Kifner (3), Buford had, by that time, already given her trusted lawyer, Mark Lane, all the bank account numbers and locations.

Even though he was still Lane's client, Jones was kept in the dark. But, he still retained an abiding faith in his honorable attorney's integrity as he once had in his trusted second in command, Terri Buford. Jones was to learn a lethal lesson.

Eventually, Mark Lane was invited to accompany Rep. Leo Ryan when he made his doomed investigative trip to Jonestown. Lane was not afraid of his own murder since he knew that Jones needed him both for his legal protection and his skills at writing interpretative history in blaming the C.I.A. to defend clients.

At a press conference at Peoples Temple, October 3,1978, Lane said that "Jonestown was similar to what Dr. Schweitzer had established and that it made him almost weep to see such an incredible experiment, with such vast potential for the human spirit and soul of this country, to be cruelly assaulted by the intelligence organizations". Lane then launched yet another vicious attack upon the C.I.A.

As the massacre was occurring, a young journalist, Charles Krause (4), describes how Lane deftly persuaded the murderous armed guards to let Lane escape so that he would be able to tell the world all about Jones' eternal greatness. The publication, *Facts on File* (5), also supports Krause and mentions that the guards told Lane and Garry that all of the cult members were going to die, but they specifically allowed the two lawyers to escape into the jungle. Lane was spared even while six reporters and the congressman were murdered.

The armed assassins were under orders to protect Lane. If Jones had wanted Lane to die, he would have had no compunction about giving the order. Less than two years later, Lane did write a book, *The Strongest Poison*, in which he attempts to exonerate only himself and Terri Buford for their own roles in Jonestown.

Preceding the murders, Lane kept Buford's information confidential, never informing anyone about her fear of imminent death. Unlike Ryan, he was fully briefed about the true dangers that awaited the group, which included: U.S. Congressman Leo Ryan, Jonestown's former attorney Charles Garry and a dozen reporters.

They never had a chance to take proper precautions to protect themselves against the life-threatening situation. In fact, according to Reiterman (2), instead of warning Rep. Ryan about danger in Guyana, Lane wrote a threatening letter to him.

He informed Rep. Ryan that if the Temple was investigated, the 1,200 members would leave for Russia, a mass defection which could potentially create an embarrassing situation for the U.S. Government.

Lane was threatening the Congressman because he wanted to prevent his investigation. Leo Ryan angrily wrote Mark Lane that no persecution was intended, but that Lane's vague reference to the creation of an embarrassing situation for the American government didn't worry him. If Lane's comments were to be intended as a threat, Ryan was not to be intimidated.

Accompanying Congressman Ryan to Jonestown, reporter Charles Krause flew in from Venezuela. In covering the Jonestown story, Krause states that on the hour's flight to the airstrip nearest Jonestown, Port Kaituma, he sat right next to Mark Lane. Lane was full of praise for Jones and the commune he represented. He never warned Krause, nor Ryan, about any armed guards or weapons.

On the contrary, when asked about possible danger, Lane denied to Krause that any force was being used in Jonestown, even though a trembling Terri Buford told him otherwise.

Lane insisted to Krause during the flight that nothing more than mere peer pressure was being used to keep the people in Jonestown denying that there were any armed guard, torture or beatings. Lane said he had visited Jonestown a month before the flight and had been extremely impressed, praising the incredibly peaceful society in the middle of the jungle.

Krause bitterly relates how Lane stated that he was particularly impressed with Jonestown's medical staff. Ironically, that staff, the **very next day**, would prepare the cyanide potion that the resisting residents would be forced to drink.

The medical staff to which Lane referred wasn't even a real medical staff at all. The only doctor available, according to Tim Reiterman, was an unlicensed medical student named Larry Schacht. Nevertheless, Lane told Krause that he had the best medical exam at Jonestown that he ever received anywhere.

Though Lane never told Charles Krause, the Congressman, the other doomed reporters, nor anyone else about the dangerous trap that awaited them, he revised his position. He later admitted to Krause (3) he knew strong depressants and tranquilizers were used to keep the people at Jonestown against their will.

According to writer, George Klineman (6), Lane even added that people who were emotionally disturbed for their entire lives were now happy. According to Lane, America couldn't help these unfortunates, only Jim Jones could.

The reasons for Lane's earlier fabrications were never examined. One of those reporters, Reiterman, also confirms that Lane also later admitted he was warned before hand that the grilled cheese sandwiches served by the waiters at the Peoples Temple to Congressman Ryan and others in his party were laced with tranquilizers and other mind controlling drugs.

According to Lane's (1) own statements at that time, he brought along cough drops, which contained a lot of sugar, to provide his own nourishment. Lane admitted that he had no intentions of eating the same drugged sandwiches that the others were forced to share.

Lane did share one confidence with Jones' former lawyer, Charles Garry. He finally disclosed to Garry that Buford was now his client and had entrusted valuable information to him. Garry had been the original Jonestown attorney for many years and knew much more about its inner workings, people and history than Mark Lane. According to Lane, Garry cautioned him about trusting Buford.

However, Lane did not caution Garry about the danger of eating the drugged Jonestown food. The food was not drugged to kill people, only tranquilize them. Afterward Garry had already eaten the food and it was too late, he asked Lane why he did not warn him that the food was drugged.

Lane (1) laughed at Garry, saying that at the time they weren't speaking. Garry had been angry with Lane for replacing him as Jim Jones' attorney. Garry's lack of information about the drugged food was shared by Leo Ryan and the reporters.

In fact, it was the precariousness of the situation which was the original reason why Terri Buford had decided to defect. It was obvious through her actions that Mark Lane was directly exposed to the true conditions of life in Jonestown.

Krause writes that an infuriated relative of one of the murdered victims, upon learning of Lane's claim to having prior knowledge, bitterly accused Lane of complicity in murder. The claim was never examined in a court of law.

Herb Caen, in an article in the *San Francisco Chronicle*, February 5, 1979 described media reaction to a Mark Lane claim that he had tried to warn Congressman Ryan not to go to Jonestown: "KGO's Jim Eason couldn't believe his ears last Tues. when he heard Mark Lane say, in an interview, that he warned Congressman Leo Ryan not to go to Jonestown. On Eason's program last October, 3, Lane had described Jonestown as a 'Paradise on earth' and invited him to visit the place. 'Any danger?' asked Eason. 'Nothing more harmful than a little kitty cat,' smirked Lane...' "

Yet, during that time when he was misleading the public, Lane carefully collected sensitive information from both his new client, Terri Buford, and his former one, Jim Jones, with both their interests in direct conflict. Jones still believed, even in his final moments, that Mark Lane was still actually acting on his behalf.

As his lawyer, Lane was pledged to keep Jim Jones' many secrets. Once Lane began to cover up the true nature of Jonestown, he was compromised, caught within his own web of attorney complicity. It was too late to divulge the entire truth without subjecting himself to scrutiny.

Jones died screaming that he was betrayed. Eventually Lane (1) claimed that Ryan was comforted in the safety of his own arms. No witnesses were left alive to dispute that allegation.

During the crises, Terri Buford was safely tucked away in Lane's home, drinking heavily, in a state of paranoid shock over the situation, fearfully awaiting the revenge of Jim Jones.

CHAPTER 3

QUADRILATERAL

Destiny is not a matter of chance, it is a matter of choice.
William Jennings Bryan

Mike Prokes, Jones most loyal bodyguard, survived the holocaust at Jonestown. He soon showed up at Georgetown, Guyana, with his pockets lined with large sums of cash. He was apprehended with a suitcase...loaded with money.

This was not the first time Prokes stole money from the Temple. A letter was found written by him stating: "and I certainly hope that Jim Jones doesn't somehow find out that I've stolen substantial amounts of money on various occasions from the temple." (1)

Buford's fear of Jones was greatly relieved by the support of Michael Prokes, her boyfriend before they joined the Temple together. Prokes pledged to protect her and was in a perfect position to fulfill that vow. Prokes served Jim Jones both as bodyguard and media chief.

Prokes was a crack shot, and always carried a loaded .38 caliber revolver. Totally trusted, Jones considered him to be his best friend. However, Prokes secretly hated Jones for stealing his girlfriend, Terri, after they joined the Temple together. Jones then further degraded Prokes. Reiterman (2) states Prokes was accused by Jones of making plays for teen-age girls.

Prokes was ridiculed in front of the entire assemblage. They came to the conclusion that Prokes did not feel comfortable with women his own age and, therefore, was really homosexual. To prove his thesis, Jones converted Prokes into one of his many male lovers.

Mike Prokes was also a licensed airplane pilot. Jim Jones never intended to die in Jonestown. On November 18, 1978, the day of the bloody murders, Jones spoke of being the last to die, which would have allowed him to flee as soon as the deed was done. Jones' plan, *The Last Stand*, was modeled after Hitler's own escape plan.

Jones kept a small Cessna hidden in the jungle with enough power to fly him to the nearest Guyanese coastal town of Port Kaituma. As his pilot, Mike Prokes was essential to Jones' escape plan.

However, since the Cessna could only fly as far as the coast, a boat was needed for the plan to succeed. For that, the Temple's trawler, the Cudjoe, also known as *Marceline*, the name of Jones' wife, lay in waiting, piloted by the only Englishman in the group, Captain Phillip Blakey, the husband of Debby Blakey. Captain Blakey spent most of his time hauling equipment and people around the Caribbean for the Temple.

Fellow Englishman, author John Peer Nugent (2), states that on November 17, the day before the murders, Phillip Blakey and a three-man crew were strategically moored in Port-of-Spain, Trinidad, which was about two hundred miles from Jonestown.

Captain Blakey was rumored to have been in radio contact with Jonestown, awaiting orders to pick up Jones with his select band of key aides along with several suitcases of cash.

According to ham radio operators who were monitoring the transmissions, the secret destination was to have been a prearranged, secret, Caribbean port. Even though *The Last Stand* was dependent upon him, Phillip Blakey had heard about the massacre over the wireless and wisely changed his direction.

29

After years of amassing huge untaxed profits from drug and gun running, it was finally time for the captain to retire. Following in his wife Debby's lead, Phillip Blakey also defected. He never arrived to rescue Jones and Blakey totally disappeared.

Prokes began to realize that things looked hopeless. After their preplanned escape, he realized that he would be expendable. Why should Jones share any of the loot with him?

Prokes had just witnessed a thousand murders. He realized that his life was in serious danger. As chief personal bodyguard to Jim Jones, Mike Prokes was the closest person to Jones when he was shot. According to Reiterman, one of Jones' mistresses, Maria Katsaris, ran up to Prokes for help at the time of the murders. She told him that a group of armed members had gone after Congress-man Leo Ryan to murder him. She pleaded.

Reiterman (3) states that Herb Caen, of the *San Francisco Chronicle* wrote a commentary specifically mentioning his feeling that Prokes had evil intentions. Caen stated that he could well imagine Prokes being able to kill, basing his intuitive feeling on a dinner meeting that he had with both Jones and Prokes.

Al Mills, the top level defector who had earlier warned the public about Jones' escape plot, also believed that Jones was murdered by someone very close to him. Mills conjectured that when Jones' escape plan went sour, one of Jones' inner guards shot him. One deadly bullet from a .38 caliber revolver ended life for Jones. He was shot in the right temple from a distance of about sixty feet by the expert marksman.

Jones' screeching pet monkey, Mr. Muggs, had his screams silenced by the same weapon that killed Jones, a .38 caliber revolver. Whomever it was that killed Jones had also taken deadly aim on a harmless monkey.

Immediately after Jones was murdered, Prokes fled from the scene with the suitcase full of money and a thermos filled with survival water. The sturdy steel thermos could also double as a blackjack in case of any trouble. His gun was left at the murder scene. Fingerprints on that gun were never checked. Reiterman states that according to reports, Mark Lane was hiding safely in the bushes during the massacre and saw Prokes carrying the heavy suitcase of money while making his getaway into the jungle.

But Prokes didn't walk through the jungle. Instead, he flew the small Cessna to the coastal town of Port Kaituma and ditched it. Then, he anxiously waited for the Captain Blakey's *Cudjoe* which never arrived.

Captain Blakey's wife, Debby, stated that so much money was stored in trunks hidden in the Jonestown area that mothballs were ordered from the U.S. The treasure was starting to mildew and insects were feasting on the greenbacks.

Prokes buried part of his stolen money in a chicken coop and then hid the suitcase. He was apprehended in Port Kaituma by the Guyanese police where, Reiterman states, Prokes admitted he was sent by Jones to board the Cudjoe.

The police found Prokes with $48,000 stuffed in his pocket; a letter of introduction to a foreign country and two passports registered under different names. Why would Prokes, only one man, have needed two passports in the first place? Jones and Prokes prepared their escape together, well in advance.

The New York Times (4) reported that Jones did have a plan to move the group to Cuba, or Russia. Members of the Soviet Union's delegation had met with leaders of the Peoples Temple to plan such a move and Jones had started to teach his people Russian.

But their actual secret destination was not Cuba. Nearer to Guyana and Panama where their money was stashed in Swiss affiliated banks was their real port of call, Costa Rica, which had no extradition treaty with the U.S.

Eventually, the Guyanese government recovered Prokes' money from the chicken coop. They let Prokes keep his thermos. Krause states that the ditched suitcase originally contained about $550,000 in United States currency plus around $130,000 in Guyanese money. That was in addition to the $48,000 Prokes had stuffed into his pockets. There had also been a treasure in gold and jewelry within the Jonestown safe.

Selwyn Daly, now a transit worker in New York, worked in the Guyanese airport during the time of the murders. He states (5) that he was taken by a chief detective who was his personal friend to see the gruesome sight of Jim Jones' dead body as well as those of the two murdered mistresses as they lay rotting in the Guyancse sun. As there was no gun nearby, he assumed that Jones was murdered.

He also remembers what happened to most of the money that the Guyanese government confiscated. Daly alleges that the Guyanese Chief Detective took Prokes' suitcase and there was a *free for all* for most of the remaining cash in Jonestown as well. The Chief Detective disappeared. The money, according to Daly, was not recovered in Guyana.

Daly also confirms the knowledge that the Guyanese investigators had of the Cudjoe's planned return to pick Jones up as part of the failed inner Jonestown escape plan.

Prokes is mentioned prominently in the newspapers of Guyana as they conducted their own investigation of Jones' death. Guyana's assistant commissioner of crime, Cecil Roberts, listed the various valuables Prokes' was caught with on his report.

Prokes had told Roberts that the treasure of cash, jewelry and gold that was given to him was not delivered because he allegedly found it too heavy to lug through the Guyanese jungle; so he buried it for safekeeping.

The money was confiscated by the Guyanese government. Prokes left for the U.S. to meet up with Terri and Mark Lane to futher the alibi of labeling the mass murder, a mass suicide. No one would ever learn the inner details, unless one of them squealed.

Certainly, helpless monkeys like Mr. Muggs, can be considered to be as incapable as the Jonestown infants of committing suicide. Yet, experts have claimed that Muggsy, like Jones, the children, the infants...everyone killed themselves, on the same day, at the same time.

Jones was finally forever silenced. His *Last Stand* had turned out like Little Big Horn. Just before his own murder, Jones cried out to his people, "we've been so betrayed." Jones was triple crossed by his most trusted associates: lover, lawyer and bodyguard.

Jones died without ever learning of the Lane-Buford connection. If he had been left alive, he would have eventually stood trial in the United States for his part in the conspiracy, therefore, Jones' death was necessary to protect the upper members of the plot from exposure.

According to *Facts on File* (6), Michael Prokes, was reported to have quietly slipped into the U.S. on December 29, 1978, a month after the massacre. While they were in Jonestown, ex-lovers, Buford and Prokes, had conceived a plan to meet together after Jonestown expired. Prokes too was unaware of the Lane-Buford connection. He was supposed to have brought the suitcase that Lane witnessed him carrying into the jungle with him to the secret meeting. Buford was to bring the bank account numbers.

Four months after the massacre, their secret meeting did occur in California. However, Buford did not show up alone. She brought her lawyer and new lover, Mark Lane (7). After waiting for Terri Buford for seven years, Prokes was shocked and severely disappointed. He had always been in love with Terri Buford.

This trio of Jonestown survivors discussed their strategies in a hotel room in California. They had to get their alibis straight for the press and government. Lane, (7) himself, admits that when they talked their meetings were marked by a lack of trust.

Prokes had been reading the newspapers and was stunned. *Facts on File* (8) states that The U.S. Justice Department had received a report on December 15, 1978 indicating that Buford and Lane went to Switzerland right after the Jonestown murders to try to retrieve cash from the Temple's Swiss bank accounts.

Walter Cronkite was beginning to investigate the Buford-Lane connection.

Since the money was spread over many countries and different banks, it was very difficult for Cronkite to determine where it was laundered after Jonestown. The amount in question was also being pinpointed. *Facts on File* (8) reports that former Temple financial manager Terri Buford told a federal grand jury in San Francisco on January 17, 1979, that the Temple had about $10.5 million: $ 7.5 million in Panamanian banks accounts and the rest in cash.

That leaves $3 million dollars in cash alone! However, *Facts on File* (8) further reports that the Guyanese government said that more than $1 million in cash belonging to the Peoples Temple had been deposited for safekeeping in the bank of Guyana. Thirty-eight pieces of gold jewelry and about $65,000 in Social Security and Veterans Administration checks also had been found at Jonestown.

The actual Temple assets were probably ten times the amounts originally estimated. The final financial tally of the death lift operation by the U.S. Government in Guyana was $4.4 million or $4,800 per body. But there had been twelve million dollars, alleged to be hidden within secret bank accounts around the world.

According to an article written less than a month after the massacre by David Binder (9), eight million dollars had been removed from a bank in Zurich. Binder got that information from the Swiss authorities who checked the accounts and told him that they had been emptied. Binder adds that a Justice Department spokesman said that there were reports that Mark Lane and Terri Buford had gone to Switzerland to remove the secret Zurich assets.

The only other financial advisor from Jonestown to be questioned was Debby Blakey whose accounts of the money had been stated a full six months before Buford's defection. Furthermore, Blakey always knew very little about Jonestown's inner finances. Buford kept her underling, Debby Blakey, totally uninformed.

Prokes, who was uninformed as well, was reassured by Lane and Terri. Lane blamed the C.I.A. and the press for misinformation. Lane, while never retained as Prokes' lawyer, managed to keep his confidence, his girlfriend and the account numbers. Lane now knew everything about the Temple's finances.

Facts On File (10) describes a report commissioned by Secretary of State Cyrus R. Vance and made public May 3, 1982, which charged the State Department with errors and lapses in handling and evaluating information about the Peoples Temple before the mass murders.

The State Department never questioned Mark Lane even though, according to *Facts On File* (11) Jones told Lane that he was certain that Larry Layton and several other cult members were going to shoot Ryan. It appears that Lane had advance, personal knowledge that Jones, his client, had dangerous intentions.

While the heroic congressman was slaughtered, Lane was allowed to remain alive on Jones' orders, since Lane agreed to write Jones' memoirs.

Soon after their meeting, Mike Prokes began to question his *friends*. Feeling he was used as their puppet, he decided to cut his own string. Only a few short weeks after the meeting with Terri Buford, several months after Jonestown died,

Mike Prokes, Jones' bodyguard and press secretary for ten years, called a news conference. His agony translated into another death.

On national television, he finally gave up, by firing a bullet from a .38 revolver into the right temple of his head. He died instantly ending his life by the same caliber weapon that killed Mr. Muggs and Jones.

By exhibiting his death publicly, he was demonstrating that he was not a murder victim of any Jonestown hit squad. A week before his death, San Francisco Mayor George Moscone and his assistant, Harvey Milk, were assassinated.

Prokes made his final statement to Terri Buford, as she was comfortably watching T.V. with Mark Lane. In Prokes' confusion, even though he was severely pained by her betrayal, he corroborated the Lane legal defense strategy by blaming the C.I.A. for everything, ultimately protecting Buford.

However, Prokes left behind no shred of evidence to prove his allegations of C.I.A. involvement. That was because none ever existed.

Prokes did leave a very pathetic, prophetic personal letter to his friend, Tim, regarding his despondency while at Jonestown in which he states:
"Dear Tim,

I don't know how much longer I can take it. I mean the witchcraft. I feel like I'm programmed. I enjoy violence when I do it—like all those dogs I mutilated, but sometimes-like right now-I feel sorry I did it. I think I'm going to end it all with my .38, I only wish I could see my brains blown out. Maybe I'll try someone else first. Just didn't want you to be concerned if you don't hear from me.

Thanks
Your friend,
Mike Prokes   (12)

Prokes, who admits he enjoyed violence and relishes the thought of shooting someone with his .38 achieved his goal of ending his own troubled existence with that same gun.

Clearly Prokes was very disappointed in his failure to escape without some of the fortune. He preferred death to the prospect of spending his life in jail. Ironically, Nugent believes that Prokes had probably been the F.B.I.'s candidate to be offered immunity in return for his testimony. They had flown him down to Guyana to identify the bodies. Besides Buford, who was protected by Lane, Prokes could have provided a major link to the Jonestown mystery.

Nugent explains that the questions that the government were to have asked Prokes included the location of the money, the identity of Jim Jones' killer and whether Jones actually was planning to survive the November 18th massacre with a select cadre of overlords and escape to live in secret luxury.

If Prokes had lived, the government might have pieced the puzzle together. But with Prokes' death, the answers had to come from another high echelon source.

In his Last Will and Testament, Prokes explains his motive: his intense hatred for Jones. He claims that he never liked Jim Jones' authority over people. In his suicide note, Prokes pleads for an investigation of the Jonestown murders. Lane writes that Prokes called for an eventual *deep throat* type of secretive investigation of Jonestown. His request was made over ten years ago and is now long overdue. Terri Buford finally responded to Prokes' dying wish.

Actually, the trio, Prokes, Jones, and Lane, never realized the whole picture that was carefully drawn for each of them. In this complicated love quadrilateral, Buford accepted three dangerous dates: Jones was first, Lane was second and Prokes was last. Buford was linked emotionally and sexually to each one of them.

At the convergence of this quartet's locus, Terri was fully prepared for any contingency. If Jones had successfully escaped, she could have gone with him and his millions. If Prokes was successful and if Lane didn't work out, she could go with her former boyfriend. However, her highest hopes were with Lane, knowing how badly she would need a lawyer's protection in the future. Her counterpoint succeeded.

The only souvenir Terri Jean Buford has from Jonestown is Mike Prokes' sturdy thermos (13) which survived the massacre. She borrowed it for coffee during the secret California meeting intending to return it one day to Mike. With his death, she kept it as her private link to him, she mysteriously carrying it with her at all times.

Lane quotes Terri Buford as stating that Jonestown would have been a nice place to be without Jones. Eventually, she proved to play a pivotal role in her fantasy's realization.

Terri ultimately spent a few years working with Lane on a number of cases. They plotted to write an anti-C.I.A. book together about Jonestown. She learned his private strategies and, in disguise, even interviewed James Earl Ray as well as others. Finally, in secret, she conceived Mark Lane's daughter. Then she disappeared.

Who is Teresa Jean Buford? She looks like a sweet teenager, a typical all-American girl. In fact, she creates the vulnerable image of the archtypical fairy princess that any red-blooded man would be only too glad to rescue in his wildest fantasy.

Tall and straight-standing, embodying the freshness of youth and the strength of a mountain woman, she possesses exquisitely balanced features. She's a trim 5'9", with lightened blond hair and piercing deep-set eyes that gaze steadily out beneath gracefully arched brows, high cheek bones, long aquiline nose; a vision of fair, arresting attractiveness.

She wears long dungaree country skirts, L.L. Bean shoes and even plays a great game of double six dominoes, taught to her by her Texan grandaddy, a railroad conductor from Fort Worth. She speaks with a honeysuckle sweet, southern accent. The package is so deceptively attractive. Like hot butter to touch, any man would desire her.

How had her inner heart frozen into stone? What furnace had forged her will into iron? Did Jones and Buford share the same dreams and goals? How did a sweet young Teresa Jean Buford ever take hold of the Devil's hand and enter within his abode of weeping skulls, to enlist as his second in command.

CHAPTER 4
COMMANDER

Those who have gone before, backward beyond
remembrance and beyond the beginning of
imagination, backward among the emergent
beasts, and the blind, prescient ravenings
of the youngest sea, those children of the sun,
I mean, who brought forth those, who wove,
spread the human net, and who brought forth me;
they are fallen backward into their graves
like blown wheat and are folded under the
earth like babies in blankets, and they are
melted upon the mute enduring world like
leaves, like wet snow; they people the silence
in my soul like bats in a cave; they lived
in their time as I live now, each a universe
within which, for a while, to die was
inconceivable, and their living was as bright
and brief as sparks on a chimney wall, and
 now they lie dead as I soon shall die;
my ancestors my veterans. I call upon you,
I invoke your help; I desire to do you honor,
you are beyond the last humiliation. You are my
fathers and my mothers but there is no way in which
you can help me, nor may I serve you soon;
meanwhile may I bear you ever in the piety of my heart.
                                        -James Agee-

The past can be a prologue to the future.

Virginia (Jackson) Buford, James Agee's niece and Terri Buford's mother,
was a beauty contest winner. She grew up near the small town of Cleveland,
Tennessee not far from the Kentucky State line where she received a strict

religious upbringing.

Virginia was justifiably proud of her lineage which included religious leader, William Jennings Bryan, the populist candidate for president, who wrote the famous *Cross of Gold* speech. Her family's religious beliefs were modeled after Bryan's staunch fundamentalist views.

Author Louis Koenig (1) examines the core of Bryan's political philosophy. Bryan proposed that the government was manipulated by the rich and that the common people, especially the farmers, were getting the short end of the government's stick. He felt that the common man was being crucified by the Eastern Bankers and the *Eastern* Press.

His political philosophy assumed a cult- like religious fervor. The *common people* of the Midwest considered him their champion. Like Jim Jones, Bryan's oratorical style was a mixture of political demagoguery combined with passionate evangelical fervor.

Koenig describes Bryan's physical appearance with his eyes flashing and his, as described by Koenig, "raven" hair tossed with an actor's skill to underscore his argument. Jim Jones himself was nick named, *Raven*. Jones eventually copied many of Bryan's numerous and powerful speaking skills.

Ironically Reiterman, even though he coincidently named his book, *Raven*, never realized any hidden connection between Jones and Bryan, through their link, Terri Buford.

Bryan fought vehemently against Charles Darwin's theory of evolution. Darwin's views were pure blasphemy according to Bryan who is most vividly portrayed in the book and movie, *Inherit The Wind*, by Jerome Lawrence, as the prosecutor in the famous, *Scopes* monkey trial.

In the movie, he is viewed as the staunch anti-evolution political/evangelist lawyer, battling against the clever Clarence Darrow, the defense lawyer who espoused and defended the progressive scientific thinking of that era.

This one pivotal issue led to Bryan's tragic downfall. His religious beliefs were defeated and ridiculed in the courtroom.

Bryan, an extremely intelligent and gifted man, took the position that Darwin's new scientific thesis, specifically, *Survival Of The Fittest,* could be potentially dangerous if misinterpreted by power hungry politicians. Bryan was enormously influenced by an American war relief's worker's account of his conversations with German officers during World War One.

The war worker's disclosures about the German interpretation of Darwin's theories explained the direct influence on shaping their militaristic philosophies which developed via an unbroken pattern through Nietzsche and other philosophers, to intense German nationalism, and then, into their war machines.

Bryan then linked Darwin's theory to possible future World wars and mankind's subjugation through political elitism. He had predicted a type of Jonestown, one hundred years before the event occurred. In an address to the World Brotherhood Congress in 1920, Bryan condemns Darwinism as the most damaging influence which human civilization will ever have to contend with.

Yet, for his justified concern for mankind, Bryan was widely feared and labeled as being a socialist, an anarchist, and even a Communist. Koenig disclosed that *The New York Times* printed letters from a reader who expressed his opinion that Bryan was insane.

These anti-Bryan opinions were supported by a very hostile *Eastern* press with whom Bryan had an ongoing war. His economic programs had mostly blamed the New York bankers for the country's economic troubles. He also alleged that the industrialists were pushing the nation into war for their own selfish economic purposes.

The majority of Bryan's progeny sympathized with him in his view that the Bible must be interpreted literally. To them, science had to be false since it conflicted with the Bible. Sex was considered sinful, unless it was strictly for procreation. Virginia Buford, Terri's mother, was utterly loyal to these fundamentalist religious beliefs.

Bryan would never imagine that one of his descendents, Terri Buford, would rebel against his values to eventually contribute to the very type of violent tragedy (Jonestown), that he was desperately trying to avoid.

The paternal side of Terri Buford's family stems from France. The Buford name is the anglicized version of Beaufort: strong beauty. Terri can trace her ancestors to their proud participation as revolutionaries in the French Revolution.

After the French Revolution came the *Reign of Terror* during which all traitors to the *cause* of that day had to be tortured and mercilessly killed. That terror would be reincarnated in the steamy jungles of Guyana.

Original motivations for the French Revolution were forgotten and cast aside. Preserving the new order was all important. Loyalty became a matter of survival. There was no mercy for dissidents. Over the centuries, strong family loyalty was passed down from generation to generation and became as important to the Buford clan as their loyalty to their new country, The United States.

Terri Jean Buford's father, Charles Buford, a Naval Commander, shared his intense family loyalty with his total devotion to his country. Buford functioned as the Ollie North of his era, Vietnam, sharing the maverick philosophy: *the ends justify the means*, during their respective military careers.

Terri's father did considerable intelligence work. *Intelligence service* is a polite expression for spying. He was trained at the Naval Base in Newport, Rhode Island, where on February 4, 1952, Terri was born.

Gone from home for six months at a time, he was sent on covert missions to meet with pro-U.S. governments around the world. This would include personal dealings with the Shah of Iran with whom he was photographed (2) in a brotherly embrace. Buford's extensive scope of operations included the entire Mediterranean.

He desperately wanted a son to follow in his *super-spy* footsteps. Instead, the couple produced two daughters. Four years after his eldest daughter, Caroline, was born, he was blessed with Teresa Jean, whom he named after his favorite country music singer, Teresa Brewer.

Terri abhorred getting the hand me downs and taking orders from Caroline. The name, Terri, from the latin *terra,* means *earth.* Charles wanted his youngest daughter to always stand on firm ground, knowing quite well the dangerous and manipulative ways of the world.

Realistically, Terri sadly faced the cruel realization that she would never realize her father's dreams. As a woman in America, the odds were stacked against her ever becoming a Naval Commander, Secretary of State, or President, no matter how bright she was, or how hard she tried.

Commander Buford was blessed with a photographic mind. Terri was blessed with the same incredible ability, along with rigid self-discipline. She soon was able to perform amazingly prodigious feats of memory.

By transferring an item to be memorized onto a third object, she was able to retain total recall of numbers and other vague information that most people would have a difficult time remembering.

Terri also describes her father's method of rapid advancement in the U.S. Navy. If in the course of performing his duties, Charles made an error, he would zealously turn himself in to his superiors for a reprimand.

He also spied upon his fellows secretly turning them into their superiors in order to attain his own promotions as well as their trust. Eventually, Terri would use the same tattling tactics in Jonestown.

His loyalty to his Naval superiors was legendary and he expected the same total quality from his own men. Defending his friends and death to all enemies, a commander must be fully loyal to the nation's cause, sometimes having to operate covertly without even his own superiors knowing what his entire plan of action will be. Thus, the leader is protected from any possible failure and exposure.

Commander Buford's specialty was cracking enemy codes while developing his own ingenious ones to baffle the enemy. After World War Two, where he worked for naval intelligence, he and his wife were stationed with their children in northern Norway. Before she reached four years of age, she learned to speak a bit of Norwegian in this bleak climate.

According to Terri, her dad's job was to intercept and decipher codes sent by the Russians across their far northern frontier. He became a staunch anti-communist.

The entirely conflicting philosophies of both Commander Buford and William Bryan mixed together within Terri Buford's heart, generating a vexing disharmony.

For instance, Bryan had been a staunch prohibitionist, pushing through the amendment against alcohol. However, Terri's parents drank to excess. At times in her life, Terri has resorted to heavy drinking and then, total abstinence.

Furthermore, Commander Buford was, a warrior, whereas Bryan was a total pacifist. In fact, as a three-time Secretary of State, Terri's great uncle William Bryan was a major force in keeping America out of World War One. Terri is a pacifist, yet could accept extreme violence in Jonestown to justify her revolutionary positions.

Bryan's position on human rights, woman's suffrage, and civil rights has been called communistic and Terri shares that philosophy. Yet, her own father fought communism with all his strength.

Terri attended the all important Army-Navy football games, debutante balls and was only allowed to date officers during her teenage years. Charles Buford lived with an inborn sense of eliteness. Yet, ironically, Bryan supported the common man. Terri, whose rhetoric often copied Bryan's, acted as an elitist in her true activities.

According to Terri, her father considered certain targeted ethnic groups to be inferior. For Commander Buford, the atomic bombing of Japan presented no great moral dilemma since he practiced what he preached. The ends justified the means and, in his opinion, Americans were much more important than Asians. Bryan's fears concerning the usage of the *survival of the fittest* dictum were realized by Commander Buford.

A central conflict for Terri was religion. The beliefs of her mother were consistent with William Bryan's in their staunch fundamentalist dogma. Since Bryan's beliefs were proven in court to be legally and logically inconsistent and he was further embarrassed by the press and general public, according to Terri, choosing her father's atheism seemed to be the only path to follow.

Her mother was totally rejected as father and daughter, together, would ridicule her religious concepts. Virginia grew to become bitter as her staunch beliefs were challenged within her family. Caroline stayed neutral in this family struggle. This active alliance between Charles and Terri became a betrayal to Virginia causing a rift that would never heal.

Pure atheism, without any moral base to replace lost religious precepts, left Terri with a shallow moral core. Into this void lept faint echoes of William Bryan's eloquent political pleas. Terri eventually would be curiously drawn to explore various political/religious organizations for their possible final resolution to a variety of unconscious inner conflicts.

Bryan believed that a union between church and state was not only possible, but immensely preferable to the constitutional American governmental system. He envisioned himself as a combination of messiah, politician, religious leader, and prophet. His ultimate goal was no less than the American Presidency.

For Bryan, like Jones, religion and politics were closely intertwined. Critics at the time felt that the moralistic, evangelical fervor of his politics lent him a distinctive vitality which captivated a devoted and massive following.

The type of political/religious marriage that Bryan so yearned for could be easily achieved by a charismatic leader of a cult such as Jonestown.

Bryan ran for the Presidency three times in 1896, 1900, and again in 1908. His death and subsequent burial service reflects his lifelong inconsistencies within his belief system. The burial was at Arlington Cemetery, by his own request, thus presenting an interesting final paradox to his life. This ardent pacifist choose a soldier's grave. He was honored with a military burial.

Reverend George Stuart of Birmingham, Alabama, made a final prayer in Bryan's honor. Stuart thanked God for this great hero of the common people.

Buried nearby Bryan's gravesite, are the remains of one of his in-laws, military hero, Commander Charles Buford. Linked through eternity, America's final homage is paid to the both of them.

While Bryan is revered for his statesman's role as a peacemaker, Commander Charles Buford, the fighting hero, is honored for the important and top secret role he eventually would play in the Vietnam war.

PART TWO

AXIS

CHAPTER 5

KAMIKAZI

Deru kugi wa utareru.
"The nail that sticks up gets hammered down."

After his stint in Norway, Commander Charles Buford and his family were transferred to the naval base in Sasebo, Japan, a town near the strategic harbor of Nagasaki on the southern island of Kyushu. Asia was in turmoil and Vietnam was in danger of falling to the communists whom he hated.

The cherry blossoms were in full bloom releasing their sweet aroma throughout the air. Every day, Terri walked two miles to her little schoolhouse. At the age of eight, she began to think and speak in fluent Japanese in addition to her second language, Norwegian. Her revered Japanese teacher, called *Sensei*, or master, was very strict, focusing mainly on mathematics.

Terri became the teacher's pet as the sensei's humble wife, became both mama-san (nanny) and personal tutor to her. With her assistance, Terri quickly showed a superior aptitude for education. She was especially adept at math, treating each problem as if it was a code that had to be solved.

Terri's mother, Virginia, a country girl who could quickly bake a delicious homemade cake, felt uneasy in Japan and wanted to return home to the U.S. Furthermore, she was constantly ill with severe manic-depression which triggered recurring alcoholism, a common problem for isolated military wives abroad.

Terri claims that she suffered from severe physical abuse. She was woken up in the middle of the night by her mother and beaten, for no apparent reason, causing her to become very angry and confused. Developing an ear infection that her mother left untreated, she lost most of her hearing in one ear.

To soothe her mother, she had to participate in deluded imaginings. To win her father's confidence and approval, she had to demonstrate a sane outlook. Terri grew accustomed to living in the world of madness and sanity at the same time.

Still, she could not comprehend her parents betrayal. How could her father allow this abuse to occur? Virginia's alcoholism also lessened her capacity as a wife. Terri began to fill in for those shortcomings.

The relationship between father and daughter infuriated her mother's already intense rage. Terri learned the special tricks of preparing his food exactly as he liked it, creamy soft scrambled eggs with milk and country biscuits covered with thick, white country gravy on the side. She learned to massage his back to ease his tension.

Young Teresa sat piously in church, ever ready to explode, but she learned the art of gentle deception as she kept a coy smile on her face and basked in the special relationship she had with her father who understood her.

In stark contrast to her own mother, her mama-san took wonderful care of the little girl and gave her pretty *hakata* dolls and delicious miso soup. It pained her greatly to realize that her angel was being beaten regularly by her biological mother.

To mama-san, like the Japanese people, this sweet little girl was being victimized. To protect her, mama-san taught her the secret of the survival of her people, psychological karate, handed down for centuries in Japan:

Hide your inner heart well, child, disarm your opponent with your mind, trust no one fully, learn how to please, quietly and submissively, never display your anger and speak softly. Plan a course of action after quietly examining your options and then act swiftly, never looking back. If you fail, move on ahead.

This type of behavior was deeply ingrained in the Japanese character. According to the President of the Sony Corporation, Akio Morita (1), it is very difficult to argue in the Japanese language because of its very structure and character. The language is very indirect and nonconfrontational and forces politeness upon the speaker, unless he wants to get physically violent. There is no compromise between the two positions, explains Morita.

Japanese is a monotonous language full of harsh sounds and is best spoken in whispers. Speaking Japanese, Terri learned their inscrutable manner of understated behavior. Identifying with Japanese culture, she began to hide her emotions, act very respectfully and politely to others, and speak quietly, nearly always in a soft whisper.

Terri developed great respect for the power of the group. Working together as a team, Japanese style, much energy could be harnessed, with limited resources.

An essential key to the Japanese success, as in the Buford family, was utter loyalty for each other within the atmosphere of an extended family, with the emperor himself, serving as group father. For the good of the group, people were expected to lay down their life, *Hari-Kari* style, with utter devotion. The legendary *Kamikazi* pilots were so effectively conditioned that death for their emperor was considered their greatest honor.

When a Japanese emperor dies, people commit Hari-Kari even to this day. Actually, the people of Japan were the focus of a cult that was foisted upon them. In fact, Shinto, the central Japanese religion, is a particular, carefully contrived version of Japanese culture that has been turned into a religious cult for political reasons.

That blind, utter loyalty was also a key to their failure in World War Two. Like carefully trained soldiers, Japanese schoolchildren, at the mere mention of the word *Emperor,* had to stand instantly to attention.

The Japanese emperor, like the feudal kings of Europe, is a priest king, supposedly deriving his power directly from God. Eventually, this concept was utilized by Jones, as well.

However, the emperor never wielded actual power. That was in the hands of the shoguns, who used the imperial mystique to legitimize their rule. True power lay with the overlords: safely hidden behind the facade of the emperor.

Since the shoguns had the true power which was hidden, the emperor wasn't held accountable for what others did in his name. Hirohito escaped censure through this clever system which caused the worst tragedy in Japanese history, World War Two. In Jonestown, the system was cleverly reversed. Jones got all the blame and his shoguns escaped.

Morita explains how Japan functioned during World War Two. Everything the military-dominated government did was made to appear as a direct command order of the emperor.

Special thought police roamed the country arresting people on the slightest suspicion that they were not reverent enough to the emperor. The nation was totally in the grasp of the military. Dissension was extremely difficult and dangerous. All families had to go along with it or risk their children's death.

Wartime tension was increased by the difficulties of everyday life in Japan. The environment was a hostile one, constantly threatening disaster. The entire populace suffered from earthquake anxiety. Tokyo was hit with earthquakes of such magnitude that the San Franciscan tragedies seem minuscule by comparison.

Every time an earthquake would strike Tokyo, the city would burn from massive fires and have to be entirely rebuilt. Within fifteen seconds, an entire family's home would be destroyed. The eventual atomic bombing at Hiroshima and Nagasake seemed to be just a continuous link in the Japanese chain of catastrophes.

School field trips to these bomb sites made a dramatic impression on young Terri Buford that would affect her all her life. Seeing the photographs of the victims of the American bombing through her classmates eyes was chillingly instructive. Some of the images were too brutally graphic for any sensitive little girl to absorb.

Terri Buford, who began to not only speak, but think and feel in Japanese, felt overwhelming sadness for the people of her adopted land. Furthermore, she felt totally alienated from her native country, America. Her father seemed to be the enemy of the Asian people, especially the Japanese. Every night she had the most terrifying nightmares of nuclear destruction.

Constant reminders of the U.S. bombing of Hiroshima and Nagasaki affected Terri at her most suggestible childhood years of development. Her older sister, Caroline, who was four years her senior, was affected much less since Caroline spent her formative years in Norway. Eventually, according to Terri, her sister, Caroline would marry four times and eventually become a nuclear physicist engaged in weapons research.

While eavesdropping on the phone, after a school trip to Hiroshima, Terri claims she was mortified to discover that her own father was directly involved in the planning of an unauthorized bombing raid upon Laos.

For Terri, it was another genocide of Asians. She now knew the absolute truth about her father and country. Not only was she being victimized at home, but in her eyes, her father was part of a plot to destroy and control the entire planet.

Asians, whom she identified with, were being slaughtered by Americans. Terri lost all faith in her father, God, American politics, the capitalist economic system and standard moral behavior. After the feelings of pain, shock, and numbness subsided, she was overwhelmed by seething anger.

With its many roots shaping the tree of her anger, defiant rage began to be expressed in direct action. Joining with other rebellious navy brats, they planned clandestine graffiti raids on U.S. airplanes right in their hangers. Terri claimed they spray painted boldly emblazoned testimonials to *Jefferson*, not in tribute to Thomas Jefferson, but in reference to the rock group, *Jefferson Airplane.*

Jefferson Airplane's song about powerful jet aircraft affected these alienated, young navy brats with its forceful, emotional message. Any danger resulting from the consequences of this action brought extra exhilaration.

Near the Sasebo naval base, there were many Japanese prostitutes openly carousing with the soldiers. What were their secrets of love, a budding, adolescent Terri wondered? These Japanese women pleased the sailors so fully, in stark contrast to the cold manner in which her mother was treating her father in their conjugal bed.

Terri heard her parents in the next room constantly arguing over sex, her mother refusing to satisfy her father at all. Sex, itself, was presented as a crime. Parental policing caused her to feel a shame, a nameless guilt over anything sexual. She decided to emulate those accommodating wartime Japanese women in their total administering to their foreign boyfriends' needs. She refused to ever become sexually stingy, like her mother.

According to Terri, her family had taken temporary custody of a teenage boy, Mike, whose own father was serving on active duty in Vietnam. He became an integral part of the Buford family. Commander Buford treated him like the son he never had.

Like the beautiful cherry blossoms all around her, Terri slowly developed into a sensuous young woman. Her sexual fantasies revolved around Mike until soon, during hot, lunchtime trysts, her fantasies became realities.

The young lovebirds had their first, teenage sexual experiences without their parents ever realizing. This affair was the first time sex and rebellion would blend for her into the perfect revenge against authority. Sexuality would become the focus of great drama, eventually mirroring Terri's politics. The tension between sexual danger and sexual pleasure is a powerful one for some women. Sexuality can be both restrictive, repressed, and even dangerous, while at the same time for some, explorative, pleasurable, and urgent.

Escaping the misery of her home through Mike's embraces, Terri fought a secret war against both Vietnam, and her parent's religious hypocrisy. As her first lover, Mike now became dearer to her than a brother. Pleasure and danger were, thus, juxtaposed.

This was a dangerous game, however. If her parents ever found out what she was up to, they would severely punish her. Certainly, the Oriental attitude towards sex that she witnessed firsthand on the naval base seemed to be a lot more fun than the strained relationship between her parents in their dull marriage based upon their western religious ideals and spiced up by their inordinate amount of alcohol consumption.

Far away from their homes, Terri reminded the lonely young sailors of all their sweet girlfriends left back in the states. On the canteen's jukebox, her father's favorite, Hank Williams cried out the most popular ballad of the time, *I'm So Lonesome I Could Cry*. Commander Buford anxiously noticed the hungry stares that his daughter received as she walked around the base.

Terri was finally given the love and attention she lacked within her own family through the sailors' constant attention. She shared in the use of various drugs abundant on the base. Relations between Teresa and her sister became estranged. Caroline's age advantage allowed her to take Terri's favorite suitors.

To add fuel to her smoldering fire, Commander Buford, in jealously trying to protect youngest Terri from the constant advances of all these lonely sailors, restricted her movements much more than Caroline, causing deep resentment.

"That's not fair," she cried.

But being fair was not the commander's primary concern. Being a Navy man, himself, he was well aware of precisely what those boys wanted from his youngest daughter and he was determined not to share her with the any of the ensigns. In fact, she began to notice a strange pattern emerging.

Terri relates that when any of the Navy men showed any interest in her, Commander Buford would immediately order them sent directly to Vietnam, earmarked especially for front line duty.

Terri felt that her father, in his jealous rage, was deliberately destroying her potential suitors. His explanation was based upon the excuse that she was embarrassing him in front of his naval superiors.

In her horror, she began to realize that her father was in full command of her sexuality, and furthermore, in his military position, he had an awesome power over the very lives of her boyfriends, those same men he was sending off to war. She felt a murderous guilt.

Finally, the Buford clan was sent back to the states. Terri always had a book in her pocket, a literary security blanket to make up for her loss of friends she suffered through as her family moved from base to base.

Now stationed in Toledo, Ohio, Commander Buford requested the gruesome task of going personally to the homes of newly deceased soldiers to console their distraught parents. Terri was morbidly forced by her father to attend countless funeral services. Her silent rage was infinitely kindled as she suffered through the endless agony of witnessing bereaved family members. The void left by their sons untimely demise was felt by brothers, sisters, mothers and fathers, grieving family members left with only their hearts silently pounding in anguish.

Furthermore, seeing boys much like the ones she had spoken to and cared about now laying dead in their coffins totally overwhelmed her. Attending their services and watching boyfriend after boyfriend lowered into their resting places, Terri began to experience nightmares in which she wept and kicked the coffins of her close friends and lovers imploring them to arise and wake up from their eternal sleep. In her dreams she was also in a coffin and felt the unbearable claustrophobic fear of being forever trapped alive, hopeless, dazed in guilt, angry, wanting to run, faraway. She heard a high pitched wail of a chorus of cries and screams from the pain of people dying too young, too soon before their time was up, violently ripped from their lives prematurely, The Commander's implied message had been clear to everyone else on the naval base as well, **don't mess with my daughter if you value your life.** Ultimately, her father's actions bonded death with sex.

Terri was being taught a brutal lesson by a powerful sadist who wanted nothing more than her total domination. Her rebellion was essential for emotional survival.

Terri's family moved to Philadelphia and she graduated from the Philadelphia H.S. for Girls in 1970. She said that she danced on Dick Clark's *American Bandstand* T.V. show.

Eventually, Charles Buford retired from the navy and became an English professor at a small college in the Amish haven of Indiana, Pennsylvania, a town that claimed the actor, James Stewart, as one of its native sons. Commander Buford retired from warfare.

Sharing the traditional Japanese respect for the teaching profession, her father's new role appeased her smoldering hostility and Terri was able to direct her energy into a positive channel. She studied photography and took award winning photographs of the area around her town. Her self esteem and confidence soared. She attended Indiana University from 1970 to 1971.

Totally dedicated to pacifist principles, Terri eagerly joined the *Society of*

Friends, more commonly known as the Quakers. The small group met in various homes in the area. She agreed with their criticism of U. S. exploitative military policies. Before the Civil War, the Quakers provided refuge for many runaway slaves and other fugitives. In the Vietnam era all war dissenters had the Quaker's assistance.

Commander Buford was not pleased with his daughter's new friends. However, Terri related to this very decent group and their sincere efforts on behalf of the homeless, the drug abusers as well as their assistance for all underprivileged people. She felt as it she was now a part of a new, benign family.

In 1971, sincerely believing in nonviolent political transformation, she started a regular Quaker center within Indiana, Pennsylvania which is still in operation.

Furthermore, in opposing capital punishment as well as discrimination based upon sex, race, economic status, nationality, and education, the Quaker ideals greatly appealed to Terri. Eventually, the rhetoric found its way into the tenets of espoused Jonestown rhetoric. Unfortunately, Jim Jones never practiced what the Quakers preached.

Through this reborn religious affiliation, Terri began to flourish emotionally as well as academically, scoring an amazingly perfect 1600 on the S.A T. and achieving a full scholarship to Penn State University. She also excelled as a master gymnast. She sprained an ankle during a competition. Enduring incredible pain, much to the astonishment of her coach, she finished the performance.

Possessing great ability to plan complicated military strategies, this sagacious Naval Commander's daughter also excelled as a leader of the college chess team.

Meeting a young student named David, she fell deeply in love and was soon engaged to be married. Serious trouble was brewing in America at that time. She was deeply affected by Kent State. She stated that those students were murdered because they were demonstrating against other murderers in Vietnam. Having grown up in Japan, she felt a particular responsibility to help end the war as soon as possible.

Like many other people of conscience, watching American soldiers killing

Asians on television in the name of some vague Domino Theory was impossible to accept. Even though most Americans certainly seemed to want the war stopped, the government seemed unresponsive to the people's voice. The peaceful Quakers were not militant enough to counter that oppression in Terri's view.

To complicate her life even further, following a pre-marital vacation that he took alone to the Caribbean, her beloved boyfriend, David, came home to announce he met someone new. Their engagement was off.

The wedding invitations were already sent out. A hurt Terri was looking forward to finally leaving her parents and starting a new life as a respectable married woman. She was embarrassed in front of all her relatives and crushed by disappointment.

The situation was deeply strained in the Buford household. Her sister, Caroline, was already happily married. Terri's rage against her family resurfaced.

Soon after the shock was absorbed she began dating once again. One day, she brought home her newest boyfriend, Ben, and was caught in a compromising situation by Commander Buford. He furiously threw her out.

Finally, she had no choice but to leave her home and family forever. Terri Buford's odyssey was about to begin.

CHAPTER 6
DIVINITY

I have the answers to the problems of society.
Someday I will be the ruler of the United States.
I will eliminate racism, political oppression,
ecological imbalances, and the problem of the
super rich and the super poor. I will make the
whole country become like our community.
I call this... Apostolic Socialism.
Jim Jones

In her painful confusion, just before her graduation from Penn State University, young college senior, Terri Buford, dropped out and escaped across the country in a camper with Ben, her newest beau, to join forces with the rebellious spirits during the tempestuous early 1970's.

There was no way home now, knowing her intractable father would never forgive the perceived disloyalty to his family. Beautiful California looked like a promised land until her young beau, Ben, promptly kicked her out into the *Haight Asbury* night, cruelly explaining that he was only with her for sex and now he wanted his freedom.

She became a lost street child, being handed drugs and used for quick sex in the name of *revolution* and *flower power*. The *Haight* was home to a weird assortment of degenerates such as the infamous Charles Manson gang. Terri's pride prevented her from ever calling back home.

Weary of searching, she ran from the pressure cooker of the big city and decided to hitchhike to pastoral, northern California for a new start. A young driver picked her up for a lift that was to prove providential. His name was Mike Prokes and he worked himself up from reporter for station KXTV-TV in Sacramento to assume the position of Stockton Bureau Chief.

He had graduated from the University of California at Fullerton with a degree in Communications. Prokes was headed for Ukiah, a small town in Northern California near Redwood Valley, on an interesting assignment to investigate a handsome new faith healer named Jim Jones.

His pretty passenger, Terri Buford, was particularly interested in this story. Prokes began telling her about the group known as Peoples Temple. He said it was an integrated group of working people who supported the same general political beliefs that she seemed to hold.

Mike and Terri checked into a motel for the evening and got high on a variety of drugs. Terri was accustomed to being used by many men for impersonal sex by this time.

A letter found in the rubble of Jonestown describes Terri's feelings at that time regarding her experiences with men before she joined the Temple:

"Every male face I see reminds me of the culture I came out of, eating out their asses, swallowing their piss and sperm, getting my ass ripped open, beat up, getting police called for prostitution etc. This wouldn't bother a good socialist but it's a nightmare to me." (1)

Terri felt abused both as an adult and during her childhood and was very interested in Jim Jones' generosity in adopting and caring for so many lost children.

She understood that it was less of a church than a political organization. In 1966, Jones had become chairman of the Mendocino County grand jury by judicial appointment. In this era when people were searching for new leaders, especially religious ones cast in a Martin Luther King mold, this seemed to be an exciting road upon to embark.

The church impressed Terri Buford and Mike Prokes as they eagerly joined its ranks. By October, 1972, Michael Prokes joined the Peoples Temple to become its chief media spokesperson. He resigned his financially secure television position even though the Temple paid no salary.

However, Prokes realized that joining up with Jones, he would never have to worry about where his next dollar was coming from. He never would have quit his lucrative position at C.B.S. unless he saw a great money making potential in becoming Jones aide and manipulating the media.

"War mongering America must be destroyed," Jones preached, as he substituted his new order of socialism and equality for the world's survival. Jones' alleged, apparent love for black people came from his mother. Jones' mother, Lynetta had attended college and was interested in anthropology. She specialized in the study of African tribes. In her twenties, she went to Africa to live with natives. There she worked in the field of animal behavior, observing monkeys and other animals in their native habitat.

In Africa, she had a dream, a vision, that she would have a son who would right the inequalities of the world and unite black and whites together. He would be important and famous. Soon after her dream, she returned to America and married James T. Jones.

James Jones, Sr., was gassed with poison chemicals in World War One. As a result, he hated war as well as the country of his birth which sent him to Germany. In his hometown, which warmly welcomed the Ku Klux Klan, James Jones became an active member.

This marriage of opposites, James and Lynetta Jones, was a disaster. Like his father, their offspring, Jim Jones, grew to hate America. Jim displayed an interest in blacks. He falsely claimed mixed parentage of black and Indian blood and at times he exhibited his mother's love for blacks to gain their trust. Jim Jones reminded Terri of her own father with his superior attitude towards people of different backgrounds. She addressed her letters to Jones as, *Dear Dad.*

Upon observing Jones perform, Terri imagined her political mentor, William Jennings Bryan, with his superb oratory skills, jet-black raven hair, sharp, flashing eyes, combined with his entire political/religious philosophy. Jones seemed to be a reincarnation of this secret inner flame. She was greatly attracted to this new, wonderful hero. This was an opportunity to further develop Bryan's old platform along with his visionary religious/political ideals.

Jones stated that he was in favor of feminist rights. He claimed to be a pacifist, against alcohol and for the common man. Bryan's strong animus stirred like a magnet within her breast. Through Jones, Bryan's long silenced voice cried out to enthrall her.

But unlike Bryan, Jones only posed as a true religious believer, while having no faith in God whatsoever. Jones was fiendishly clever, a total atheist using the powers of religious beliefs to promote his own political concerns and eventually to control people's lives. Jones' soulless atheism was more chillingly sincere to Terri than any real religious belief might have been. She had no more religion than a bird.

Jones had learned the tricks of psychic healing developed by Margaretta Fox Kane. During the William Jennings Bryan era, she was the most popular psychic of the day. When Margaretta was a child, in 1848, her parents heard loud rappings coming from her room. Soon their house was filled with curious people who were convinced that their deceased relatives were speaking through Margaretta.

By the early 1850's more than a million people had accepted the strange knocking as proof of her supernatural ability. They had wanted so much to believe in the teenage girl's power even if on blind faith. Margaretta is considered to be a founder of modern spiritualism. But in 1888 poor Margaretta's conscience could no longer stand to hide her secret trick.

Margaretta held a large press conference and admitted that she had a big toe that was unusually double-jointed and, at will, she could make it bend, creating loud clicks. She and her sister Katie had decided to play a joke on their mother. The teenage sisters had no idea that the joke could ever go so far.

Before he embarked on his long and successful career in the clergy, psychic Reverend Jones had once been a successful monkey salesman in Indiana. Even when he became a minister, he sold monkeys door to door to raise money for his ministry.

It is not easy to sell monkeys to poor people, but Jones was very successful. Beneath his new display of holiness, beat that same expert huckster's soul. He claimed no one could refuse to buy a monkey from him.

Jones had obtained his monkeys from the laboratories of companies hired to do experiments on them. He continued to experiment, train and control these doomed for death primates through his own style of behavior modification.

He and Mr. Muggs, his favorite pet monkey, had moved from Indiana with their entire flock. Like his mother, Jones surrounded himself with pets to experiment upon. He loved to train monkeys. Mugg's nickname had evolved from the venerable J. Fred Muggs, the chimp that made his name on Dave Garroway's *Today* show. Jones used Muggsy to make people feel at ease so he could gain their trust.

During a time when people felt they were on the eve of destruction through nuclear war, Jones frightened his flock by telling them that he had seen a vision of a big flash of light in the Chicago area. Prone to painting colorful imaginings, Reverend Jones described this insight as proof that Indianapolis was going to be destroyed by nuclear holocaust.

To his religious congregation, this picture of an approaching apocalypse summoned up horrifying images. Throughout the ages, men have been panicked by the notion of impending doom and felt an need to do something immediate to alleviate that fear. A planned society that put power into the hands of an elite few eased the panic for some of the congregation.

By *preying* upon these terrors, Jones then easily convinced his followers to immediately abandon their homes in Indiana since had read in many magazines that northern California was a nuclear free zone and a safer area.

In 1825, another Hoosier, Robert Owen, who was originally born in England, had attempted to set up a model socialist community at New Harmony, Indiana. Jones intended to improve upon Owen's model.

He used the psychological *carrot* and *stick* approach to get his membership to follow him all the way across the country. His behavior modification technique used terror as a primary force to control the flock.

The effective use of terror is usually dependent on the use of violent weapons. The more horrible the threatening force, the better the control. Jones often employed threatened governmental hydrogen bomb usage to scare his congregation. Jones had even once predicted that nuclear warfare would begin on January 16, 1964 at 3:09 a.m. His false predictions were quickly forgotten by his congregation.

But their imprinted fears remained. Remembering the horrors of Hiroshima, Terri was deeply moved and easily manipulated by this fearful vision of nuclear doom. Her anger at her father transformed into a desire for revenge upon America.

Her savior's new home was to be the Redwood Valley of Northern California. The beauty of this area near the Russian River in California reminded Terri of her peaceful days in Indiana, Pennsylvania. She was fearful of the possibility that her father would find out where she was and pressure her to return home. She felt safe under Jones' wing.

In quiet northern California, the Temple quickly gained political steam. By 1967, less than two years after his arrival, Jones had been appointed foreman of the Mendocino County Grand Jury. Then he became the director of the Mendocino and Lay Counties legal services foundation.

Jones' wife, Marceline, became a state nursing home inspector. Old people were to be included in the master plan. Tim Stoen, a Temple member, was promoted to the rank of assistant pastor. Stoen was also the county district attorney, thus, all criminal prosecution was controlled by Jones! The Temple was above the laws of the county. Temple members in Ukiah accounted for 16 percent of the voting turnout as well.

By 1972, a weekend take at the small church usually totalled in excess of $15,000. All of the patients within the Mendocino State Mental Hospital were released into Jones' care since he offered drug and psychological treatment programs. Jones accepted all the payments that the state would pay and promptly built a fence with guard dogs to ensure privacy for his victims. However, there were not enough people in Mendocino to please Jones' greed.

Quickly, the Temple outgrew its northern California base and moved its ruling staff to San Francisco. A church was founded in San Francisco in 1971 as original motivations of nuclear safety were forgotten. No one even questioned the move to an area known for severe earthquakes. Along with the new converts, the Indiana faithful were transplanted once again, more dependent upon Jones than ever.

The central base of the expanded Peoples Temple was an old Jewish synagogue on Geary Street, in the center of the Fillmore section of San Francisco. All the Temple's bases back in Indiana had also been converted Jewish synagogues. He kept the Jewish symbol of the eternal flame lit in place of the traditional Christian cross. The Jewish Star of David and Menorah were still part of the building's structure; however, the former Jewish Temple was now transformed into the new, interracial, Peoples Temple.

The impoverished, surrounding area was now primarily Black, Mexican and poor white hippies. The hippies disdained money and jobs, often living out of sleeping bags with few possessions. The Temple was strategically located near the Fillmore West Theatre, their most popular haven for acid rock music. Alcohol and drugs like pot, L.S.D. and speed freely flowed. Huge, drug infested crowds gathered nightly to hear the music of groups such as Jefferson Airplane and Jimi Hendrix.

Next door, within their new Temple preached slick *Father* Jim, the people's new voice. Jones didn't speak in Latin or use expensive vocabulary that his congregation didn't understand. He spoke in plain, everyday English and sprinkled his sermons with street lingo and ghetto expressions that swept his audience into his clutches.

By offering them all free food, gospel music and kind understanding, many of them were vacuumed into the flock to kick their drug habits and accept his religion as a substitute. They were grateful to their generous savior for restoring their self esteem.

The word was out that a touch from Jim's fingertips was all that was needed for their cure. The gospel choir cried out for Jim to lay his healing hands on each one of them.

When those lonely, tired, poor men and women wandered into the Temple, they were welcomed by Jones' handsome disciples with open arms to draw them in and keep them returning. Jones specifically *called out* drug and alcohol addicts to come forward. These lost souls were tired of the mainstream church's usual hard pews and boring hymns.

They looked for a strong, committed leader, who was truly concerned with their needs. At the bottom rung of the economic scale, this emotionally rootless group was highly susceptible to the raging winds of fortune. Their need denied any possibility of perceiving that Jones' cause was merely a hook for their eventual control.

The promise of a close community, a meaningful life, spiritual salvation and a better world drew the best and the brightest of these vagrants into Jones' arms and his religious recruiters. The most bloodthirsty of all beasts can be a new faith.

To operate, Jones needed young, attractive disciples. Terri and Mike fit right in. These new missionaries were instructed to look clean-cut, wholesome and trustworthy. Their clothes were ordered from mainstream American clothes catalogues, like L.L. Bean, to project a respectable image.

With their assistance, Jones became more powerful. Buford quickly understood and related to the disguised psuedo-religious front and decided to join the group. By doing so, she resolved deep personal conflicts.

Her mother and father, representative of two opposing strains in her family's history, were finally philosophically united through the love of Jim Jones. She felt peaceful for the first time in her life.

Deciding to hitch her wagon to Jones' star, she fully realized that the leaders espoused socialism, as she did, and that the tax exempt status afforded to a church made it a lot easier for them to operate.

She was intrigued with this idea of a socialist organization functioning through the guise of an evangelistic type of church. Protected by the First Amendment, even the U.S. Government could not easily interfere. Here was a cosmic change to get even for all the wrongs of her life.

Jones' hybrid philosophy had followed Bryan's vision. She realized early that Jones was selling what people wanted, packaged with a powerful lie and that they would have no power to refuse due to their religious beliefs.

Furthermore, their church permitted diversion of some of the federal governments war expenditures. By not paying taxes there would be less for Uncle Sam to spend on weapons. Besides, most people might not contribute much to a political movement, but religious people are more easily parted from their money and Jones was glad to *liberate* his people from their life savings.

An accomplished illusionist, Jones studied magic tricks. His skills were ideally suited for the business of faithhealing. He developed terrific schemes to accomplish his goals.

Discovering that phony healings with selected accomplices easily tricked gullible suckers and quickly separated them from their money, he gave people *the business*. The vast multitudes that began to follow Jones were nearly all, on some level, people in crises.

Jones learned his subtle religious craft from other fellow phony preacher/ healers such as Daddy Grace and Father Divine, otherwise known as plain old George Baker. Baker was an ex-con, convicted for fraud.

According to author, Robert Weisbrot (2), posing as a religious leader, Baker combined faith healings with the right words and phrases in order to swell his own bankbook. His devoted flock believed every sacred word he told them as if their very souls depended upon it.

Healing cards were passed out to gain private information of those seeking healing. Small index cards were secretly prepared to give Jones secret data. Terri, an expert in sign language, stood in the auditorium and used special hand and body signals to communicate with Jones at the podium. Eavesdropping on conversations in the audience was a cinch.

Jones appeared omnipotent. The infirm were told that every doubt directed toward the healing Powers of Christ and especially of his agent, Jim Jones, would prevent effective treatment by their inner physician. Dr. Jones was practicing medicine without a license.

To succeed, his patients had to totally submit. For Jim Jones as well as Father Divine, women formed between seventy five and ninety percent of all members, an imbalance common among both white and black disciples. Weisbrot suggests that, in his opinion, the feeling of inferiority manifested by women in society was a contributing cause of their prominent numbers within unconventional cults.

The relationship between these women and their doctor, Jones, followed another pattern set by Father Divine. Their surrender was a total one, both soul, and body. A few of these women, black as well as white, appeared to experience sexual ecstasy and even orgasm during the healings.

Jim Jones started to attract a spellbound following with his theatrics. The women followers fell madly in love with their savior.

Eventually, however, these women's minds, bodies, and very souls would merely service the insatiable pleasure of this one, deified man. Ultimately, the avant-guard recklessness, bisexual orgies, and sexual fireworks that finally ensued, weren't necessarily going to lead any of them to their enlightenment, only into darkness. The price of membership was far more than money.

Jones, a truly great orator, deduced that psychological phrases and razzmatazz images could work better than reality. His religious people were very susceptible to his magic act, since their trusting eyes searched for God and their hearts were more open than doubting nonbelievers. Trust is the con artists greatest ally.

Jones believed that religious people make the best followers because they were the most easily conditioned to devotion, self sacrifice and discipline. His goal was money, fame and power. If anyone doubted him, they were warned that their doubt was the voice of Satan. Who would dare to investigate a preacher, the perfect cover for a con man?

Jones also emulated Father Divine, in especially targeting the black churches, even though Divine was black, himself. He stole many of Father Divine's members, among them two women named Truth Hart and Mary Love. Jones' white missionaries set a tone of trusting, caring love to lead their poor, black victims into their clutches. The real object, money, was always the same color. That was what really counted, as Jones converted their faith into his own prosperity.

Since, according to Reiterman, Jones' own father was suspected of being a loyal Klansman, Jones readily agreed with the theory that the black race was more susceptible to religious oratory. Posing as the white savior of blacks and comparing himself to Martin Luther King, he drew them in by performing his sensational magic shows...in God's name.

Reiterman also describes how Jones would steal black converts directly from the black churches. For instance, at one black service in the Macedonia church, Jones went into a healing performance, using one of Reverend Bedford's own members as his subject.

When the member emerged from the restroom, Terri Buford, dressed as a nurse, displayed a red blob supposedly passed from the rectum. It was actually a chicken gizzard drenched in the animal's blood, one of Jones' many tricks. The victim was told that a cancer had passed out of their body and that Jones healed them of the illness. Pastor Bedford's congregation watched in shock, convinced that Jones had performed a miracle.

On other occasions, a nurse would put a finger down the mouth of the victim who would vomit up the cancer in public.

Reiterman estimates that almost two hundred of Bedford's black congregation eagerly joined the Peoples Temple for life and eventually death.

The black ministers could not protect their flock without seeming jealous of this white preacher. They would certainly appear to sound racist and petty themselves, therefore they had no choice but to keep their hostility to themselves.

Who would listen to their bitter complaints? There is no organized legal body that investigates phony faithhealers. Even Congress is powerless due to the restrictions of the First Amendment. With his religious education, Jones had a knowledge of good as well as evil. He mingled the precious with the vile, and this is what gave him power to deceive.

Reiterman mentions that Jones also cultivated alliances with many black church leaders, in particular, Archie Ijames. Jones made him feel especially needed and invited Ijames's two oldest daughters to join. Their presence served as a positive reminder that Jim Jones' was a friend to the black race. Ijames served as an associate pastor to Jones' flock.

Jones' collaborators each had his own personal agenda. For Buford, this was the opportunity to mold this *Church* into a quasi-political, anti-U.S. organization that eventually would have a destructive effect on the country for many years.

Jones personally instructed Buford to coordinate a revolution against

America through his movement. He sensed a larger following and more profit with this new political orientation. Terri was dazzled with his utterly pragmatic approach, as he admitted to desiring power.

Jesus had increased his followers by using his powers of healing the infirm. To add new followers to his Temple, Jones utilized his most successful weapon, staged faith healings. To accomplish this, Jones' loyal disciples acted as what he termed, *Heavenly Deceptors*. Terri Buford was granted the opportunity to become one.

Jones' proposal was tantalizing. It wasn't only the money; it was the devilishly exciting *game*. Teresa was on the inside of one of the biggest scams of all time. A moment of truth had arrived. The key choice of her life hung precariously in the balance.

She consented to become one of the angelic *Deceptors* in Jim Jones' church. Her joy was inexpressible. Everything that had transpired before this momentous act pushed her toward that decision. She was to prove such an enticing recruiter that men found it difficult to resist joining the cult.

As accomplices during the phony faith healings, the deceptors put on disguises and pretended to be elderly, ill, black and/or crippled to demonstrate that Jim Jones had the power of God to heal them. Through their clever use of makeup, these mostly young, white women would be magically transformed into elderly black women. Complete disregard for their fellow human beings was essential for success.

A Church promotional film (3) shows Buford at one of these faith healings. In the huge crowd she sat next to an old crippled woman who was Linda Dunn, a friend of Terri's, as well as another heavenly deceptor. Dunn, only 22 years old, was disguised in a grey wig and theatrical makeup. Jones had paid theater makeup experts on his payroll.

A very nervous Linda Dunn's disguise was composed of old Salvation Army clothing, a wig, cheap shoes, napkins in her cheeks, and powdered makeup to make her young skin appear to be wrinkled. She spoke with a quiver in her voice. Jones paid her well.

Jim Jones put on a great show. His kindly voice soothed her troubled soul.

He pleaded with her to try and get up and walk. She strained with her broken legs with all her might and appeared to use her *elderly* arms for leverage. She gritted her teeth as the audience pleaded with her to try and walk.

Then, Dunn slowly stood up. It seemed to be a miracle, certainly appearing that this poor, sick old lady walked fort he first time in many years. Captured on promotional film, desperately ill people all over the nation believed that Jones was blessed with a great power. They flocked to California seeking help.

The audience was caught up in the pretense. They tacitly participated in the hypnotic ritual by remaining and enjoying the full spectacle. If they condemned the preacher's sincerity, they condemned themselves. By defending him, they ultimately defended their own behavior. Any doubt was unthinkable sacrilege.

Even if a miracle failed, it was perceived as the members lack of total faith and submission. To increase their submission became their holy duty. Furthermore, on that particular day, the Holy Spirit might be drained of its power.

One successful faith healing could wreak havoc upon more people than an arsenal of machine guns. In this electrifying drama, among the throng next to the *old*, crippled woman, Buford is clearly seen on Dunn's right side. Jones heals the woman and the camera stays on Buford, as she pretends ecstasy over Jones amazing *heavenly power*. This was a clear message to her family. The videotape mortified Terri Buford's family. Her father gave her up for dead. Her mother disowned her.

After the healing service, the disciples quickly changed their outfits to pose as nurses and doctors to verify the authenticity of the cure. With so many people participating in the lie, the audience's minds were seized with amazement.

Dunn and Buford laughed at the gullible masses and were overjoyed at the full coffers as thousands of dollars rolled into their hands. No one was healed that night, but people were cruelly hoaxed and paid dearly. Some merely wheeled out in agony because Jones' cure was too expensive. The others that bought the miracle cure paid a high price for nothing.

When the adopted son of Jim Jones, Steven Jones, and his friends eventually saw the footage of Terri Buford acting enraptured and nearly fainting over the supposed miracles, they laughed uproariously. They all knew exactly what was going on behind the scenes.

Reiterman mentions specifically that Mark Lane eventually was shown the videotape of the *show* when he first took the job as Jones' attorney. He was well aware of these deceptive tactics and approved. He enjoyed the entertainment while keeping these despicable methods top secret.

It rained a flood of money after the Jim Jones' fake healing service. Only by surrendering all their ethics could these Jonestown deceptors lure poor, mostly black victims to this *church* and strip them entirely of their meager possessions.

Terrible acts of cruelty to members were compensated for by loving gestures, personal acts, that on a small scale, like a gift of a cake, or a get well card, show care to someone afflicted with an illness. However, merely taking the possessions of these relatively poor subjects was not the final goal. Capturing their souls was the *end* for those *means*.

Teaming up with Jones, Terri agreed to try and create a new political state based upon Jones' *religion*, which simply declared that he was GOD.

Reiterman portrays Jones crying out to his flock that even after America had failed, he would still be standing. He screamed that he was freedom, peace, justice, and finally...GOD! The massive crowds went wild.

Reverend Jones, seemed actually to have the power to heal. He derived a shocking source of control as people submitted totally to his every order. People who are sick with a horrible cancer or a variety of other illnesses can be quite desperate. Jones simultaneously prayed and *preyed* upon them, his very favorites.

Jones' insatiable greed had to be concealed carefully into coded language. Behind the pious scenes, Teresa Buford, who had personal expertise in that field from her father, the expert code breaker, diligently invented a new vocabulary.

The code, *Mr. Hill* meant Jim Jones and *Mrs. Frazier* meant death. Robin Hood robbed from the rich and gave to the poor. Jones reversed the concept. *Socialism* was just another code that really meant that everyone in the flock would donate all their assets to Jones. He was otherwise known as...the *cause*. The Temple's take was called the *offerings*. *Suicide* would eventually mean...mass murder.

In their perfect crime, nothing could ever be proven. All correspondence letters written to politicians and other allies were also carefully coded as well. Jones kept records of that correspondence for future leverage.

Politicians were cruelly compromised by the deceptors as sex squads were sent out to ensnare politicians through sex and alternate forms of blackmail. Reporter Steve Stanek of CAN, the Cult Awareness Network (4), describes how Jones ordered two 15 year-old girls to perform oral sex together on a San Francisco politician. The two underage girls were foster children that Jones had adopted, trained, and controlled.

With that type of oral persuasion, Jones put those politicians into his back pocket. The minors were Jones' *Trojan' Horses*, infiltrating the political structure as sexual gifts bestowed for favors.

When they got to a new city, Reverend Jones' select inner core group deceptively called his angels, would then photograph or tape record people sexually. The pornographic pictures would be used to blackmail officials. According to Tim Stoen (5), Terri Buford headed this group.

Buford and Jones melded into quite a formidable duo. To enhance his attractiveness to female parishioners, Jones dyed his graying hair black for his sleek, raven Elvis image. He began to dress like the *Las Vegas* Elvis with the long capes and cool, dark sunglasses, hiding his lying eyes.

Like the *King* of rock and roll, he even claimed to have American/Indian blood running through his veins to enhance his status as a member of an oppressed minority. This, Jones later admitted, was a blatant lie.

Terri lightened her brown hair to play the sex goddess for potential male converts. Her innocent, pretty face belied her sharp manipulative mind. She graduated in 1976 with an 'A' average from the University of California at Berkeley.

Originally, Terri had studied Chemistry at Penn State, graduating with straight A's in that area. Jones planned to use her expertise in chemistry for his own purposes. Each person was to be examined as a formula. Combinations of induced drugs were given with the intention of control.

Jones' flock contained many former substance abusers. San Francisco's government officials, in their inability to help those unfortunates, began to recommend that they join the Temple to submit to Jones' religion as a substitute for their drug *fix.*

People who were dysfunctional for a variety of reasons try to compensate by trying to *fix* their distorted *reality.* Combinations of psychological profiles were juxtaposed to create clever interactive systems between victims for further domination.

Jones ordered Terri to change her major to journalism. She began to function as Prokes' primary press aide. The art of successful communication was studied very carefully. Whatever Jones ordained was immediately accomplished. Terri's razor sharp lips were now fully honed to create biased news bulletins for Jones' yearning masses.

Soon, she had a new job. Terri functioned as a newscaster for a small, local television station in Ukiah, slanting and manipulating the news into a pro-Jonestown point of view. On her show, Jones could do no wrong. Prokes had many solid connections in the media having been a powerful bureau chief. They proudly watched their own propaganda on T.V.

Reborn into his *church* she was now both elated and motivated with her new mission. Bending over backwards to please Jones, she fell head over heels in love. The fact that Jones was already married was not an issue since the holy *Reverend* was beyond any earthly reproach.

In becoming Jones' lover, she achieved another personal victory. She now proudly had the man everyone else wanted, the most desirable man in the country. Jones was the *dream father* she was searching for. She finally felt at peace within this new interracial rainbow family's bosom. Buford, who had been cut off from her entire biological family, had found a home at last.

He was forty and Terri was only twenty. Jones particularly attracted young runaways who shared an *Electra* complex. Old enough to be her father with his physically intimate and dominating manner, Jones infantalized her as well as most of his flock.

Jones knew that no one could ever be as loyal as daddy's little girls. Coming to him for food, shelter and money, he developed a parent's absolute control. Like children who learn from omnipresent parents, they gave him total loyalty. Unfortunately, children have no rights. They have no money, no status, and no place to run. Their dependency is both emotional and psychological as well as physical.

Children were forced to beg on the streets of San Francisco to raise money for the Temple. If they failed to meet the $100 a day quota, they often received severe beatings. Child abuse charges were filed against Jones and the Peoples Temple, but because of Jones' political connections, the charges were dropped. There is no other sanctioned relationship where one may strike others, prepare them for formal sadistic beatings, and deprive them of nourishment. Children can be mutilated and even beaten to death by sadistic parents. Jones developed that power. Loyalty to the cause meant loyalty to Jones as a *Father-God* for the servile rank and file party members. As to the Japanese Emperor, this absolute obedience must be great enough to require the ultimate sacrifice if necessary; death, itself.

Terri Buford totally submitted.

Now, serving Jim Jones and becoming his lover, she passionately bonded her philosophies together with his, blurring any differences and blending roles of father and lover. He was as ruthless and sadistic as Commander Buford but, in her opinion, Jones fought on the right side. She had yet to realize in her ultimate horror that she had met a more brutal sadist than her father could ever be; she was soon to become her own worst enemy.

Remembering her childhood, Terri related to the terrible beatings that Jones administered to his closest disciples, including the women, done in the name of God for their own sake. Furthermore, Jim and Terri's sexual unification created an intersection of the political, social, economic, historical, personal and experimental, linking together behavior and thought, fantasy and action.

Jones' ancestral conflict between mother and father mirrored Terri's. According to Tim Stoen, Terri was put in charge of the *Planning and Manipulation Section*, functioning as Jim Jones' lieutenant colonel in the same manner that her father once did for the American government during Vietnam.

The Planning Commission met twice a week and contained from 40-80 members. The exhausting meetings lasted all night. The Planning Commission

(PC) was the central branch of Jonestown's incestuous family tree. Tim Stoen was her superior in that office. Planning Commission membership also was a symbol of status and a measure of Buford's trustworthiness.

Driven by the triple demons of lust, greed and power, Jones would awake from his sleep with Terri at his side and, with insatiable energy, issue fanatical, fantastic orders for the flock to act upon. Their dreams would then shape reality. Thus, the inner unconscious mind motivated the entire operation.

Events were determined during sleep, created within dreams and transformed into reality, which quickly sped into the external manifestation of this tragic inner nightmare. A web spun out gradually from this distorted inner self that pathologically trapped others easily within its compelling grasp.

This giant extended family quickly turned into a dysfunctional nightmare as confusing, conflicting orders were constantly given and then contradicted. People were asked to perform savage, demeaning rituals and were punished severely for not carrying out impossible commands.

Terri followed like a sleepwalker in a trance.

Acting in the mirror opposite role of her father, instead of meeting with the Shah of Iran and other Pro-American dictators, Terri personally contacted all the most radical, anti-U.S. groups available, such as the Black Panthers through direct contact with Huey Newton via Charles Garry, the P.L.O., the S.L.A. (Symbionese Liberation Army, the group that kidnapped and raped Patty Hurst), Dennis Banks (The Indian rights leader who was wanted by the F.B.I.), Laura Allende (the daughter of the Chilean leader), Cesar Chavez (the farm union leader), and Angela Davis (the black communist leader).

Some of these people had genuine grievances with America. Opposing wrongs does not automatically guarantee that they were right in their beliefs. Included among the extended group were drug dealers and murderers. As long as anyone was against the United States, they had the support of the Peoples Temple. That was the only criteria.Revolutionaries were aided with a bit of small change and cheap rhetoric while they were used for their political value.

All the outcast groups of society began to trust the Peoples Temple due to their various associations and they began joining up in vast numbers. When the revolution came, Buford wanted to be a key operative in the new order, with input that would forever put war mongers like her father out of business.

Jones became a choreographer of emotionally laden faked attacks from imaginary enemies who, supposedly, were out to destroy the Temple. This tactic was to attract and indoctrinate new converts and raise new funds.

For further theatrical effects, he used the tactics of planting stooges in the audience during his sermons. Jones would yell at them; *Drop Dead* and they would fall down. Then he would raise the dead by yelling; *Arise*. As they got up, he appeared to have the very power over life...and death, an ultimate gift reserved only to God. Terri participated with glee, finally able to bring the dead soldiers her father had sent to Vietnam back to life, even in her fantasies.

But Jones' imagined power finally led to its ultimate synthesis: mass murder! For particular target groups, Jews and blacks, that were especially selected for slow eventual genocide, Buford, as the head of planning and manipulation, would devise staged clandestine attacks featuring the evil deeds of the Nazis and the Ku Klux Klan.

As the Nazis burned the Reichstag while falsely blaming the communists and Jews in order to gain support for their movement, Jones staged Klan attacks against the Blacks and Jews to gain the trust of both of these groups and convert them to his cause. These clandestine attacks in various disguises portrayed phony assaults from all sorts of imagined enemies. After the target groups joined the fold, their own assets were utilized for their eventual destruction. The Nazi's had utilized the same tactic, by cleverly appropriating the Jew's own finances to operate their concentration camps.

America, the Nazi's mortal enemy, was also Jones' main target. Heading the list was the C.I.A. Of course, to effectively fight against this invented threat, more and more money was needed. Where was that money to come from? Uncle Sam and its taxpayers.

CHAPTER 7
TAPESTRY

"What shall I say about him who borrows from me the money
to buy a sword with which to attack me."
Kahlil Gibran

To raise money, Jones began raiding the foster care agencies and taking the unwanted children into his church. He also deduced that the loyalty and love that parents have for children could be transformed into a most powerful weapon.

Jones was able to enrich himself with millions of dollars in welfare and Social Security payments. Sixty five thousand dollars in Social Security money rolled in every month. Jones encouraged Temple members to become foster parents and to hand over the bulk of state payments they received for support of their wards.

Members also were tricked into giving Jones legal control of their own children by signing agreements that placed many of the youngsters under the guardianship of Jones' most trusted followers.

He began to arrange foster care adoptions by the staff and members to insure their loyalty, as well as to gather as much money as the U.S. would generously provide in benefit payments.

Many staff members were placed in key positions in these government agencies to ensure their financial support. According to journalist, Thomas MacMillan (1), a former public servant from Ukiah, a list of Jonestown members included some workers from the Ukiah Department of Social Services, the Juvenile Hall, the Public Health Department, and the Offices of County Government. Basically, the entire local government was on Jones' payroll.

Jonestown guardians of the foster children eventually had total financial control of all of their assets and income. Temple attorney Eugene B. Chaiken, for whom Terri Buford worked as an aide, filed to adopt two black children, Georgiann Brady, 10, and her sister Michelle, 9, both of whom died at Jonestown.

These two children had an annual income of $2,844. The expenses were padded. Former Temple members describe the statement as fraudulent. Most of the food was free such as day old doughnuts and powdered milk. All the children's clothing came from Goodwill. Some of the children had trust funds that were taken by the Temple-some of them in six figures.

After Jones had possession of the children, the parents signed away their property as well. Once destitute, the parents were fully in his grasp. If people wouldn't sign over their deeds, Jones would have blank papers notarized in advance-and then sign them himself. Forty thousand dollars rolled in a month.

That's close to half million a year and this was only the smallest scam among dozens of others. Over ten years, it translated into more than five million dollars.

When any real parents of these foster children wanted them back, they had to ask *Father* Jones, even if it eventually meant going to Jonestown, Guyana, *one way*, to get them. After these people had been robbed of their houses, their life savings and their children, they eventually became the lost hostages of the Peoples Temple in order to be near their biological offspring.

Terri Buford joined in by adopting one of these foster children. As an abused child herself, Terri did not believe that the family unit functioned for the welfare of children. She felt that she could best protect her new charge. No one ever checked out whether or not she was a fit parent. It was simpler to adopt a child than to obtain pet monkeys from scientific laboratories since the workers in the state agencies who did the checking for adoptions were all under Jones' employ. Jones became known simply *as Father* to everyone.

Terri's new ward, was eventually kidnapped, illegally, in her opinion, by his own biological parents. If they hadn't taken that action, their child would have died in Jonestown along with the other, almost three hundred children, that were eventually murdered.

Undaunted, with Jones' help, Terri adopted yet another little boy, Newhuanda Darnes, renamed Dietrick Walker. The children were all renamed to destroy their identity and make it easier for them to be remolded. Unfortunately, Dietrick's real parents never came back for him and he was sadly left to perish in Jonestown, while his foster mother, Terri Buford, fled for her own life.

Actually, it was not unfortunate for Dietrick's parents that they didn't fly to Guyana to try and rescue their boy. They would have perished there as well, trapped there along with their son. That tragic fate eventually did befall many biological parents of the Jonestown hostage children who would all be listed as suicide victims after the murders.

By planting his own members within the agencies that made the fitness decisions Jones had total control of the legal documents. The real parents were always deemed unfit when they came for their offspring no matter how fit they were. There was not one child freed by Jones once he had them in his grasp. Jones knew that love for children is one of the most powerful emotional bonds that people possess. To control children guaranteed power over their parents. Families were forced to go to Guyana in order to remain together in the hope that someday, someone would rescue them.

Children within cults exist for the good of the group, not the good of the child. With religious protection, these children's rights to eat properly and not be tortured were superseded by the Constitution which guaranteed Jones' protection under the freedom of religion clause.

Jones' religious classification deflected any serious investigations, especially since the Constitution is quite vague about explaining exactly what a religion is. In their zeal to protect religion, the founding fathers had neglected to imagine the specter of Jim Jones.

People generally have a need to join something greater than themselves. In the age of the nuclear family, the individual often feels isolated, alone. Many others felt the same urge as Terri Buford in joining this new family. Jones held on to his flock tightly since they were bringing him a fortune.

To further increase the membership, obituary columns were scanned daily and aggressive Temple agents were quickly dispatched to attend to the grieving mourners. By checking information in the relatives homes while they attended their loved one's funeral, they gathered information for future reference. When any of the deceased friends and relatives attended a faith healing, that information was used to draw them into a new family.

Enriched by new converts, Jones claimed to his congregation that he was aiding the avowed enemies of America, but it is doubtful that a large part of the money ever got into their hands. Jones' pitch was mostly for its propaganda value to draw more unhappy members of society into the Temple's clutches.

Buford actually gave small donations to Huey Newton (five thousand) of the Panthers and Dennis Banks for the Indian movement, but the paltry sums were just for a show of conscience to justify the bulging collection plates. Loans to creditors went unpaid since Gods, like Jones, were beyond their earthly claims.

Jones was lavished with praise for his concern for the unwanted, especially the black children he was *helping*. Reiterman even cites a commendation from President Carter's wife who met with Jones and wrote him a personal letter. She stated that she enjoyed being with him during her husband's campaign. She had hopes that Carter's suggestions could be acted upon in the near future.

Jimmy Carter didn't realize that Jones supported both candidates in every election. Jones couldn't lose. A new *American Hero* had catapulted into the center of the political arena.

CHAPTER 8

EXODUS

The Lust for power, for dominating others, inflames
the heart more than any other passion.
Tacitus

The whole plot fell under media scrutiny. Finally, reporters like Les Kinsolving and Tim Reiterman were asking pertinent questions. Reiterman interviewed Jones on February 22, 1978, asking some key questions. (Jonestown Files, California Historical Society) Jones had to leave town quickly to keep the scam going. He decided to move to Guyana, a nation eager to develop its poverty stricken interior.

Jones stated, enigmatically, to his aide, happily married Al Mills, that if they went to Guyana, any man can have two wives. Eventually, Jones had an entire town of wives to entertain him. The harem women of Jonestown were trained to please Jim Jones. The faith healing technique of the laying of hands were applied for Jones' sexual pleasures.

He dispatched Terri Buford on a key mission accompanied by three other Temple deceptors as bait for his many hooks. Their mission was to sexually subvert the upper members of the communist government of Guyana, a nation predominately composed of poor blacks, led by Prime Minister Forbes Burnham.

Terri, with her bleached blond hair, was able to subdue the politicians especially since fair-haired white women were considered to be rare objects of desire in Guyanese culture. She checked into the centrally located Pegasus Hotel and prowled the top nightclubs in search of political prey. With a team of women that included Paula Neustel, she made the contacts necessary to pave the way for the exodus from San Francisco to Guyana.

Five years after Jones' final sunset, intriguing facts began to surface. Journalists Nancy Lewis and Joanne Ostrow(1) state in an article published in the *Washington Post* that a woman named Paula Neustel admitted having a long-standing affair with the Guyanese ambassador to the U.S., diplomat Lawrence *Bonny* Mann. Neustel said in a December 5, 1978 interview that she was aware that Jones had said she had been assigned to seduce the Guyanese official.

Jones was granted 27,000 acres of inland Guyanese jungle territory. Now Jones had his own unrestricted and unmonitored empire. There were no inspectors of buildings, health, or even police to worry about. His Georgetown, Guyana, based headquarters was a veritable private diplomatic embassy. Jones was seriously considering opening his own diplomatic mission in Washington.

Jones had his own army, navy and merchant marine. He had his own carefully censored newspaper and his own broadcasting operation. And while Jonestown had no chapel, or bible classes, they were allowed membership in the Guyana Council of Churches.

Finally in Guyana, Jones could drop his pretense of being a pious religious believer. In his transition, he openly declared himself against religion, cursing God and stomping angrily upon the Bible.

Brindley Benn, leader of an opposition group in Guyana, began to demand an official investigation of Jonestown after U.S. press reports cast suspicion on Jones and his practices. Benn said that Jones had the Guyanese government in his pocket. Benn expressed fear that Jonestown was becoming a state within a state.

Among the charges made by Burnham's opponents was that the Temple seemed exempt from many Guyanese laws, particularly those governing the payment of import and export duties and the regulation of firearms. No one in America ever even questioned why the *Church* needed weapons.

Guyanese fears would prove to be justified. Jeannie Mills, a former member of Jim Jones' inner circle, revealed Jones' true motive for his move to Guyana describing a staff meeting when she was in Jonestown. According to her testimony, Jim Jones said that if he could ever get the members over to Guyana, he would always be able to keep them in line.

Jones told her that while they were in the States the members could always protest and leave, but when they're in the jungle there wasn't any place for them to go. No one would even be able to complain in Guyana.

Mills believed that Jones was planning to take his people to a concentration camp, where he would have full authority over them without ever having to worry about any possible legal repercussions or U.S. Government interference.

The Mills figured right. They ran away from Jones as fast as they could even though they realized their lives were in danger. They opened up an awareness center in California for others who wanted to escape from the trap Jones had set. They spoke the truth at the risk of death while most other staff members profited greatly from participation in the scheme.

Al and Jeannie Mills were murdered.

Lewis and Ostrow reported another murder victim, Paula Neustel, Jones' liaison to and secret lover of the Guyanese ambassador, Lawrence Everil Mann. She had survived the bloodbath and had changed her name while in Guyana to Paula Adams. In 1983, she was shot to death with Mann and her infant son. Neustel (Adams) was one of Jones' most trusted aides.

According to Yee, Debby Blakey stated that when she arrived in Guyana it was Paula (Neustel) Adams who was in charge of confiscating the passports. Debby's passport was locked in the Lahaina Gardens strongbox.

Coincidently, Neustel's alias, Paula Adams, was utilized by Herman Ferguson, otherwise known as Paul Adams, for his work within the government of Guyana. Reporter Peter Blauner (2) states that the former American, Paul

Adams (Ferguson) began working for Guyana under Prime Minister Burnham.

Paul Adams (Ferguson) spent his first few years in Guyana trying to develop the interior region. Through the seventies, Ferguson continued his rapid rise in the Guyanese government. Ferguson was a fugitive from the United States involved in some of the most explosive episodes of the sixties including the Ocean Hill-Brownsville crisis, Malcolm X's assassination, and the black-separatist movement, according to Blauner.

Even though Ferguson returned to the U.S. to face trial, any hidden connection between Paul (Ferguson) and Paula (Neustel) Adams has yet to be investigated in connection with the Jonestown deals they devised.

Due to their work carried out in the bedrooms of the Pegasus Hotel in Georgetown, the faithful flock followed their modern day *Wizard of Oz*. In his domain, Jones achieved total control over all, demanding absolute fidelity.

The mind-raped women had to share each other in sex orgies with him. Every attractive woman was turned into a bisexual object for Jones' perverted desires. Jones especially liked young, tall, slim blondes for his pleasure.

In all, the masses that left America to finally live in Guyana included 296 foster children along with another 700 adults, a full assortment of society's misfits, including prostitutes, drug addicts, many debilitated elderly, the emotionally disturbed and the physically handicapped.

From the airport at Georgetown, the capital of Guyana, they were transported by buses to the port in order to board the *Cudjoe*, also known as *The Albatross*, the rickety, Temple trawler manned by Captain Blakey. Terri Buford states that the trip to Port Kaituma was so stormy and brutal that she thought she'd never arrive. The boat pitched for 11 hours and nearly capsized in the stormy waters until it finally reached its destination.

The unfortunates that walked off the Cudjoe's plank onto a dump truck for a two hour ride into the jungle could now be easily molded by the Jones overseers into total submission. The majority of the members were black while the leaders were all white. The San Francisco city government's agencies picked up the tab.

It has been estimated by Joe Klein (3) that the Peoples Temple was receiving an average of $250,000 per month into P.O. Box 893, Georgetown, Guyana, from its various sources of income. Much of it was funneled into secret bank accounts overseas. Jones built a financial empire through welfare fraud and federal assistance, ironically, all of which enhanced his humanitarian reputation.

In San Francisco estimates were made that the Temple's assets were to the tune of hundreds of millions of dollars. The cradle of Guyanese' communism now rocked to a new beat played by a modern Pied Piper. Jones had a new ambition. Here was an entire country laid before him. Why should he not be king? No one questioned Jim Jones, after all, he was a man of *God.*

PART THREE

THE LAST STAND

CHAPTER 9

OBLIVION

Fly with me then to all's and the world's end...
Blind Satan's voice rattled the whole of Hell.
William Empson

In the brutal hell of Jonestown the commanders stopped at nothing, using murder, kidnapping, torture, rape, and drugs to dominate their flock. The children and elderly in this village of the damned were kept awake and forced to work 16 hours every day.

To further ensure the loyalty of the followers, Jones and Buford studied Freud's essays, particularly those on sexuality, and applied those ideas to control people. Freud felt that being in love is a form of hypnosis and that the self-love that a person possesses can cleverly be transferred from the person's own ego to the sexual object. According to Freud, through sexual repetition, one can actually gain possession over another and eventually hypnotize and manipulate them.

Jones especially preyed upon submissive women and homosexuals, groups he secretly abhorred. Gays are often scapegoats of mainstream society. They are forced to play roles and publicly limit their tendencies. Often they become rebellious against a society which seems to be their enemy. Jones preyed upon their weaknesses by feigning sympathy.

All sex, hetero/homosexual, was limited to and controlled by Jones and his partners, assuring control. The chained members' desperation became his aphrodisiac. If a member was ill, Jones convinced them that sex with him would cure their ailment. People were made to believe that his sex organ was a holy instrument. In their desperation, people lost all their discriminatory powers and submitted blindly. He then broke their spirits by making them perform perverted acts. In some cases, their belief in him actually made them temporarily feel better, especially if their original problems were psychosomatic to begin with.

Furthermore, steroid hormones normally released during sexual activity, combined with the elevated positive outlook of new hope, helped his victim feel better...temporarily -- as Jones put them on his own brand of sexual drugs.

Then Jones would brag about his magic sexual powers to the entire group. No one seemed to resist the forceful process and speak out, as more and more victims fell under his total dominion.

The Temple did not believe in the traditional family unit. Their goal was to smash it. This idea springs from an intensive study modeled upon Aldous Huxley's *Brave New World*. Within its futuristic visions of behavioral conditioning are fertilizing rooms with their directors of sperm bank hatcheries.

Their design was to produce scientifically developed humans who would be in the total control of their leader. Jones took Huxley's ideas seriously, studying his plans like an architect would a blueprint.

Furthermore, another of Jones' heroes, Karl Marx, had called for the total abolition of the family. He stated that the bourgeois family will vanish as a matter of course with the vanishing of capital.

Since Karl Marx had died before his philosophical theory was ever fully completed, the further application of the manner in which the bourgeois family unit was eventually to be destroyed was completely open, first to Stalin's imagination and then, for its penultimate perfection, to Jim Jones' mad interpretations. Without any parents to protect them, the entire minor population within Father Jones' grasp were put into grave jeopardy. Quickly, entire families were viciously shattered.

Jones realized the power of sex in destroying stable family relationships. Jones had his secretary arrange trysts for him with both men and women. When asked why he had sex in this way, Jones reportedly answered that he had to since sex focused all the member's interest on him. He boasted that he could engage in sex for up to six hours at a time. He stated that sex with him totally obliterated the personality of his followers. Jones ordered many of his followers to commit homosexual acts because they were then easier to manipulate or blackmail.

Jones would arrange peepholes to photograph sex scenes to control his consorts. He especially enjoyed threesomes with two woman to entertain him, especially daughters of ordained ministers, like eighteen year old Maria Katsaris, as well as Carolyn Layton, who became Jones' favorite victims.

After young Carolyn and Maria were totally compromised there was no turning back. Lost, they believed that their pious families would never accept, nor understand their behavior. According to Guyana court reports based upon their medical investigator's reports, these two women, Katsaris and Layton, were the only two actual suicides of Jonestown.

By utilizing compromising sex pictures, Jones would manipulate loving couples into hating each other such as: former lovers Mike Prokes and Terri Buford; Tim Stoen and his beloved wife, Grace; as well as Larry Layton and his wife, Caroline. These couples were all turned into adversaries, their solidarity with one another broken by their own weaknesses and temptations. These terrible jealousies exploded into hatred and distrust, eventually leading the broken hearted victims directly to Jones' waiting web.

Usually, a new member was courted by one of the inner circle in a sexual relationship.   It wasn't that Jones and Buford were so physically attractive. The game that was played was one in which the highest victory is to be loved or desired while feeling nothing oneself. Bursting with plans and stratagems, inexhaustibly productive of lies, feints, and impostures, these experts were energetic scoundrels who possessed skills almost military and diplomatic in scale.

These strategists also had an ability to astutely predict human behavior and maneuver the conquest of their victim. Once resistance was overcome, the subjects were turned into sexual masochists.

Freud explains how sexual masochism can create a passive attitude in the sexual object. In its most extreme form their gratification is connected with the suffering of great physical or mental pain at the hands of the sexual object, driving these victims to their knees. Diplomats and politicians were especially compromised by using crafty techniques of sexual subversion. Besides sexual methods of control, other primary drives were utilized.

Hunger, itself, was a force that brought many poor people into the fold through the kitchen where the smell of Terri's freshly baked banana and carrot cakes filled the room. In the spirit of generosity, anyone that was hungry was given a free feast and became indebted to the Temple. Eventually, in Jonestown, these victims were trained like monkeys to obey Jones, their sole source of food.

Love bombings was another popular cult technique: prospective members are welcomed with open arms, free food, advice and understanding. Jones appealed to all the human appetites. He had their senses working overtime. He was doing more for his poor flock than all of San Francisco's social welfare agencies. In every regard, people were treated as a social experiment by applying the pragmatic scientific concept that humans are fully programmable biological and psychological machines.

Members were trained to believe that other groups, and especially their own families, did not have Jones' New Testament vision. Members became self righteous and judgmental, puffed up with their new religious elitism.

Other people weren't edifying enough to be around. Any negative information was considered slander. Personalities were shattered, creating spiritual cloning.

The fiendish leaders also utilized other ideas borrowed from Karl Marx, who described the effectiveness of phony religious rhetoric in controlling of the masses. Other communist theories were borrowed, specifically, the intensive study of the brainwashing techniques of the Chinese communists and the North Koreans.

Aldous Huxley (1) describes the brainwashing techniques that were implemented during the Korean War on military prisoners. Within the camps, the captives were constantly subjected to stress, publicly humiliated, and continually harassed. The victims were bewildered and suffered from chronic anxiety.

Then they were required to confess their sins and tattle on their fellow prisoners. A nightmarish society emerged in which everybody was spying on, and informing against everyone else. Prisoners were deprived of food and sleep, resulting in physical and mental illness.

Similarly, in Jonestown, all of their victims' ties with the past were totally severed. Friends, families, morality, religion, and all customs and habits were stripped from them until they were recreated in the image of their new lord, Jim Jones, and totally dedicated to his service. With their ball and chain secured anyone within the group who spoke out against Jones was crucified by the entire flock.

Terri wrote a note explaining her feelings toward her family: "...and I hate my mother more than him. I could kill her easily for going to bed with me when I was little. If I never saw the name of my mother Virginia Buford again I would be happy and my father, Charles, is a bastard too, I'd like to hack him up with a hatchet. Last but not least I hate my sister, Carolyn, she's the worst. She is solely responsible for the dike that I turned out to be. If I ever see my mother, father or my sister again I'll kill them all with pleasure." (2)

Reiterman describes Jones' library as containing books on Hitler, Marx, Mao and the Mafia. He had another shelf with books studying nuclear war and the creation of a nuclear bomb. Tim Stoen mentioned that Terri Buford had confided in him that she was working on the creation of a nuclear bomb for Jim Jones.

Yet another library shelf contained information about psychology and mind control. Jones had especially loved Hitler, whose plans he idolized, examined and copied. According to Reiterman, Jones worshipped Hitler as a young boy. He usually claimed positions of superiority in all his childhood games. He made believe that he had special godlike powers, even in those imaginary youthful days. The boys used a password when they wanted to enter his house. The password was *Heil Hitler*. Jim used to part his hair like Hitler and issue commands to all his friends in a harsh manner.

The goals of the Nazi concentration camps were adopted in Jonestown. Most of the literature on the camps has tended to stress the role of camps as merely places of death. Very few political theorists have paid attention to the highly significant idea that these camps were actually a new type of human society with a world all their own. In these camps, the society of total domination evolved directly from another of mankind's institutions: slavery.

Human life became worthless as the Nazis turned people into things that responded like zombies, to all their masters' wishes. Like chattel, the children's very lives were bought and sold. Even when ordered to dig and then lie down in their own graves, this victimized human livestock did not question the orders, their minds already murdered.

Ultimately, Jones, with his own consummate craft created a living death which was even more terrible than death, itself. The ultimate cruelty is that few of those doomed souls were even aware of it at the beginning, on their very first day in Guyana. Their torturous slavery was leading to their own premeditated murders.

The world wondered why the Jews seemed willing to march toward their own gruesome deaths in the Nazi camps. The same world accepted the premise of a willing mass suicide of the Jonestown holocaust victims.

Jonestown was far more of a permanent threat to society then previously realized. If it was only a place of death, an extermination center, it would not have been so frightening. The world has seen death throughout its warlike history. However, Jonestown was the land of the entranced zombie, the living dead.

Jones had improved upon the Nazis. Thirty years later, he had more modernized, subtle psychological techniques to employ. He harnessed the mass mind by utilizing Buford's expertise in Japanese group psychology through repeated words, slogans and visual effects.

Contradictory concepts from George Orwell's nightmare vision, 1984, such as *WAR IS PEACE, FREEDOM IS SLAVERY, IGNORANCE IS STRENGTH* were played on a continuous loop to the flock over loudspeakers to drive them insane. Big Brother had come to life.

A chemist whose interests lay in achieving power over others could make everyone a subject for drug experimentation. The Jonestown medical staff had enough behavior controlling drugs to medicate the entire city of Georgetown. According to radio researcher, David Emory (3), in a *Radio Free America* broadcast, Joe Holsinger, aide to Congressman Ryan, stated that according to his information, the population of Jonestown were treated in the commune's medical facility every day for some sort of dubious ailment. Holsinger believed that they were victims of a mind control experiment through secretly induced doses of various drugs given during these checkups.

Among the drugs later recovered by the U. S. investigators were: 20,000 doses of the pain-killer Demerol™; 3,000 liquid doses and 2,000 tablets of Valium™, 10,000 injectable doses and 1,000 tablets of Thorazine™, 200 vials of injectible morphine sulfate; and thousands of doses of other extremely powerful hypnotic sedatives such as Quaaludes™, Vistaril™, Noludar™ and Innovar™.

Aldous Huxley in his prophetic horror, *Brave New World*, warned of a mythical drug he named, *Soma*. In that far off fantasy-nightmare, the doctors and engineers used *Soma* to control people. Huxley's fantasy had become a reality in Jonestown.

With the realization of the horrible uses of their drugging techniques, Temple insiders, Al Mills and his wife questioned their purpose and were told that the Temple nurses were ordering a vast quantity of medical supplies in liquid form.

They wondered why drugs in liquid form were necessary! They spoke with a Georgetown pharmacist who agreed that their requests were peculiar. He noted that such medicines are usually taken in pill form. The pharmacist speculated that the only reasons anyone would need them in liquid form was if they were to be injected or if they were to be given in drinks such as Kool-Aid™, in which case the victims would not realize they were being drugged.

The pharmacist was right. Terri Buford was asked by Jones to administer drugs to a troublesome member named Sandi Bradshaw. Buford, who had studied chemistry, responded in a letter marked personally for Jim Jones that it was going to be very difficult to secretly administer any drugs in Sandi's food because she ate mostly potato chips. Buford added that the job of drugging Sandi was unnecessary since Sandi was very ill and dying anyway.

While under the secret influence of a variety of these liquid drugs hypnotized victims were bombarded with subliminal messages with a lower threshold than the human ear is capable of detecting. Programmed commands were whispered over the loudspeakers night and day. Huxley explains how a suggestion above the threshold of awareness is more likely to take effect when the recipient is in a light hypnotic trance. Under the influence of certain drugs, people can actually see and hear a great deal more than they consciously know. Suggestions are recorded by the subconscious mind and may affect conscious thoughts, feelings and behavior. The conscious mind hears only the loudest sound, whereas the subconscious mind hears all of the sounds: everything. Because the subconscious mind believes everything, obeys all commands, behaves as directed and says *yes* to all requests, it evades the conscious mind. Erotic suggestions are obeyed because the victim believes they originated in their conscious mind.

The scientist, Dr. To. Poetzle, an associate of Freud, was the first to demonstrate the similarity between post-hypnotic suggestions and subliminal stimuli. *The Poetzle Effect* is described as a time delay reaction. The doctor called it a *time clock* phenomenon, in which subliminal perceptions might take weeks or even months to surface in actions.

Jones used subliminal messages to create strong sexual desires for him from others. His commands demanding surrender easily overcame any pre-conditioned resistance. Eventually Jim Jones had to have personal secretaries make appointments to allow the throngs of begging, pleading men and women enough time for his sexual healing encounters. They were paying Jones for their allotted time through hefty donations made out generously to his *church*. Besides, it was a religious tax write-off.

These followers were already convinced that Jones was a god. Huxley states that direct commands such as *buy popcorn* or *vote for Jones* are likely to take effect only upon those minds that are already partial to Jones and/or popcorn. For the would-be dictator the moral of all this is plain. Under proper conditions verbal suggestions passed through the somnolent cortex to the midbrain can trigger posthypnotic commands especially in captive audiences found in prisons, labor camps, military barracks and in Jonestown.

Jones' captive audience finally had each and every freedom stripped from their grasp, as Karl Marx (1932) had suggested when he wrote: There are *eternal truths, such as Freedom, Justice, etc., that are common to all states of society. But communism abolishes eternal truths, it abolishes all religion and all morality.*

Certainly, Jim Jones was one of Marx's best students.

CHAPTER 10
JUMBLE

> I have a lot of respect for my uncle James Agee,
> who was a very sensitive author. When he was
> asked if he was a communist on one occasion,
> he answered, 'I am a communist by sympathy
> and conviction'. That meant a lot to me.
>
> Terri Buford   1980

A superb Jonestown intelligence system was created and conceived by utilizing the techniques employed by Terri Buford's great uncle, James Agee, the famous Pulitzer Prize winning writer, while gathering data for his book, *Let Us Now Praise Famous Men*. Terri's kinship with Agee, through her Aunt, Omega Agee, also included Walt Whitman. Agee's own mother, Laura Whitman Tyler Agee, had Whitman's last name proudly added to the middle of her own. (1)

James Agee's poetic writing style is strangely similar to Whitman's in its biblical grandiosity and extensive poetic descriptions inserted into a prose format. Like Terri, Whitman had Quaker religious roots.

One of Whitman's finest poems, *I Sing The Body Electric*, praises the full, unrestrained, bisexual expression of physical love. In harmony with those passions, Terri hummed a similar tune, enjoying a full range of sexual appetites. Walt Whitman traversed the length and breadth of America while recording the common folk with his unique style of poetry during the Civil War era. Following in his illustrious footsteps by also writing and photographing the poor, mostly black share cropping tenant farmers of the deep south during the era of the great depression, James Agee, along with photographer Walker Evans, befriended and lived with poor people while studying them.

Agee never disclosed his true intentions while he wrote magazine articles about his victims. According to Hersey, Agee began to think of himself and Evans as spies for God. Furthermore, Agee (1) admits and rationalizes his unethical behavior by blaming his superiors in apologizing for his technique calling it obscene and thoroughly terrifying. He claimed that his bosses instructed him to pry intimately into the lives of his undefended sources merely for profit. He admits he acted as a literary spy.

Agee simultaneously does the spying and passes the blame. The poor farmers Agee wrote about were only too happy to be photographed and interviewed, charmed by Agee and his easy country manner, never catching on that he was a city reporter only using them for personal gain.

The sharecroppers generously invited him into their homes and fed and entertained him. When some of these people found out the truth they were furious.

In the same soft spoken manner as her uncle James, Terri Buford acquired her information by befriending each person in Jonestown with the spirit of her trusting love. Buford, with the sophisticated computer files at her disposal, suggested to Jim Jones that she could undertake the responsibility of establishing records about the history of every person in Jonestown. Jones approved the idea as an excellent way of obtaining more information for control.

Like Agee, she began to collect short histories of the inhabitants of Jonestown. Most of the residents wrote out stories of their lives. Others dictated their stories verbally as Terri recorded interviews with the citizens, some of whom were illiterate.

She, as Uncle James, also began to think of herself as a spy for God, or Jim

Jones, in his battle against evil. Quite the opposite effect was achieved as every person's dreams and weaknesses were quietly exposed, eventually to be utilized against them.

With those Jonestown biographies, the inner most fear of the victims was catergorized. The worst thing in the world varies from person to person. It may be burial alive, or a fiery death, or drowning, rats, or whatever. Jones could now call up computer files to know one's innermost secrets to bring his gothic nightmare into fruition.

Scrupulous records were kept to locate every possible nickel of revenue. Form letters were found in Jonestown files inquiring about pension funds and retirement benefits from organizations including the Railroad Retirement Board, Veterans Administration, Public Employees Retirement System, YMCA and the Dry Cleaning Pension Fund.

Information was even smuggled out of their garbage cans from within their own, before they even entered Jonestown. Al Mills explains the system. He recalls a Gene Chaiken who died while drugged in Jonestown. Gene and his wife Phyllis were spied upon by information gathered from an *IV*, code for an *indirect visit*, made by Linda Amos, one of Jones' staff, to their home. The date was February 14, 1973. An indirect visit implies entering when one is not invited, like a thief.

In their garbage can, Linda Amos had found such items as a box of Hostess donuts, an envelope addressed to Gene's wife, Phyllis, from *Ms. Magazine*, an envelope addressed to Phyllis from the Gray Panthers, an advertisement cut out from a local newspaper advertising rooms at the Sheraton Hotel. When Al Mills went over the list, he finally understood just how Jones was performing his fake show. Jones' revelations were based on his garbage picking accomplices.

Jones had predicted at one time, for instance, that Phyllis had wanted to go to a Sheraton hotel and she liked to eat donuts. It was suddenly very apparent to the Mills exactly how people were so easily convinced that Jones had the powers of extrasensory perception.

Temple spies followed people and went into their houses when they were not home. Then they would look in their medicine cabinets to find out what medicine they were taking. From that information, Jones knew which ailments to pretend he was curing. A follow up to Agee's book, *Let Us Now Praise Famous Men*, was ingeniously undertaken by two investigative authors, Dale Maharidge and Michael Williamson for which they won a Pulitzer Prize. Their study, *And Their Children After Them*, returns this duo to Agee's original tenant farmer victims of his originally unsolicited, voyueristic scrutiny, fifty years later.

They realized the deep resentment these poor farmers had for Agee. Even their children felt exploited by having their parents and grandparent's poverty put on display in Agee's print and Evan's pictures.

In their study of the long term effects upon victims, they discovered that suspicion about Agee's actual motives was widespread among these once naive tenant farmers. Dire consequences resulted. Maharidge describes the suicide at age 45 of George Gudger's daughter, Maggie Louise. Maharidge implies that Agee's tactics were at least partially to blame for her death. Maharidge felt Gudger died because of a deep sense of betrayal.

Hersey quotes Gudger's suspicions that Agee was a communist, trying to provoke people against their landlords and the country. According to his victim's testimony, Agee did much more than innocently observe the poor. Buford, as well as Agee, didn't merely sympathize with the downtrodden. They had political agendas. They brought their communist political convictions into those wretched lives. Buford repeated the myth of the educated savior of Jonestown, projecting her own values upon less literate people.

Buford inherited more than Agee's blue/grey eyes, as she emulated his communist bent and secretive political activities. During the sixties, when America's social consciousness was seething, Agee was resurrected as a counter-culture hero.

Those were the days when *Let Us Now Praise Famous Men* became a kind of bible, especially for bright young people who, like James Agee, had the privilege of attending good colleges. Those children understood Agee's irony, idealism and guilt.

In Berkeley Terri Buford was proudly leading cheers for her own blood relative. In fact she went further than him in creating her own revolutionary role. Hersey explains that Agee's political consciousness was that of a revolutionary, but one who saw that all revolutionaries turn wicked, cruel and power-mad.

However, not grasping his sad vision and the possible consequences of a real revolution, Terri took him quite literally, extended her Jonestown spy system far beyond the Agee technique to turn the art into a more precise science.

Besides just merely gathering essential information, it became a weekly routine for Terri or Jim Jones to invent some new confession or threat for the other leaders to write. Al Mills states that he was instructed to write a letter saying that he and a friend were conspiring to destroy America.

Soon Jim had a huge file on all his members that included confessions about illegal and perverted acts such as blowing up banks, conspiring to overthrow the government, raping their own children, killing the President, belonging to the Communist party or bombing a train. If a member wouldn't sign the document admitting their guilt, then they would be considered guilty of *NOT* signing! Either way, the victim was trapped.

Blank sheets of paper were signed and notarized by each member so that even in the event of defection, things could be invented to blackmail and eventually destroy the person's life. The top agents within the organization were put under scrutiny, spying on each other.

Terri Buford was specifically assigned to be a spy/aid to San Francisco District Attorney Timothy Stoen, who worked for Jones. Later she worked for and spied upon Temple attorney Charles Garry. They were under the impression that she was assisting them. However, her real assignment was to watch them and report directly to Jim Jones. Through these tactics, she was directly responsible for both of their dismissals from the Temple. Charles Garry disclosed that Terri had personal keys to his office with 24 hour access to all his files. His own legal associates were furious with him. They considered this a breach of lawyer-client confidence.

Eventually Garry was replaced with Lane. Tim Stoen was replaced with Buford, herself, as she rose once more through the ranks. Neither Stoen, nor Garry were ever willing to compromise themselves to the extreme lengths of depravity and eventual murder that Jones eventually would demand.

No one could realize at the time what Buford's secret function entailed. She was silently following in her superspy father's footsteps in Vietnam. Like her father, Terri was willing to do any task to further her cause. In Jonestown's early days, Terri volunteered to work on the electrical crew, making herself look good in the eyes of the others by doing her share. But she managed to avoid doing any heavy physical labor required of all in the Guyana heat. She then moved into the control room, working at night to beat the heat. Her total loyalty was well rewarded.

She was soon promoted to be Jones' second-in-command, making independent decisions, controlling sensitive information, creating secret codes for the computers and rising in status to become the all-important financial manager of the entire operation.

According to high ranking member Tim Stoen, Buford always operated on the principle that the ends justified the means. Stoen reaffirms that Terri was the highest top echelon person in Jonestown, next to Jim Jones, running it when Jones was unavailable and states that she was Jones' arch manipulator and strategist.

Stoen states that Terri was the head of a sex team to entrap men into Jonestown. These cult prostitutes were instructed to give their bodies for the *cause.* Stoen explains that Terri Buford ran courses in the *church* on the covert uses of sex and drugs for the revolution, teaching women how to manipulate men. She, with her fellow women members, would put on sexy outfits to lure men into the Temple through sex.

Stoen stated that Buford was not only a member nor a mere victim. She was a brilliant operative in charge of administering drugs into people's food to manipulate them.

According to Reiterman, two people were murdered while drugged in Jonestown. Stoen has also stated that he considers Mark Lane and Terri Buford to be moral degenerates. In awe of Buford, he says that she has the highest I.Q. of any woman he has ever known. Stoen ought to know, since prior to her meteoric rise to power in the Temple, he had been her superior. Stoen also states that Terri told him that she was building an atomic bomb for Jones.

Mark Lane describes two documents signed by Terri Buford. In the first, she confesses to attorney Charles Garry that she was the mistress of Jim Jones. The second document according to Lane, was a one-page notarized confession admitting that she personally smuggled the sum of one million dollars into Jonestown from San Francisco.

In a letter to her sister, Caroline, Terri writes:

> "Well, see you later and I'll tell you how I ripped off that
> Jim Jones church. I got so much $ off them it is incredible."
> Teresa J. Buford (2)

Another of Buford's many functions, according to Tim Stoen, was as the head of the *Diversions Department*. The Department had three sectors:

a) Defectors and Critics Division: To divert individual persons, particularly ex-members of PEOPLES TEMPLE and outspoken critics thereof, from publicizing and from organizing in opposition to the practices of defendants JONES and PEOPLES TEMPLE, by threatening such persons with death and injury to their persons and properties, including threats that their homes will be burned;

b) Government and Media Division: To divert agencies of government and of the media from investigating the practices of defendants JONES and PEOPLES TEMPLES by;

(1) *Bombarding* them with continual mass volumes of letters written in longhand by PEOPLES TEMPLE members conscripted as part of *letter-writing committees* which allege various types of unjustified harassment; and

(2) Making anonymous telephone calls to agencies of government and the media which accuse totally innocent persons selected at random of heinous crimes and immoral acts (particularly crimes and acts related to those for which defendant JONES feared he was about to be accused); and

c) General Public Division: To divert the public from focusing upon the questionable practices of defendants JONES and PEOPLES TEMPLE by publishing press releases and other communications which falsely accuse the critics of such practices as being sexual deviates, terrorists, drug traffickers, or child molesters.

Lane admits that since he was not present at the meetings of this Jonestown Planning Commission with Stoen, he cannot be certain that all of the allegations made by Stoen against his client, Terri Buford, were *not true*.

But Lane admits they might be. Tim Stoen, who lost his son in Jonestown, is labeled and dismissed by Buford and Lane as another C.I.A. operative with no proof to show for their conjecture. Since Stoen had access to more information than the average victim, he knew he had to defect from Jonestown. However, within the master computer room at Jonestown, all information shared with the general population was limited to Terri's discretion. Unlike top leaders like Stoen, the people of Jonestown shared the same ignorance of their fate as those dumb animals of Orwell's 1946 fantasy, *Animal Farm*, as they mutely awaited their inevitable slaughter for their owner's insatiable appetite.

On the Jonestown farm lived the prized male pig, Charlie. With the same name as Terri's father, this important hog enjoyed the sexual favors of the entire group. Charlie was the sole stud, like Jim Jones. Charlie, through his progeny, created all of the pork that was served in the Jonestown kitchen.

One day tired old Charlie couldn't perform his cheerful duties and was slaughtered. That night the entire starving commune feasted hungrily on Charlie while Mr. Muggs screeched gleefully.

An exhausted Terri Buford went back to her coded computers and her intelligence files. She kept the Jonestown's sensitive information safe and secure within the computer room where she slept.

CHAPTER 11
TEMPEST

Our love became a funeral pyre
Jim Morrison

The operation was proceeding so smoothly for Jones that a new long-range goal was developed. It was decided to try to take over the entire country of Guyana for eventual use as a base of operations against the U.S. By moving the group to Guyana, Jones achieved total control over them. Guyana was so remote that the nation had no roads or railways linking it to its neighbor countries.

With total faith in her loyalty, Buford was given the position of the top courier,ferrying the money from Guyana all over the world. She claimed $250,000 upon entry into Guyana on her customs declaration.

Terri deposited funds in banks in Switzerland, Panama and Venezuela and other havens of laundered money. Tim Stoen formed two corporations in Panama, Bridget and Association Evangelica de Las Americas. Terri signed on a Box number 86 in the Banco Union Sucousal of San Pedro. She deposited five million dollars into the Union Bank of Switzerland in Panama: account # 121-00-191A.

Another safe deposit box #14665/Huk was held in Buford's name in Zurich, Switzerland.

She rented a house for three months in Panama City, Apartado Postal 1824, Panama, 1. Panama. Her purpose was to make contact with the heads of state and clear the way for more massive deposits in the banks there. The Panamanian Government worked closely with the Jonestown people. The tactics used by Terri and her group in Guyana were similar to the methods developed in San Francisco. Wild parties were held for friends of the Temple. Allies were rewarded handsomely with financial and sexual favors.

The necessary security of this financial operation was achieved through Terri's photographic memory. If anything were to be written down concerning the banking deposits, anyone else might be able to withdraw the funds. She memorized all the numbers for safety so only she had control of the money.

Currency sent to Guyana was earmarked for bribes to various politicians. While these deposits were being made, children were starved, brutally tortured and put into small boxes within the hot Guyanese ground for days. They emerged crushed. People back in the Jonestown concentration camp were slowly starving to death.

The mass of people in Jonestown were poor black pseudo-slaves who were totally exploited by their new masters on the Jonestown plantation. Jones convinced black Temple members that if they did not follow him to Guyana they would be put into concentration camps and killed. However, once in Guyana, victims were brutally beaten and worked unmercifully with no place to hide. It was set up in the style of a quasi-military camp. The victim's passport and money were taken immediately.

Jonestown developed into a uniquely self contained para-military ghetto utilizing a mainly black work force on the front lines. The same discrepancy that exists in the armed services held true between the leaders of Jonestown and the masses that served them. Jones and his elite group of cohorts enjoyed steaks, caviar, all night parties and hearty laughter.

This plantation's hierarchy made all the decisions about the general population, while utterly disdaining them at the same time. These victims' assets were cleverly appropriated under the guise of socialism.

A deeply troubled Charles Garry was becoming very difficult to work with. He was asking too many questions. Lane states that soon after Charles Garry was retained as the Jonestown lawyer, Terri Buford began to share with him vital information about the shipment of weapons to Guyana, the foreign bank accounts, and other crimes that Temple leaders were committing. Lane states that when Charles Garry asked Terri why so many weapons were being stored in San Francisco, Terri explained that it was for shipment to Jonestown.

Garry asked her how the weapons in Guyana arrived there and how additional weapons were to be smuggled in. He was concerned about the welfare of the people in Jonestown. Buford told him that weapons were placed in false bottoms of crates that were manufactured in the woodshop at the San Francisco Church. Then, she explained, various belongings of the people on their trip to Guyana were placed in those boxes. Rifles were broken down into small components and hidden into a duffel bag that contained clothing. The clothes used to smuggle those guns were the same pathetic rags the unfortunate foster children were forced to wear in Jonestown. Guyanese officials were rewarded with small bribes for their assistance.

According to Lane, when Garry asked her if she thought all of the actions were morally correct she reported that she wasn't critical of the group since she was a revolutionary and realized that these things had to be done.

Charles Garry would never have agreed to the theft of money from the Jonestown project into any private hands. Garry had made his reputation as a passionate defender of underdogs, misfits and unpopular causes for a very personal reason. He grew up at a time when discrimination was rampant against his own American heritage. Garry's real name was Garabed Garabedian. At Selma High School in the San Joaquin Valley of California he was the brightest boy in the school, but was bypassed by the principal because of his background. Charles decided to spend his entire life defending anyone who was a victim of discrimination. That included the Panthers.

Teresa played the spy for Jones, tattling on Garry, while she worked with him as his trusted aide. Garry had explained to her that Newton was co-opting the

Black Panthers with his drug habit and would use the money for that purpose.

If Garry were ever to try and seek revenge for being pushed out of the Jonestown picture, a complex plan was worked out to discredit and silence him. Lane writes in *The Strongest Poison* that Garry pocketed $5,000 dollars to be delivered to Huey Newton of the Black Panthers, a fugitive in Cuba. Their defense against Garry was to be a strong offense. Garry's alleged indiscretion over a measly sum came at a time when millions of dollars were secretly funneled into Swiss bank accounts by Terri Buford.

Garry was proven correct about his assessment of Huey Newton. Newton's drug habit had caused his death. He had crossed a notorious street gang by stealing their drugs and finally paid with his life. Through Buford's tactics, Garry was branded a thief and a traitor and ostracized by Jones.

With Garry out of the way, the project flourished. It took many hands to store the illegal guns in California; to smuggle them out of the United States in violation of Federal statutes; to get them into Guyana in violation of that nation's laws; and to keep them at Jonestown. Heads were turned all along the way.

Elderly people worked as much as sixteen hours a day even though they collected social security. Jones even collected welfare and social security payments for dead people. Janie Brown died in 1974, but checks in her name continued to roll into the Temple coffers until the very end.

Hospital records and obituary columns were scrutinized for the recently deceased. Then credit cards and benefits were applied for in their names. No one would ever realize that these cards and payments were still being paid to deceased people since bribed Temple members were placed into the offices that made the payments.

Member Peter Holmes handled burials in Jonestown and worked in the San Francisco morgue. The offices that were supposed to protect the foster children turned a blind eye to their brutal plight. Alot of those children were unwanted black emotionally disturbed youths.

Reporter Stanek (1), describes the abuse of Michele Brady, 12, who had a history of mental instability, and was punished for misbehaving. Jones ordered that she be put in a plywood box 3 feet wide, 4 feet high and 6 feet long with two hooded holes to let in air but no light. Kept there for more than a week with a small can for a toilet, she was given only water to drink.

After that she turned into a living zombie, never misbehaving again. Eventually, she drank her cyanide without a struggle. She was listed as a suicide.

Other children were punished at one time or another by being forced to strip nude in front of the full membership and then thrown into ice cold pools of water.

Some were given electric shocks with cattle prods. Electrodes were attached to the children and they were tortured in a variety of gruesome manners. Besides her adopted child, Dietrict whom she abandoned in Jonestown, Terri Buford worked on the committee in charge of electric wiring for the commune. She studied the use of electricity in small doses for stimulation and other applications. With a population of almost 300 children out of 900 people, severe discipline was necessary.

Anyone not grinning or applauding enthusiastically during a meeting would be punished. For the younger children, Jones threatened to let them loose in the jungle. Then they were blindfolded and lowered into a well. On Jones orders, the adults would frighten them by pretending to be scary monsters.

There were other many forms of severe abuse for everyone. Burying adults, as well as children, into the closed box in the ground was a favored method. The residents were trapped. There was the constant presence of roving security guards who reported all signs of subversive activities. All day and night sentries manned searchlight towers.

There were many elderly victims in Jonestown. All of them were black. One poor, elderly woman born in 1902, Hyacinth Thrash, survived the Jonestown tempest by hiding beneath her bed. Reporter Wes Smith (2) quotes Hyacinth as she began to suspect that Jones was trying to starve the old members. People began to realize that Jones and his inner circle were eating fresh-baked goods and big meals.

While her skin peeled from the intense Guyana heat, Thrash reported that Jones had a fan and an air conditioner. She could also see that their *Father*, was attended to by nurses who sometimes wore only bikini tops and bottoms.

Even though Hyacinth was afraid, there was no way out. Vicious techniques were utilized both to appease and entertain the masses and especially to keep them in fearful awe of their master's total power over their very lives.

The most frightening cadre of killers was Jones' elite personal armed guard. This army, totally loyal only to Jones, was culled from the desperately poor, exploited, foster children, forcibly abducted from the U.S. and now carefully trained to be ferocious killers.

He applied a grotesque application of communism's traditional deformation of family bonds. These warrior children were trained to commit murder without conscience. They had no regard for the people in Jonestown, only disdain. They were manipulated to hate America and enjoy violence, these orphans of a storm, abandoned by their country to find their destiny or death. In the jungle, these armed guards surrounded the entire compound on that final fateful day.

They were armed with semi-automatic weapons, shotgun, and crossbows. According to Lane, a private investigator named Louis Gurvich, whose own daughter perished in the murders, carefully examined the site. He refused to believe that his daughter killed herself. His investigation shows that she was murdered.

Upon close investigation Gurvich found bows and arrows still lying around. People don't use arrows to commit suicide. Gurvich, from hard evidence, concluded that at least two-thirds of the people had been murdered.

He saw bodies that were obviously dragged after they were killed. There were track marks on the ground. The bodies were all neatly laid out. Others were injected in their backs, foreheads and arms. Needle marks were all over their bodies. Furthermore, Gurvich was convinced that Jim Jones had been murdered. A solitary .38 revolver was found 60 feet away from his corpse.

Guyana's government investigation agreed with Gurvich. Bruce Buursma quotes the chief medical examiner in Guyana at the time, Dr. C. Leslie Mootoo, a key eyewitness who was immediately on the scene, who estimated that more than 700 of the victims were forcibly injected with poison. To kill the infants squeeze bottles were utilized to squirt the poison down their throats.

Ken Wooden (3) quotes Cecil A. Roberts, the Deputy Police Commissioner of the former British colony of Guyana who also agrees that murder occurred in

Jonestown especially since legally, under English common law, a child cannot consent to suicide. He concluded that many of those children had been sent to death in Guyana by the courts of the State of California. Roberts feels that those courts and California officials were engaged in a conspiracy of silence to cover up their culpability in the deaths of the children. Roberts realized that Jones kidnapped the children of some parents who would not have otherwise joined the sudden 1977 exodus from San Francisco to Guyana. Wooden (4) quotes Roberts as feeling that many of the younger children were actually tricked at first into taking the poison. What child would refuse a sweet cool drink on a hot day? They thought it was a fun game. These children perished without any knowledge of the reason why they were brought there.

Facts On File (5) quotes another eyewitness to the murder, Odell Rhodes, who escaped death by hiding under one of the camp houses. Rhodes had been a green beret. According to Rhodes' eyewitness testimony some shots rang out as other camp residents fled into the jungle. They were shot by the guards. Rhodes observed how the murderers then started with the babies as at least 80 infants were fed the deadly potion. In America, the officials and public would eventually consider these injected babies to be suicides. According to reporter, Jon Nordheimer (6), even Jim Jones' own son, Steven Jones stated that he felt that there was no possible way the deaths at Jonestown could be labeled suicides. Nordheimer further states that two young women and two children had their throats slit at the Jonestown headquarters in Georgetown, Guyana. Those women and children never even got to drink the Kool Aid™ at all. Even though their throats were slit, their deaths were also listed as suicides.

Wooden (3) describes Stanley Clayton, another survivor, who told the *Sun Times* that security guard Johnny Brown instructed his men over the loudspeaker system that if they saw anyone doing a suspicious or a treacherous act like trying to leave, they would be shot.

Stanley Clayton survived because he was Huey Newton's nephew and had the respect and protection of the Black Panther element of the armed guard. Furthermore, Clayton was himself, a guard. Wooden (3) quotes Clayton describing what happened to the extremely frightened teenagers.

Force had to be used on the more rebellious ones. Clayton described the death of Judy Runnels, described by survivors as a spunky girl with a real desire to live. Clayton said Runnels absolutely refused to take the poison. He said she was grabbed and held by an older woman, Paulette Jackson, who poured poison into her mouth.

Judy Runnels spit it out five times. Two women then beat her. Once more they poured the poison into her mouth. This time they covered her mouth and nose with their hands so she could not breathe, forcing her at last to swallow the poison. Runnels was listed as a *suicide victim*. Wooden describes other murders of other teenagers. Fred Lewis, 15, struggled against swallowing the poison. The injected him with a needle. A Guyanese teenager, 15 year-old Jimmy Gill, didn't want the poison. Security men grabbed him. He struggled and then gave in. Nurse Annie Moore injected him.

Unpublished Guyanese police photos portray the final agony the children endured. Wooden describes Dr. Mootoo who almost fainted when he first viewed the dead children. He said there was pain written all over their faces. One photo shows a teenage girl clutching a blanket in her death grip.

Reiterman states that Clayton had passed through a group of about a dozen people armed with crossbows to escape from the massacre. These were Jones' select inner guard. According to Reiterman, Stanley Clayton fled into the darkened jungle, hid for an hour or two and reported hearing something very weird. At 9:00 P.M. he apparently heard the final cheer of Jones' armed guard!

What were they possibly cheering? The guard was described by Debby Blakey in her disclosure to Congressman Ryan as encircling the camp. She numbered them at about fifty. She reported that they had weapons including handguns and rifles, but no machine guns. They had twenty-five guards in the daytime and another twenty five at night posted to guard Jones' house, twenty-four hours a day.

Guyanese special surveillance teams spotted, by helicopter, a group of fifty armed men heading through the jungle directly for the Venezuelan border soon after the mass murder. They were Jones' elite guards, running with their booty. Furthermore, according to Lane, the Venezuelan border patrol revealed that surveillance aircraft had observed about forty people moving in a group toward their country shortly after the massacre. The Guyanese choppers could not land in the thick terrain to capture them. Originally, the Jonestown site was chosen precisely for its proximity to the Gran Chaco area of the Venezuelan frontier with an escape plan carefully conceived. The distance between Jonestown and Venezuela was only a 13 mile hike. According to Nordheimer, Steven Jones claimed that 500 members eventually escaped into the jungle. To execute their plan, *The Last Stand*, all the witnesses had to be silenced.

Jones had promised to provide for his followers for the rest of their lives providing they gave him everything they owned. After surrendering their homes and bank accounts, *the rest of their lives* proved to be not very long at all.

In the judgment of the Guyanese Government, Jonestown was considered a calculated murder plot, not a mass suicide as most Americans were led to believe. All over the Caribbean, people believe this was absolutely true. Since the crimes occurred in Guyana and the Guyanese were the first eyewitnesses on the scene their reports should be examined. Furthermore, the governments of both countries were culpable in allowing Jonestown to occur, but the United States agencies that sent foster children into their demise have yet to be investigated.

Facts on File (7) reports a headline from a Guyanese newspaper that stated that a Guyana jury found that the *Cult Deaths Were Murders*. A Guyanese coroner's jury investigating the death of more that 900 persons at the Peoples Temple commune in Jonestown ruled on December 22, 1978, that all but three of the victims had been murdered. The jury initially ruled that Jones too had committed suicide, but it changed its mind after the investigation's Magistrate, Harold Bacchus cautioned them to look closely at the facts.

After the jury stated that Jones had shot himself in the head, Bacchus asked, shouting: "What evidence were the findings based upon? Why was the weapon so far away from his head? How could anyone claim it was suicide?" The jury deliberated briefly and ruled that Jones had been shot to death by some person or persons unknown.

British researcher Nugent (8) states that the U.S. Government did not examine the bodies for cause of death at all. According to Nugent, Army spokesman Lt. Colonel Brigham Shuler claimed that no autopsies were needed. He believed that the causes of death were not an issue.

In spite of the glaring evidence, even Tim Reiterman (9) does not give any credibility to Guyanese eyewitness accounts. He writes that in Guyana, the political opposition merely seized on the tragedy only to embarrass the regime of Prime Minister Forbes Burnham. He discredits the Guyanese inquest by calling it laughable.

In dismissing Guyanese reports by implying that a small country is incapable of conducting a thorough examination, Reiterman has lost valuable and objective testimony. Guyana should not be criticized, nor ridiculed.

Their view that the event was a murder plot is proven by Jim Jones' own words. He discussed his plan to kill the people and make it appear like suicide. Reiterman (9) explains how Jones asked Dr. Larry Schacht how they could get everybody to *commit suicide*.

According to David Emory (10), Dr. Schacht received his *education* in Guadalajara, Mexico, at a technological school, nicknamed, *Los Tecos*. Emory states that he was actually trained there by a fascist group promoting death squad tactics as a method of fighting communism.

Reporter Arthur Crewdson (11), confirms that Schacht had studied *medicine* for three years at the University of Guadalajara, Mexico. Author Michael Meiers states (12) that Jones himself ordered Schacht to study there. Meiers also mentions that Schacht might have been a direct descendent of the Nazi doctor, Hjalmar Horace Greeley Schacht. In the same capacity as Terri Buford served under Jim Jones, Hjalmar Schacht was the chief Nazi Minister of Finance under Hitler.

According to various Mexican journalists *Los Tecos* has harbored about 5000 Nazis that escaped Hitler's regime in an attempt to create a Fourth Reich using Mexico as their base of operation. They have a certain amount of power within Mexico and are considered very dangerous. Their main tactic is assassination.

According to Reiterman, Los Tecos graduate *Dr*. Schacht, suggested to Jones that the best way to kill everyone would be sedation and then injections into their hearts. Jones objected. That would not appear to be suicide, even though many of those adults and children were later found to be injected after the mass murder.

To Schacht's idea, Jim Jones replied that he would personally be glad to shoot everybody. At which point, according to Reiterman, Jones' own son, Steven, asked if his father was serious. Steven mentioned that it wouldn't be easy to kill a thousand people, trying to talk his father out of mass murder.

Jones asked his son and Schacht how many bullets they had in Jonestown. He ordered them to count their ammunition. Then he said that he would shoot the thousand people himself. According to Reiterman Jones stated that he would actually walk around and put a bullet into everyone's head. Ironically, the statement to Schacht prophesied precisely how Jones himself would be killed.

Schacht, an unlicensed doctor, was typical of the medical staff. Reiterman describes this staff at Jonestown in a statement by a member, Mike Touchette. In Mike's judgment the Amerindians (natives) that lived in the surrounding jungle had better medical care then the people of Jonestown. If he had a choice between doing without treatment or visiting the quack, Dr. Larry Schacht, Mike would rather suffer.

Touchette once watched Schacht stitching up a finger. Reiterman states that according to Touchette, Schacht's hand was vibrating so much he looked as if he had Parkinson's disease.

Schacht would throw crazed tantrums, ranting about minor problems. He was also a former drug abuser and lived on the edge of paranoia. Jones had also sexually abused him as his personal lover whenever the mood hit his fancy. Schacht got very little sleep.

Anytime Jones had one of his attacks, Schacht was called for immediately to administer one of the many illegal drugs available at Jonestown. Jones had become addicted to drugs and was getting more and more insane from their effects as Schacht kept feeding his leader whatever he desired.

Ironically, since Schacht was not a licensed doctor, and never swore the *Hippocratic* oath, he did not have *medical ethics* anyway. Schacht, was in charge of treating everyone in the compound, even the sick, helpless children. He carefully placed poison into the Kool-Aide in this planned genocide.

Since everyone was seen in the medical facility everyday, a file was kept on each person in the compound. In her statement to Congressman Ryan, Debby Blakey stated that illness was rampant in Jonestown and that more than one half of the population had severe diarrhea and high fevers.

Furthermore, the blood supply was used by all the Jonestown members and the population had a high percentage of homosexuals and drug users. It has been theorized without any proof or facts that the people, especially the black inmates, might have been suffering from an early version of AIDS without their ever realizing it.

Jones' strict rule in the camp was that no white top echelon overseer was permitted to sleep with any black worker. The only instances of sex between blacks and whites occurred when the girls were sent out to compromise Guyanese diplomats or in the one instance when Jones had intercourse with Shanda James. To prevent contamination, Guyanese Prime Minister Forbes Burnham ordered all the personal effects, even the beds, burned immediately after the murders. Why was this necessary? Were the black people contaminated? Jonestown's final solution, mass death, focused mainly upon blacks, homosexuals and drug users whereas the white leaders that planned the operation have survived except for Jones, himself.

In spite of the rampant illness at Jonestown, Jones' lawyer, Mark Lane, at a pre-massacre press conference, described the medical staff of Jonestown as giving him the best examination he ever received. Lane countered what he described as unfair attacks upon his client by the San Francisco media with his eyewitness description of Jonestown as a *paradise*. Even though there was not one licensed doctor, Lane claimed to Charles Krause on the airplane going to Jonestown that there were actually seventy people on the Jonestown medical staff.

According to Klineman's (13) study, Lane was careful never to divulge any facts or specifics about his alleged U.S. Government C.I.A. conspiracy against Jonestown. He didn't because he simply couldn't. He was unable to produce one single fact to demonstrate any C.I.A. complicity.

Lane even added to his list of conspirators. Besides the C.I.A. he added more names of Jones' supposed other enemies including The Treasury Department, The

Internal Revenue Service and even the Postal Service. Lane had planned to sue these and other government agencies on behalf of Jim Jones.

Lane also fantasizes a press coverup. He labels *The New York Times* and the U.S. Department of Justice as the enemy. However, upon examination, it remains clear that the murders were set into motion from within the Jonestown hierarchy, itself, and certainly not solely by Jones whose very own death weakens that myth's false assumption. Jones had become a mere puppet, a figurehead, providing a convenient scapegoat. The *mass suicide* cover had worked.

But, no one would have taken a weapon from Jones' hand and moved it sixty feet away after he was shot during the bloody carnage. For what purpose? Obviously, Jones' murderer was a proficient marksman from that distance. Jones' killer dropped the gun and vanished, only after killing Mr. Muggs. Certainly a monkey could never be considered a *suicide* victim. This was the act of emotional vengeance done by someone very close to Jones.

The majority of the dead were life's perennial underdogs, helpless black old women and helpless children. Certainly, the tricky tactic of using suicidal dress rehearsals as constant threats served only as their contrived cover enabling the perpertrators to forever, remain free.

FOUL MURDERS, declared Magistrate Bacchus of Guyana as he examined the details of the largest mass murder of American civilians in history. This chilling verdict was dismissed by American experts such as author and Jonestown authority, Tim Reiterman, who declared Guyana to be a mere *backwater* country. After that, the official story presented to and accepted by most Americans was one of an amazing, simultaneous mass *suicide*, which even grade school children know is absurd.

Unlike America which swept the story under a rug of Hollywood glitz, backwater Guyana did have their own comprehensive internal government investigation during which heads did roll.

CHAPTER 12

SNOWBALL

Comrades, I pronounce the death sentence upon Snowball
Animal Farm, George Orwell

One of Jones' major personal targets for exploitation was Larry Layton, a Jew, whose mother had been a victim of a Nazi concentration camp. In fact, Israel was branded a major enemy of Jonestown since it is an ally of the U.S. A political alliance between Jones and the P.L.O. was formed. As its courier, Terri Buford was sent to donate funds to the P.L.O. from Jonestown.

Larry Layton's father, Laurence, attended the same Quaker church in Berkeley as Terri Buford when she first arrived in California. Reiterman states that in spite of his Quaker beliefs, Laurence worked as a scientist, developing various kinds of biological warfare, nerve gas, missiles and other military hardware.

Like Jones, Laurence often used monkeys and other animals such as dogs for his experiments. It is worth noting that the entire Layton family also professed to be Quakers as did Terri Buford and many other Temple members. Moreover, Jim Jones' father came from a Quaker background.

The senior Layton first worked at Penn State University and then moved to Berkeley. Terri left Penn State as well and settled in Berkeley. Larry Layton studied at Davis College in California where Terri Buford enrolled as well for some military training courses. Davis was the place where the Jonestown armed guard received their paramilitary training.

Layton's father was the Chief of the Biochemistry Branch of the Chemical Warfare Division for the U.S. Government. He was appointed Director of Chemical Warfare for the U.S. Army. He was one of the developers of a chemical process used in the Manhattan Project assisting in the development of the Atomic Bomb. Terri's sister, Caroline, was in the same field. She was a scientist using her chemistry background for military purposes.

Terri Buford followed the spiritual, ethical, religious, occupational and geographical patterns set by the Layton family for years prior to Jonestown. With her mathematical and chemistry background, Terri obtained jobs in Berkeley working with various scientists who were also helping to develop military weapons.

Even though Quakers are pacifists, these ex-Quakers renounced that philosophy and now believed in fighting fire with fire. In those antiwar years, his father's position caused Larry the same discomfort as Terri experienced. Larry's beloved Jewish grandmother, Anita, was now a devoted Quaker. Anita's family had worked for I.G. Farben, the German chemical company, before the Nazis took control. Through that connection, her daughter, Lisa, met and later married Laurence Layton Sr.

Anita realized with horror what this research in chemical warfare could unleash. The entire family was crushed when she committed suicide at the age of 61. According to Yee, she was severely troubled over the work that her son-in-law, Laurence was doing for the U.S. Government.

Young Terri Buford and Larry Layton Jr. shared an intense guilt over their families' violations of Quaker beliefs and contribution to war. Linked in anger, they became close friends and began to abuse drugs.

Larry experimented in college with a variety of drugs. According to Tim Stoen, when Terri first joined the Temple, she had a severe drug habit. Terri introduced Larry to Jones to cure his own drug habit.

Larry had been married to a minister's daughter, Carolyn Moore. Together, they both eagerly joined the Temple and his new belief in Jones' revolutionary work quickly cured him from his addiction. Larry's new found zeal impressed not only his wife, but also both his sister and mother as well.

Severely depressed over the death of her grandmother, Larry's sister, Debby, also eagerly joined Jones. Furthermore, her mother Lisa had been diagnosed as having terminal cancer. The children were desperately searching for any possible cure for their beloved mother. They all joined faith healer Jim Jones' cult as he promised a cure.

Upon meeting Larry Layton Jr., a son of the key scientist in charge of developing chemical weapons, Jim Jones remembered his own father who was gassed in the war. Jones decided to take revenge upon Laurence through Larry, the privileged son of a healthy, wealthy father, who was destined to pay a full price for his father's activities.

In his revenge, Jim Jones devised secret plans to break up Larry and Carolyn Layton's marriage. Jones took her as his mistress. He also added Larry's sister, Debby, as his mistress as well. Larry's mother, Lisa, foolishly donated $250,000 to Jones in the hope of buying a miracle cure for her cancer. She, with her two grown children, Larry and Debby, all made the exodus to Guyana. Lisa's husband, Dr. Laurence Layton Sr., left the United States for Germany in a state of disgust.

Eventually, while Lisa Layton suffered on her deathbed in Jonestown, Jones admitted to her that he had no special power and she was an old fool for ever trusting him. Ironically, Jonestown was to be the second concentration camp Lisa Layton would experience in her lifetime.

Debby defected from Jonestown leaving her lover, Jones, as well as her brother and husband, Philip. She had been legally married to the Jonestown sea captain, George Philip Blakey, soon after joining the Temple. Pastor Jones presided at their wedding. With Debby gone, Philip defected as well during the massacre, not showing up as originally planned for Mike Prokes' getaway with the Jonestown boat for their prearranged escape.

According to tapes released by researcher, David Emory (1), Philip Blakey surfaced as an agent in Jonah Samvimbi's anti-communist UNITA organization in Angola. Because of possible links to fascist groups, assistance to UNITA had been forbidden by Congress in a piece of legislation known as the Hughes-Ryan Amendment. The legislation's author was none other than anti-fascist Congressman, Leo Ryan.

Because of his amendment, Leo Ryan proved to be a tough Temple adversary. When Debby defected, she went directly to his office to disclose the details of the operation. There she joined forces with another defector, Tim Stoen.

Jones was utterly furious at these defections. Debby Blakey's disloyalty was completely shattering to both Jones and Buford because of the information Blakey possessed. Blakey was immediately threatened with a death sentence.

Blakey's action immediately prompted Buford to quietly plot her own escape. While Buford crafted her plan for revenge upon Jones, Jones had plotted his own revenge for Debbie Blakey. Her brother, Larry, was being carefully programmed. The first step in this process had been the seduction of Layton's wife, Carolyn, by Jones who attained total control over her body and soul. As a minister's daughter, she was one of his favorite targets for abuse.

Then Larry was tricked into marrying another woman in the cult. Jones planned in advance to destroy Layton by seducing and taking his new, second wife as well. Layton was devastated. Jones asserted total dominance over Larry by then abusing and degrading him by using him as his homosexual love object.

Totally suppliant and delusional, Layton was brainwashed to believe that the upcoming investigation by Rep. Leo Ryan, prompted by Layton's own sister, Debbie, was a fantastic Nazi plot. In this scenario, Ryan was out to destroy everybody in Jonestown.

With that thought deeply implanted in Larry's suggestible subconscious mind, he was handed a gun and sent out to do his deadly mission. Layton had been turned into a programmed, zombie-like killer.

Yet, Layton did not kill Ryan. He resisted the brainwashing. *Facts On File* (2) states that Larry Layton had been instructed by Jones to wait until Ryan's plane was airborne and then shoot the pilot, causing the plane to crash.

But Layton never did. *Facts On File* (3) states that the survivors of Jonestown testified that Layton had not fired at any of the persons who died there. The only definite time of Layton harming anyone at all was during the first ambush before Ryan was murdered. Layton pulled a pistol and wounded two would-be defectors, Monica Bagby and Vernon Gosney, as they were boarding a rescue plane.

According to *Facts On File* (4), there exists serious doubt within Guyana as to whether or not Layton even committed any of the murders. The Guyanese government had a different interpretation of Larry Layton's culpability and they were certainly closer to the event. A Guyanese jury acquitted former Peoples Temple member Larry Layton and extradited him to the United States for trial. The Guyanese vote was 12-0 for acquittal.

In 1987, seven years later, Layton was tried in the U.S. and sentenced to life imprisonment. He was convicted by a Federal court in San Francisco of conspiracy, aiding and abetting in Ryan's death and attempted murder.

In handing down the sentence, Chief U.S. District Judge Robert Peckham made Layton eligible for parole in 1991, saying a just sentence requires consideration of the environment in which Layton and other members were imprisoned.

After the murder trial, *Time* (4) quotes Fred Lewis, who lost 27 members of his family in Jonestown as saying that he felt better that someone got convicted. Larry's conviction alleviated some of the pressure the prosecutors felt from an angry public. Larry Layton is the only Temple member ever charged in connection with Ryan's killing or any other activity concerning the Temple.

The heroism of Larry's sister, Debby, as she tried to save the people of Jonestown, sealed her own brother's fate.

Facts On File (5) describes the reactions of Layton's defense attorney. They argued that the prosecutors had sensationalized the case against Layton by playing up the spectacle and horror of the mass murder and had attempted to make Layton the scapegoat. In addition, the defense attorneys argued that there was no direct evidence that Layton had fired shots at Ryan. The evidence had indicated that the shots were fired by others who later died. Thus, the defense argued, Layton could not have been part of the murder conspiracy to kill the congressman.

Layton had signed a confession in Guyana right after the murder of Ryan. *Facts On File* (5) describes the circumstances of that confession. The lawyers said that Layton was kept in handcuffs for three days in an unlighted cell infested with insects and deprived of food. Also, he was not allowed to speak to an attorney or anyone from the American Embassy in Georgetown, Guyana.

Sadly, charged *in connection* with Ryan's murder, not of actually killing him at all. However, everyone in the nightmare of Jonestown had some *connection* with the events that transpired. It is the ultimate horror to be Larry Layton.

His current lawyers, Robert Bryan and Thomas Jackson, were hired after Layton was sentenced to replace his original attorney, Tony Tamburello. Bryan (6) states that Layton's former defense attorney, Tamburello, did not call a single witness on Larry's behalf and that Larry got a *raw deal*. Even the jurors were stunned. This was highly unusual in a trial that involved the possibility of a life sentence and, even if he was guilty as charged, could he, the underling who had both of his wives stolen and his own sexuality smashed, have planned the whole thing by himself?

Layton's new attorneys are desperately attempting to reopen the case one day. According to Bryan (6) Layton's previous defense lawyer just gave up. Bryan stated that the federal prosecutor in San Francisco personally told him that he was totally baffled by the lack of any witnesses in the trial.

In prison, Layton's letters are edited and his visits are monitored. How can he defend himself without new witnesses called to clarify what actually occurred?

While the trial was going on in California, Terri Buford was hiding in her apartment in Brooklyn, New York, fearfully checking license plates of cars on her block for California tags. Her testimony might have proved Layton's innocence. Even though she felt Larry got a bad break, she was greatly relieved to learn that he was sentenced, realizing that the blame for Jonestown would be diverted away from her.

Luckily for Terri, no subpoena ever came.

CHAPTER 13
TWINKIE

Something is happening and you don't know what it is, do you...Mr. Jones?
Ballad of a Thin Man. Bob Dylan

The basic reason for Rep. Leo Ryan's visit to Jonestown was a legal one. Tim Stoen was a former Temple chieftain who had Terri Buford assigned to him as both an aide and a spy.

Terri gained his absolute trust. Her method was to insist on total honesty and display an air of complete loyalty. But then, behind Stoen's back, she rifled through his briefcase and files.

She informed on Stoen to Jones in the same way she betrayed Charles Garry. Stoen became persona non-grata within the Jonestown community, accused of being a C.I.A. informer. Again, there was no evidence. Buford then assumed Stoen's Temple duties.

Stoen was then cruelly treated by the group and defected. He desperately wanted his only son, John Stoen, returned from the Temple to his care. For Stoen's alleged disloyalty, Jones held John hostage in angry revenge as a brutal example to others.

Jones also claimed that he was the biological father of John Stoen. Grace Stoen, John's mother, denied the charge. Under extreme pressure she had signed a notarized statement presented to her by Jones to the effect that he, Jones, was John's father. This was a precaution to prevent Grace from ever defecting at the risk of losing her child.

Grace left the Temple anyway and was forced to abandon her child to Jones. John Stoen was trapped. Grace realized that even if she returned to Jonestown, she would then be Jones' prisoner as well. If she fought Jones from the states, her child would be harmed and she would most probably be murdered. However, her husband, Tim Stoen, was not a poor, helpless victim, but a knowledgeable lawyer, who would prove to be Jones' toughest adversary.

Stoen instituted child custody charges against Jones in Guyana. But Jones was used to having his way. Jones had ignored the court's orders. The court's letter was nailed to the Jonestown gate and then Jones' lieutenants tore it up and threw away the pieces.

Terri Buford had responded to this legal threat by calling up the Guyanese officials involved in the custody case and threatening a mass suicide unless the investigation was called off. In effect, Buford was issuing a veiled murder threat against a thousand people. At that point, the situation became a hostage crises.

A sworn statement by Deborah Blakey, dated June 15, 1978, described the tense situation as reaching crisis proportions. The radio messages from Guyana were frenzied and hysterical. Debby and Terri Buford, public relations advisers, were instructed to place a telephone call to a high-ranking Guyanese official who was visiting the United States.

They delivered the following threat: unless the government of Guyana stalled the Guyanese court action regarding John Stoen's custody, the entire population of Jonestown would die. After that, an incredible letter was sent to every U.S. Senator and representative also threatening mass death.

Why was the Peoples Temple so concerned about one child? The controversy over John Stoen, Tim Stoen's son, revolved around Jim Jones' claim that the boy was his own flesh and blood. However, Father Jones claimed every person in

Jonestown as his own, calling all of them his children.

Stoen's doomed son was now Jones' favorite, groomed like a prince waiting to accept the Jonestown throne. In revenge for his father's defection, John was being molded in Jones' image and, therefore, developed tremendous importance.

John Stoen was systematically trained in all the techniques of rebellion against organized government and religion. Methods of Machiavellian deception were carefully passed on to him. Even adult Temple members were afraid to reprimand him. His black hair was styled to look like Jones'. He was personally molded to be manipulative, pragmatic and ruthless.

The concept of Jones as all-seeing godfather of every soul in Jonestown was now further threatened by Tim Stoen. In this feudal domain, no man was allowed to be a biological father except Jones. When Tim Stoen declared his son to be his own flesh and blood, this illusion was jeopardized.

The image of a young, fit, black haired Jones was changing as he aged, not gracefully, and his hair turned grey. He continued to dye it raven black like a young rock star. Like Elvis, one of his heroes, Jones began bloating from drug abuse. He developed an addiction to sex obsessed with a very force he once utilized to control others.

Buford explains how she mastered a technique to stimulate Jim Jones. She carefully wired Jones' genitals during foreplay, and under the influence of artificial stimulation achieved by a low level of electric impulses, Jones was able to have continuous sex for many hours.

Jones' drug abuse, combined with the defection of many key members and lovers, so affected his ability to cope with reality that by the time Congressman Ryan arrived to discuss the custody of Stoen's son, a rejected Jim Jones was quite delusional.

Terri realized that if Congressman Ryan were to prove successful in delivering the child to his proper parents, Jones would be psychologically shattered, with his powerful hold on the group completely severed. At that time, she decided to defect. She lost complete faith in Jones, especially since she was aware that he had been lying about numerous other lovers.

She already discovered his drugging of young, beautiful, Shanda James.

Reiterman states that Shanda was only nineteen and already married to another member, Bruce Oliver, but, Reverend Jones wasn't concerned with such trivialities. He desired her body. Soon, he and Shanda were spending time together in bed with his excuse to the others that he was administering his holy sexual healing as medicine to cure her depression.

Furthermore, besides the actual infidelity, she had been more offended by Jones' ethnic abuse since Shanda was black. She was the first and only black woman that Jones ever violated. It was strictly forbidden for black and white members to have any sexual relations with each other. All Jones' mistresses had been lily white.

Terri observed drastic changes in Jones' behavior, combined with the threat of Tim Stoen and Congressman Ryan's investigation into the John Stoen child custody case. These events propelled Terri out of Jonestown. She realized that whether or not John Stoen was the biological son of Tim Stoen or Jim Jones, one thing was certain. John was certainly Grace Stoen's son. Jones was in legal trouble. At the very least, Timothy Stoen was trying to rescue his wife's son from certain extermination.

Jones, like Hitler, could not produce life, only death. When an organization is patterned after the personality of one man, his successor is of utmost importance. Jones egotism and worship of Hitler forced him to do something similar. Hitler could not produce a natural son as an heir. It was necessary to try to create or, at least, mold one. Stoen's son was to be the link to the future of the struggle. Jones would die defending this future vision of John Stoen as his heir.

Up until the moment he died, Jim Jones claimed that young John Stoen was his natural son. John had jet black hair and certainly looked like Jim Jones. Anyone that has lost a child through divorce or death can empathize with the way that Jim Jones would have felt upon having John ripped away by legal authorities. Jones certainly had strong parental feelings towards all of his followers. Terri Buford stated that the issue of John Stoen's custody was the final straw that drove Jones over the edge.

Little John Stoen died in the massacre. He was forced to drink Jones' poison of choice, cyanide, the same poison that Eva Braun, Hitler's wife drank. Grace and Tim Stoen were devastated. Jones was done in by his feelings for a child, a link to the future of his *cause*.

Jones, born in 1933, had been molded by the Nazis and their fantastic successes during the beginning of World War Two. Following the maxims of the master race and Darwin's *survival of the fittest*, the Jonestown nightmare had realized William Jennings Bryan's greatest fear.

As in the caste system of the Nazis, Jonestown particularly singled out certain minority groups for exploitation. After their goods were confiscated, they were worked unmercifully and then slaughtered to prevent their voices from crying out to the world about their tragic lives. Jones wanted to take as many blacks with him as he could possibly slaughter. Stoen's son was the link to the future of this continuing racist genocidal destruction.

The concept of mass suicide, was foreign to Jones. But he received all of the blame, while his leaders escaped unscathed.

To most Americans, the idea of suicide, especially on a mass scale, is a foreign one. Unlike the Japanese notion that it is honorable to kill oneself, the Christian notion is that it is repulsive and that the person who commits that act will go to hell forever. It would be natural for a person who was brought up in Japan rather than America to consider and conceive of *Hari Kari* for a group as a solution to an unsolvable dilemma.

Before he died Jones had been telling his people that he was taking them to Russia. This was an absurd lie. The Russians would never admit a phony religious maniac into their country. He created this deception to give the people a faint glimmer of hope.

He created an alliance with Russia in the same manner as Hitler had with Stalin. It was a strategy to buy time. His escape was planned to a capitalist country where he could continue to live in the wealthy style to which he had become accustomed.

Puerto Limon, Costa Rica, a quiet town near Panama on the Atlantic Coast, was targeted. It is only a short hop by boat from Guyana. Much of the Temple's funds were in Panamanian banks. Furthermore, Jones would be safe in Costa Rica, since it has no extradition treaty with the U.S.

Swindling is an art critically dependent upon the practitioner's ability to appear innocent. Jones couldn't fool anyone without fooling himself to an extent. However, without the bank account numbers, Jones' swindling days were numbered. If Congressman Ryan's mission had succeeded, the foster children would have been saved and the social security and foster care money supply would have been cut off at the source.

Without that money coming in, Jones wouldn't have been able to feed the population indefinitely and he would have had a violent mutiny on his hands. The revolution against Jim Jones would have spread to his inner circle of leaders as well.

Certainly then, Mike Prokes, *Dr.* Larry Schacht, Terri Buford, and all the other disciples would never have escaped alive. Without their meager food supply, the Jonestown population would have taken immediate revenge upon all of their tormentors. It became essential to plan a mass murder to cover their tracks.

Terri wrote a note to Linda Swaney explaining another motive for her defection: "Dear Linda, I think that we'd better stop the whole operation. I really think that someone in the church knows that I've been taking money. I realize we need the money to keep up our operation but someone's got to know. People look at me funny....Terri." (1)

Before conceiving her getaway plan, Buford came to the frightening realization that there were certain clear similarities between Jones and her own mother at her manic-depressive worst. This was accentuated by Jones' drug abuse which reminded her of her mother's alcoholism. That was when she realized that Jones personally embodied the worst aspects of both her parents.

She realized that in the event that Jones had escaped and not been killed, if he were captured in his unbalanced state of mind, he might have talked to the government. She, as well as the politicians in California who supported him would have been exposed.

Reporter Warren Hinkle (2) believes there was a seamy connection between the liberal establishment in San Francisco and Jonestown. There had been numerous reports that Rev. Jones had instructed his followers to work in political campaigns in San Francisco, including the successful mayoral campaign of

George Moscone. Membership in his church reached 20,000 in California by the early 70's and his church had 13 buses used to transport large groups on short notice to any political rally or demonstration that Jones supported.

In a personal letter to Jim Jones from Moscone dated December 2, 1975, Jones was asked to *get out the vote so we can achieve our goals for the city.* (Jonestown Files, California Historical Society)

Yee noted that Jones put some 800 Temple members on the streets as precinct workers to help elect Moscone. Furthermore, the Temple members went from precinct to precinct and voted more than one time. Emory confirms that Temple members voted more than one time for their prearranged friends. Officials at the polling places never confiscated the voters yellow registration forms. There were more votes cast than registered voters.

Moscone's opponent, John Barbagelata, complained about voter fraud. Candidate Barbagelata soon received a box of candy that contained a bomb sent through the mail. He never realized that it was sent by Jim Jones. Luckily for him, the bomb misfired.

Jim Jones donated his own bodyguards to protect Barbagelata. Luckily, the offer was refused. Jones' bodyguards would have been Bargagelata's assassins.

The four hundred voter registration books were never recovered. Originally they were locked in vaults in the San Francisco City Hall. In December, 1978, soon after the murders, Federal and State investigators asked for the files and the remaining doctored books vanished. Incredibly, the entire voting list of the 1975 election was gone. Hinkle noted the thousands of missing voter registration books and concluded that Temple influence swung the election to Moscone.

Afterwards, Joe Freitas had hired Timothy Stoen, Jones' right hand man, who was moved from Ukiah, as the Assistant District Attorney. Yee states that Stoen was in charge of the Voter Fraud unit. He was in charge of the investigation of the 1975 election which had originally brought Mayor Moscone into office. Terri Buford worked in Stoen's office as liaison to Jones to make certain that all went according to plan.

In effect, the prosecutors were put in charge of investigating themselves. Of course, Stoen uncovered no evidence of his own boss' tampering of the election. Moscone, Freitas, Stoen and Jim Jones had gained total control of San Francisco politics.

As of 1990, Tim Stoen is still practicing law in the state of California. In fact, according to Pricilla Coates (3), Stoen is running for elected office again. The 1975 fraud resulted in not one conviction.

John Barbagelata has eight children and now runs a real estate office in San Francisco. He has had three heart attacks in 1991. His children were threatened and had to be accompanied to school by a police guard because he stood up to the mob in San Francisco. He is still issuing statements and pamphlets trying to save his beloved city which is still being run by the same political forces that were forged in the Jonestown era.

Barbagelata, now totally demoralized, asserts that his "fight against the massive rip offs of the common folk of San Francisco by the politicians that are still in power will never stop until the city is sucked completely dry of all resources." His son Paul has courageously volunteered to continue to fight against that corruption when John is no longer physically able to continue.

In 1976, soon after Moscone had taken power by his manipulation of the vote which recorded the slim margin of a doctored victory over John Barbagelata, Mike Prokes was put in charge of a committee that screened candidates for commission vacancies. New Assemblyman Willie Brown immediately introduced legislation giving the new Mayor the power to appoint Jones without confirmation by the Board of Supervisors.

All political movement in that era started and ended with you-gimmee, you-get deals. Virtue did not matter. Choosing good over bad never figured as a factor. Everything was quid pro quo. Power and leverage obtained by whatever means determined all political decisions in San Francisco.

In a letter to Moscone from Mike Prokes dated May 13, 1976, Moscone was given a list of names of Temple members for job appointments. Among his many Temple appointments, new Mayor Moscone, through Prokes, then offered Jim Jones an appointment as Director of the San Francisco Human Rights Commission. Jones refused. There wasn't enough *dirty* money to be made from that position. Instead Jones was rewarded with the job of heading the San Francisco city housing authority.

Brave John Barbagelata protested to the federal government but they refused to interfere with local politics. What did Reverend Jones possibly know about public housing? Reverend Jim Jones accepted the lucrative position as head of the $14 million a year agency on February 24, 1977. Barbagelata knew that this plumb political job provided Jones with a scheme for attaining more power and wealth. Jones arranged free government housing for his members drawing in new victims through the legal system. Shelter is a basic human need. By utilizing computers in the Housing Department of the City Hall office, Jones now had access to the appraised value of his constituent's real estate holdings which were now wide open to his financial scrutiny.

Other public properties that were in tax delinquency, repossessed, foreclosed, Veterans Administration and HUD homes were quietly kept apart from the cities public auction block and diverted to the Peoples Temples' holdings.

Within this seemingly infinite corruption, Jones and his staff amassed a small fortune in city properties, now all considered to be tax exempt due to the religious classification that Peoples Temple enjoyed. Jones was creating a new western pseudo-religious empire modeled upon other timeworn concepts used by other successful religious organizations. The merger of politics and religion have led many others to supreme power. Moscone was able to bypass any conflict of interest charges by using Jones as his political shield.

In a letter to Moscone from Prokes, the Mayor was thanked for accepting an invitation to be an honorary guest at a testimonial dinner for Jim Jones. As an added incentive, Governor Jerry Brown was mentioned as being another of the honored guests.

Substantiated reports in the new media described political deals between then State Assembly Speaker Leo McCarthy, future State Assembly Speaker as well as future national campaign chairman for Jesse Jackson in 1988, Willie Brown, future mayors George Moscone and Art Agnos and other important democrats in 1975.

Political connections to Jones cost some of those politicians their lives. San Francisco's Mayor Moscone was murdered on November 27, 1978, only nine days after Jones was murdered.

On January 30, 1978, during the same year he was murdered, Moscone wrote a letter to Peoples Temple member, Mr. Eugene Chaikin, stating that he regarded "the Reverend Jim Jones as one of the most able and distinguished persons I have ever met."

After Jonestown's inhabitants were slaughtered, Moscone had received numerous phone calls threatening his life. The Mayor employed police body-guards twenty four hours a day to protect him. He was shot in the head along with Harvey Milk by two bullets from a .38 caliber handgun.

John Crewdson (4), a reporter studying both the Jonestown deaths and the Milk/Moscone murders notes that like Mayor Moscone and a number of other prominent California politicians, Mr. Milk had publicly endorsed the Peoples Temple and Jim Jones.

Milk had spoken often at the Temple and had even been invited to visit Jonestown as an honored guest; he declined. Crewdson quotes Milk as saying that Guyana was a great experiment that didn't work.

Milk paid a price for that opinion and so did his homosexual lover, Jack Lira, who was also found dead, listed by police as yet another *suicide* victim. A note at the scene warned Milk to beware the *Ides of November*. The threat was made by Lira's murderer to Milk, who was killed that same bloody November. Lira's murder case is, as yet, unsolved. The rubber stamp marked *Suicide* at the coroner's office must have been worn out by this time.

Milk had been certain that he was destined to be murdered by Jones. In a taped political Last Will, he asked that the bullets that will rip through his brain smash every closet door in America. When asked by his followers to run as future Mayor, he sadly replied that he *would not be around then*. Milk realized that the Jonestown political forces were plotting his death to silence him and continue their work. Meiers confirms that included in his ashes at his burial were several packs of grape Kool-Aid™ symbolically representing his murderers.

David Emory (5) says that Milk enjoyed Temple support as he was closely connected with Jim Jones. Harvey Milk took it upon himself to write a letter dated August 5, 1977 directly to the Prime Minister of Guyana to implore the *great* Jim Jones *to be allowed to operate his temple in Jonestown, Guyana*. (Jonestown

Files, California Historical Society).

People in San Francisco felt that Harvey Milk was a man with a conscience. Milk must have realized that something was corrupt at City Hall and that he was in way over his head.

The Moscone/Milk assassin was a former paratrooper named Dan White, an ex-police officer, armed with a .38 in one hand and a *Hostess Twinkie*™ in the other! White's best friend, detective Frank Falzone, made the collar.

It has been alleged by the media that White killed Milk simply because he was gay. For that, Harvey Milk has been made a martyr. In New York, a high school was even named in his honor. However the gay motive cover seems very thin when the timing of the murder is examined.

It is also assumed that White was unhappy because Mayor Moscone would not rehire him to his Supervisory post. But then, why had White quit voluntarily only a few days before he murdered Moscone? Many elements to explain the murders do exist and might have had some bearing on the case in adding fuel to White's rage, but the ties of Milk and Moscone to the Temple should have been examined more thoroughly than they were.

In court, Dan White successfully utilized the incredible *Twinkie*™ defense, claiming that he killed Moscone because he was temporarily emotionally insane after ingesting excessive sugar by eating a *Twinkie*™.

Dan White's defensive technicality was so ridiculous that soon after his trial, it was outlawed as a defense tactic in California courts. White got five years for both murders. The prosecuting attorneys office was headed by none other than Joe Frietas.

This *Twinkie*™ defense never explained why Dan White, supposedly under the influence of the *dangerous* pastry, had passed other people not harming them, including future mayor, Dianne Feinstein on his way from Moscone's chambers.

The riots in San Francisco that ensued were first *Twinkie*™ riots but later they were known as the *White Night* riots, acknowledging the connection between White, Jones, and the *White Night* death drills at Jonestown.

After his stint with the police, White had been elected to the Board of Supervisors. He worked at City Hall, with the same power clique that Jim Jones had operated from while he was the all-powerful housing Czar. Jones, Moscone, Milk and White were intimately connected through their jobs.

According to Emory (5) it is worth noting that Dan White had originally resigned his position at City Hall on the same day that Congressman Leo Ryan announced that he was going to Jonestown to investigate the abuses.

About seven weeks after his release from prison, Dan White, out on parole, was found dead in his car. He was listed as another suicide victim. Arresting officer Frank Falzone stated to law enforcement sources that his best friend, Dan White, in his opinion, was not capable of committing suicide. White and Falzone were teammates on a grammar school baseball team and knew each other intimately. But Falzone's opinion was never heard in a courtroom because Dan White's death was never fully investigated. The labeling of his death another suicide ruled out a murder investigation. However, according to Emory, when asked about the death, the San Francisco Police Chief responded: "Draw your own conclusions."

Hinkle explains how D.A. Joe Freitas was the prosecutor that enabled Dan White to go free. According to Paul Krassner (6), Freitas was in Washington D.C. conferring with the state department at the same time that Milk and Moscone were killed. Witnesses state that at that time, as soon as Frietas had heard of the murders, he immediately assumed that they were assassinated by a Temple hit squad. Krassner was baffled by this mysterious connection.

Why did Frietas mentally link up Jonestown with Moscone's murder at that time? After leaving Washington, Freitas immediately returned to San Francisco to conduct the trial and prosecute Dan White. Even though Frietas knew more than he disclosed, the subject of Jonestown was avoided in White's prosecution. The lone assassin theory stood as Temple-related questions were never asked of White and key Temple witnesses, like Terri Buford, were never called to testify.

Emory links White's death to the political Jonestown coverup in the bay area, calling it another *induced suicide*, implying that it really was yet another murder. White's death effectively silenced any serious continuing Jonestown connections within the city government of San Francisco.

These links seem to rise to the federal level of government. U.S. Attorney

William Hunter was in charge of investigating the massacre at Jonestown. Hunter had close ties with Tim Stoen since they both originally worked as Assistant District Attorneys in the San Francisco voter fraud investigation of Moscone's election. Hunter was promoted to U. S. Attorney and offered Tim Stoen a position as Chief Assistant. One of Hunter's employees, attorney Robert Dorado, eventually even prosecuted Larry Layton.

Corrupt mayors and other officials that were elected illegally, via stuffed ballots, have eluded conviction through collusion with the investigators under their own commands. According to Reiterman, Jones even bragged to possess close Mafia ties.

An honest voter fraud unit would have never been placed into the hands of the very people that were fraudulently voted into their offices. The Moscone murderer's successful alibis result directly from the false public perception of the Jonestown carnage as a mass suicide created by the politicians directly in charge. Responsibility was again shifted from the perpertrators to the victims. If the public bought the *Kool Aide*™ fantasy, then they could swallow the *Twinkie*™ defense. The public verdict of the Milk murder is that White killed him merely because he was a leader of the Gay movement in San Francisco. That does not explain the fact that Milk was murdered only nine days after Jones. Furthermore, there were many other gay leaders that could have been killed as well.

But that alibi was perfect for the Jonestown-Moscone connection's coverup. The real links had to be kept hidden at all costs. They were made to appear as isolated events, mere coincidences, even though there has been a nagging suspicion about their strange synchronicity. In time, it has been swept under the rug.

The citizens in San Francisco had a huge protest march nicknamed the *White Night* riots. They demanded the truth. No one has fully investigated this and other obvious political connections in San Francisco.

Temple member Bonnie Malman had been sent to have sex with George Moscone by Jim Jones, long before he was Mayor. She became his secret lover, functioning as a spy for Jones. She attended Congressman Ryan's funeral and sat near Moscone. She was still informing on Moscone to other Temple members

131

and was in San Francisco at the time of his murder. Jonestown associates had much to hide and protect from the public.

Besides Moscone, there had been many other politicians elected in the 1976 election. In fact, they still have a lot of power in California. Emory mentions that State Assemblymen Willie Brown, ex-Mayor Art Agnos, gay leaders, Supervisor Harvey Milk, Howard Wallace, Human Rights Commissioners Enola Maxwell and Sylvester Heering, San Francisco N.A.A.C.P. President Joe Hall and Cecil Williams, Minister of the Glide Memorial Foundation, were all staunch Jonestown supporters.

At a head table at one of the early Temple fundraising galas Mayor Moscone, Assemblyman Brown, District Attorney Joe Frietas, California Lieutenant Governor Mervyn Dymally and State Senator Milton Marks, Eldridge Cleaver and Angela Davis had all sat together.

Anyone that presented a problem to that powerful hierarchy had to be stopped at all costs. Yee mentions that State Assemblyman Willie Brown praised Jones by stating that Jones' *system* is what the whole system should be about.

Jonestown political forces had operated in the same manner in Guyana as they had in San Francisco, swinging the election of Forbes Burnham to put him into power as that nation's Prime Minister. Richard Meislin (7) notes that Mr. Burnham had increasingly come to rely on repressive acts to maintain himself in power, a charge that he repeatedly denied to his opponents.

Mr. Burnham was a sharp-witted man who would punctuate his statements with a nearly demonic laugh. He was a staunch ally of Jones. With Jones' death, Burnham lost popular support and, according to Hinkle, died suspiciously during a minor throat operation.

Through Jim Jones, San Francisco and Guyana were politically and financially raped. Politicians in both countries realized that if they were in Jones' esteem, he would send an army of his members to vote and campaign at election time on their behalf. Local Californian politicians received sexual favors from various Temple members on Jones' direct orders. All of this meant that Jones had many political favors when he wanted them.

According to George Klineman (8), black women were sent to Mayor

Moscone by Jones. Moscone enjoyed receiving oral sex in public in his car and then beating the poor women up until they were discarded.

Through his public contacts, Jones also amassed a tremendous amount of power in the courts. Throughout those years, scores of children who were poor wards of the state were quietly put into the custody of the Temple.

Stanek (9) examines how many parents were tricked into signing away their legal rights over their own children and making Jim Jones their children's legal guardian. Later on, a number of these parents charged that Jones and others had coerced them into their decisions. Yet, the California courts upheld all the questions over legal guardianship.

Child abuse charges were constantly filed against Jones and the Temple, but because of his political connections, not one parent was able to get their child out of his grasp.

According to Reiterman, the California State Attorney General's Office declined to probe Temple matters in 1972 as well as in 1977 for vague jurisdictional reasons. Under further pressure, they agreed, finally, to investigate, but only after the November 1978 bloodbath when it was too late to help the children. They did conclude that State officials failed to handle serious complaints properly.

They agreed that not one single precaution was taken to protect the safety of the children of Jonestown. But they could uncover no evidence of any crime. They did not indict or convict one person in connection with child abuse even with all the evidence of beatings and death. Furthermore, not one politician associated with Jones has ever been questioned, or indicted.

CHAPTER 14
LEGACY

"Truth is stranger than fiction, but it is because fiction is
obliged to stick to possibilities; truth isn't."
Mark Twain

A turning point for the Jonestown project was their hiring of the foremost anti-C.I.A. attorney in the world, Mark Lane. At his father's request, Jim Jones' son Steven had welcomed their new attorney to Jonestown with a statement to the effect that Lane had now given them new hope. Mark Lane echoed Steven Jones' eloquent enthusiasm with his own brand of praise. In a speech about the King assassination, Lane drew parallels between Martin Luther King and Jim Jones. Lane failed to mention to the Jonestown assemblage that he was actually the public defender of King's convicted murderer, James Earl Ray.

Mark Lane was then quoted in Jonestown by author, Tim Reiterman (1), as saying that he (Lane) would make every person who entered Jonestown go naked and that he would gladly look in their vaginas, exhibiting a display of solidarity with Jim Jones.

Jones was originally introduced to Lane through Terri Buford while she was a liaison to Charles Garry who had been the original attorney for Jonestown. In her reports to Jones, Buford had insisted on replacing Garry because he wasn't militant enough. In reality, Garry gave them a hard time by objecting to the way in which the Temple operated, questioning the ethics of some of their actions.

Unlike Charles Garry, Lane accepted all of Jones' directives fully. Mark Lane was secretly put in Jones' employ, happily accepting thousands of dollars to represent the Temple. Researcher, Steven Brill, in an article in *Esquire* magazine, describes Lane as receiving a $10,000 retainer and $6,000 per month. (California Historical Society Media Folder Files)

Meanwhile, Charles Garry was kept in the dark about his function as only a mere legal figurehead to keep the peace. He was lied to and told that Lane was only a media consultant. Jones did not want Garry to turn against him.

Even while Garry served as their lawyer, both Jones and Buford greatly admired Lane's anti-American political stance which deflected blame to the C.I.A. for any and all political problems. Lane's strategy kept their enemies off balance and added many new allies to their cause.

Terri realized that she might need strong legal counsel especially from an ally who wasn't afraid to tackle the U.S. Government. Lane was perfect. Terri felt that the attorney was sufficiently adept at stirring U.S. interest in plots and conspiracies to divert some attention from her true activities. Even though his media blitz offered much talk, but no substance, people actually began to wonder if an all powerful C.I.A. was zeroing in on preacher Jim Jones, the poor champion of the black race.

Extremely pleased, Terri wrote, in a confidential memo to Jim Jones, that Lane's work has had the best reaction she had seen. Many in the San Francisco underground community were poised to defend Jones against the C.I.A. Some of the members of the press actually flocked to Jones' defense as well, buying Lane's inventive C.I.A. threat. They played into the hands of the charismatic preacher and his flamboyant lawyer.

In reality, Terri Buford had played a complicated counterpoint with Jones and Lane. While she wrote secret memos to Jones praising Lane, she quietly lured

Lane deep within her web to serve as her new guru-mentor-savior and lover. Behind Jones'back, she confided to Lane that poor Jim Jones was afflicted with the same severe manic-depression as her own mentally cursed mother. Buford had correctly assessed Jones' mounting difficulties and decided to escape with Lane's help.

Lane extended his sympathy, eventually providing shelter to Terri from Jim Jones, as well as from the Congressional investigations which wanted to fully question the second in command at Jonestown.

In leaving Jonestown, Terri left behind all the Temple intelligence files, which she kept for safety in her small bedroom. Then she put her many keys into the refrigerator. She left the Temple secretary, Jean Brown, a goodbye note,with a personal memo to Jim Jones stating that she would continue to feed information to the Temple and continue to operate as his spy.

After her relocation to Lane's new home in Memphis, she and Lane celebrated by enjoying delicious spare rib dinners at the finest restaurants that the town could offer. With her Asiatic background, she treated Lane fabulously for sheltering her from the Jonestown storm. He had a personal *geisha* girl, totally submissive and attentive, granting his every wish.

Terri Buford was Jim Jones' most highly skilled lover. She had mastered all the secret sexual techniques of her fallen leader, utilizing them expertly. Blissfully, Lane believed his fallen angel's tale of entrapment and sex-slavery victimization at Jones' hands. He was happily lost in a state of denial while he enjoyed Terri's sensuous pleasures.

"I dreamt of Jim Jones again last night. I was trapped in Jonestown again and couldn't escape". As she trembled from her recurring nightmares, her hands as cold as ice, it was apparent that she was haunted by the ghost of Jim Jones. Her misadventures had left her with post-traumatic shock syndrome that veterans of war experience. As he comforted her, she slowly bonded Lane's political philosophies to her own, putting herself totally into his hands.

Buford began to work with Lane on his other legal cases even though she was his client. Lane's other clients were the P.L.O., James Earl Ray, and even the Iranian students during the hostage crisis. Lee Harvey Oswald's mother hired

Lane to defend her son before the Warren Commission after Oswald was killed.

Buford spent three years under Lane's wing, eventually doing some undercover investigative work for him as well. Lane had Buford investigate his, as yet, unproven theory of presumed C.I.A. involvement in the Martin Luther King murder.

Buford spoke to James Earl Ray, Lane's client, while he was in prison. She also secretly interviewed the key witness for Ray's defense, Grace Walden also known as Grace Stevens, an elderly black patient rescued by Lane from a mental institution. Grace was an alleged witness to the murder of Dr. King.

Lane, as well as Buford, promote the theory that the C.I.A. had Walden placed in the institution to silence her as a witness to the Martin Luther King murder. If that were true, one wonders how Buford was able to get to talk to her at all since, according to Buford and Lane's hypothesis, the C.I.A. routinely assassinates dangerous witnesses such as Grace Walden.

Presumably, according to Lane (2), Walden states that she saw C.I.A. or F.B.I. agents shoot Dr. Martin Luther King. To Lane the C.I.A. and the F.B.I. are interchangeable evils as agencies representative of an evil U.S. Government. How Walden might identify anyone as a certifiable C.I.A. agent is also a mystery. C.I.A. agents do not wear big badges!

According to reporter Nicholas Horrock (3), even the House of Representatives had considered Walden's testimony utterly worthless. But then, Lane would consider the House of Representatives C.I.A. stooges.

Reporter Horrock writes that to further protect Lane's theory, while still in Guyana, Buford tried to arrange a fake passport to abduct Walden into the *safety* of Jonestown to protect her from the C.I.A.

Horrock's (3) evidence is a letter discovered within the debris of Jonestown, written by Terri Buford and addressed to Jim Jones recommending that Mark Lane get a phony passport for Grace in order to smuggle her into Jonestown. Since there might be a problem, her suggestion was to tamper with another member's passport, Maxine Swaney's, since she looked a little like Grace.

Actually, if Grace was ever questioned effectively, Lane's theory that the F.B.I. killed King would have been proven false. Lane's client, James Earl Ray depended upon Grace's testimony even though Lane was trying to abduct her into Jonestown where poor, old Grace would have first provided Jones with yet another source of U.S. Government Social Security money following which she would have been murdered and labeled a suicide, or another C.I.A. *murder* plot.

Finally, even though Buford was in one of her disguises during her investigation of the Martin Luther King case, and used the pseudonym Kim Jackson, Lane had to take Buford off the James Earl Ray defense case because the media in Memphis eventually recognized her.

By exhibiting a public love for Martin Luther King while at the same time defending his assassin, James Earl Ray, Mark Lane cleverly allied himself with the forces of the extreme right and left at the same time and collected fees from both. He allied himself with Dick Gregory, on the one hand, and anti-black elements on the other.

Teresa Jean Buford's unbridled admiration for Mark Lane at that time was a reflection of the strange, wonderful and warm relationship that Jim Jones and Mark Lane had developed in Jonestown. The two comrades had gotten along so well that according to Reiterman, Jones had told his people that Lane called him *Saint Jim Jones.*

Their brotherhood was so strong that with his utmost appreciation, Reiterman quotes Jones as instructing his disciples that regardless of gender any new baby must be named after Mark Lane.

Going far beyond the call of duty, Terri not only would name her baby after Lane, but actually conceive his biological child. Their daughter is named Vita Thais (X) with an alias for her last name to hide Lane's identity.

This clandestinely conceived, cleverly concealed child claims a bloodline that includes, not only Vice Presidential aspirant, Mark Lane, but writer James Agee, as well as the former Presidential candidate, William Jennings Bryan.

Buford's pregnancy had been quite a disturbing ordeal for Lane. Caught in a dilemma, he did not want to be exposed in a media investigation. During the time of Vita's conception, besides investigations by *The New York Times*, *Newsweek*, and *The Los Angeles Times*, for improper practices regarding his alleged handling of the Jonestown money, particularly intense focus was put on

Lane's association with Buford, as well.

Within two weeks after the murders, reporter Robert Lindsay (4) accused Jim Jones of instructing Buford to deliver the money in cash to Lane, as a donation to the P.L.O. He states that the Reverend Jim Jones died with more than 900 followers and left a network of secret bank accounts around the world totaling more than $10 million.

In the article, Lindsay quotes ex-top member, Tim Stoen, who explains that Mr. Jones had spoken of sending the money to the P.L.O. Stoen elaborated specifying that two women, one of whom may be dead, appear to have the answers regarding the Jones bank accounts. The dead woman was Jones' mistress, Carolyn Layton. The other women mentioned was Terri Buford. Stoen categorized them both as being top financial advisers to Mr. Jones.

Two weeks after that probe, on December 16, 1978, Lane was accused by reporter David Binder (5) of going to Switzerland to take eight million dollars out of the Zurich accounts. A day later, in *The New York Times* (6), Lane denied *seeking* any secret funds from Jonestown.

But Lane denied *receiving* any secret funds. He also never repudiated the full accusation which named Terri Buford as Jones' courier for the Jonestown funds, or their P.L.O. destination.

Ultimately, the intensive investigation was not the responsibility of the press. That domain belonged to the U.S. Government. Unfortunately, there was never any investigations by the Government to fully question Lane and recover the Jonestown money for U.S. taxpayers, from whom the funds were actually appropriated.

More than likely, the money that was alleged to be delivered to the P.L.O. never arrived. Even if that goal was Jones' true intention, why would he have waited until his demise to donate it? The P.L.O. was merely another ruse the inner group used to hoard money for their personal gain and then justify it to their revolutionary followers. *Donate* it clearly meant to *keep it* within Jones' code of speaking in opposites. During the entire Jonestown operation, radical anti-U.S. forces as well as the people of the U.S. and their government, were embezzled.

According to Lane, Walter Cronkite also began to question these allegations with his own investigations, but he was facing tremendous difficulty. Cronkite was on the right track. However at that time, he didn't have all the facts, especially without Terri Buford, who was still kept behind Lane's bolted door.

No one realized Terri was even pregnant.

Cronkite had already exposed Lane as a fraud in his *Witness To History* (7) show that dealt with the coverage of J.F.K.'s assassination. Cronkite was incensed at Lane's charge that the Warren Commission was a C.I.A. coverup. He produced the witnesses that Lane used to make his allegations. In front of a nation, Lane's witnesses denied that their testimony was quoted accurately by Lane.

Cronkite lamented the idea that Americans were so disenchanted with the Vietnam war that they could accept Lane's accusations as valid. However, Lane gained a wealth of free publicity from appearing on the show and his book sold very well. A curious American public was being led astray.

If the Warren Commission had been hasty, and years later it is being accused of not calling enough witnesses, that is no reason to suggest an evil coverup.

Investigating Lane and Buford on a more personal yet relevant level, Lane, himself, describes (8) how an investigative reporter working for *Newsweek*, Harold Weisberg, actually phoned Terri Buford's father and asked him how he felt about the charge that Terri and Lane were engaged in sexual activity at the time when Lane was supposed to be representing her before the Congressional Investigations.

Commander Buford was furious both at Weisberg and Lane.

Naturally, the angry Mark Lane, denied any charge of sexual misconduct as being totally false. He threatened Weisberg with a lawsuit for slander. How could Weisberg's allegations ever be proved? Buford began to accuse the *Eastern* press of harassment. Beside herself with anger at the charge, she felt that the press was being totally biased. Lane and Buford accused the C.I.A. of harassment.

Mark Lane dismissed the media scrutiny as mere slanderous conjecture, continuing to deny vehemently, in public, that he was engaging in any sex whatsoever with his client. If those charges could be proven and exposed, Lane knew that he would be in violation of the code of ethics for lawyers. He would be in danger of losing both his credibility and his license to practice law.

Lane even denied living with Buford stating in his own book that he told reporter John Crewdson that his article contained an inaccurate implication. Crewdson had written that Miss Buford had begun living with Mr. Lane in Memphis. Lane objected very quickly, pointing out that Crewdson unfairly, in Lane's words, misrepresented the situation.

Lane acknowledged that Terri had been living with his extended family in Memphis, including April Ferguson, her daughter, plus Grace Walden, whose release from a mental institution Lane had secured the previous year. But Lane objected to the term: living together. Nothing *sexual* was going on, he protested.

Even though reporter Crewdson's charges and Cronkite's suspicions were absolutely right at the time, they couldn't prove a thing.

Buford's entire congressional testimony was guided by Lane in much the same manner. In fact, Buford insists that directly prior to her testimony to Congress in the ante chamber of the Congressional hearing in California concerning the murder of Congressman Ryan, immediately preceding her testimony, Lane insisted on having sex with her to calm himself.

At that critical, dangerous moment in her life, Terri Buford, with her back to the wall, certainly wasn't in any position to refuse. No birth control was used at that time. Terri Buford also insists that their daughter was conceived that very moment.

In order to hide Terri Buford's pregnancy, Terri states that Mark Lane commanded that she undergo an immediate abortion to conceal the true nature of their carnal relationship.

Furthermore, according to Buford, he proposed a financial inducement, generously agreeing to buy her a houseboat in her own name to be permanently docked on the Potomac near his mansion in Washington to secure her safety. For a man of Lane's new found wealth, money was to be no object. She would be at his beck and call forever.

A pregnant Terri Buford fully agreed that Lane's injunction was an absolute necessity. Calling the hospital, she efficiently made all the necessary arrangements.

But she had a secret plan. She fled the hospital moments before the abortion procedure was to begin and climbed out a window.

She left the amazed operating room attendants shocked. She couldn't go through with it. This unborn child was her very own. She was haunted by the memory of Dietriech, the helpless black boy she had adopted and abandoned in the death camp. According to Terri, another death, especially of her own biological child, was just too much for her conscience to bear.

Terri further explains why she turned him down. First of all, he desired to keep her in this safe love nest as his permanent mistress. She had hopes that Mark Lane would marry and make an honest woman out of her.

However, at the time, Lane was also sexually and professionally involved with a woman named April Ferguson. According to Lane, Ferguson helped him write his Jonestown book, *The Strongest Poison*. Lane thanks her for her assistance in his acknowledgements.

But after Lane's book was finished, according to Buford, he did not share any of the profits with April for her labor, as he had promised. Ferguson and Lane's sexual relationship broke up soon after that. Terri stated that a furious April Ferguson wanted to sue Lane. Buford received nothing for the book either.

After witnessing Lane not follow through on his obligation to April, Terri considered the possibility that even had she gone ahead with the abortion, Lane would have changed his mind about the boat offer anyway.

Catching him totally by surprise, she fled from him, as she had once from Jim Jones and from her own father. Terri vanished, pregnant, alone, no family, or friends to turn to.

Fully determined to survive even without the bosom of her family, who could Terri Buford give her loyalty to now? Jim Jones was gone. Her hope in Mark Lane was destroyed. All she really ever desired was a loving father. For her, that deep inner desire seemed to underline the entire Jonestown catastrophe.

The pain and suffering drove Terri back to the only time in her life that she felt decent. She went back to her old friends, the Quakers. She stayed in Wales, Pennsylvania, in a *safe house*, set up by the Quakers to protect people with political problems.

There, she tried to heal her wounds from the turbulence of the past, at least for the sake of Vita, if not for herself. She felt like giving up, but Vita had given her life new meaning. Desperately determined to continue that life for the sake of her daughter, she decided to be strong and fight on with new purpose.

Finally, overstaying her welcome in Pennsylvania, she left for New York where her notoriety might escape detection from not only Jones' hit squads, but Mark Lane's wrath.

Terri decided to stay at the legendary Chelsea Hotel, once a favorite haunt of her uncle, James Agee. Burning with hatred for Mark Lane, she retraced Agee's literary trail hoping to connect with new writers. She had quite a story to tell.

Her feminine appearance had allowed her to pass over into conventional society and make economic survival possible. But now, pregnant and thoroughly disgusted with men, she cut her beautiful, waist length hair in a crew-cut. The mix of brown and blond created an orange effect, which on her pregnant frame, made her look like a ripe, *punk* carrot, in her own opinion.

With that disguise, no man would now be interested in her, and in her defiant state of mind, that was fine. Now, determined to consort only with women, she canvassed the feminist bookstores, one of her favorite pickup areas. There, she encountered Mary Weiner, a feminist lawyer from California who was actively dedicated to helping women with political difficulties.

Terri discovered that Weiner occasionally visited a psychic. By using a technique borrowed from Jonestown, Buford introduced herself to Weiner by first getting the psychic to tell her that she was to become involved with a woman from Jonestown and eventually, help her raise a daughter.

According to Terri, Mary Weiner protested to the psychic that this was absurd since she passionately hated children. Terri claims that the session was taped, so that Weiner would never, ever, forget it.

Weiner was thoroughly touched by this seemingly poor, pregnant waif's version of her mistreatment at the cruel hands of men. Terri told her how Jones had used and fooled her. Then she followed her account with Lane's supposed *rape*.

Weiner offered Terri her full protection, hiding her within the back room of her apartment from 1981 until 1985.

For four years, Terri kept Vita's birth a secret, not only from Mark Lane, but from the press. During that period, Mark Lane had no knowledge of the whereabouts of her underground hideout, nor was he aware of his daughter's existence.

Springing from the strange parents, Jim Jones' ex-lover and his ex-lawyer, little Vita is worshipped by her mother who has to make sure of her absolute loyalty. Vita's deep brown eyes are carefully shielded from any knowledge of her mother's lurid past. Terri said that Vita had been kept from any close contact with men, even teenage boys, for the first three years of her life.

They lived in a back room in a quiet Brooklyn neighborhood, almost totally isolated, in fearful hiding.

Terri Buford knows that it will be impossible to hide everything from her daughter. Sooner or later, certain things about her life will have to be told to her.

That time would finally come in 1985. At nursery school, all the other children were asking Vita, where her daddy was and at the age of four, she was old enough to understand that someone important seemed to be missing from the family portrait. Not only didn't she realize Lane was her father, she didn't even know she had one at all.

Terri put Vita's need for her father ahead of her own fear of facing Mark Lane. Finally coming out of her cocoon, Terri contacted Lane. Vita's curiosity compelled her mother to arrange a meeting with the Lane family in Queens at the home of Mark Lane's older brother Larry, a New York City school teacher. There, father's and daughter's brown eyes finally met, face to face, for the first time.

There was no denying this child was part of the Lane family. A blood test was unnecessary. She had the round Russian face and even had thick, bushy eyebrows.

Vita was thrilled to be the only small child in the entire Lane family, radiating in the attention they offered. Mark was now forced, in private, to face up to the facts and, finally grant Vita a small part of her birthright, but to the public eye, full discretion was still essential. Terri was faced with the problem of raising

Vita alone, realizing that Lane was just too powerful to fight for any financial assistance.

Terri disclosed that Lane's Jonestown experience has enabled him to give about thirty college lecture tours at $2,750 each. Lane certainly didn't need the money. He has a beautiful mansion located near the White House. But he had to justify his enormous growth of income which had followed on the heels of Jonestown.

His mission had certain side benefits. Lane also, according to Terri, particularly enjoyed scoring with young coeds. He combined the archtypical rebel and father figure, exuding power and authority.

Even though Lane and Buford are bonded together as accomplices to their shared past, Buford disclosed that she has definite eventual plans to sue Lane's estate as soon as he dies. Lane has had delicate triple bypass surgery resulting from a massive heart attack. He is in his sixties. She has a strong claim to his estate, through Vita, even though Lane has other daughters living in Paris.

But Lane had to carefully rewrite his biography. First he had to carefully admit Vita's existence publicly. In 1986, she appears listed in the book, *Who's Who In America* (9) as Mark Lane's daughter, with no mention made whatsoever of her mother.

Mark Lane has a total of three daughters, Anne Marie, Christina and Vita. The first two were born and live in France with his French girlfriend. In 1986, the listing of Vita is directly after Christina's without the comma separating the names, making it appear to be only one child with a middle name of Vita. In fact, Anne's middle name, Marie, is listed, to further confuse the *issue*. But in 1988, the listing in *Who's Who In America* (10) is revised with a comma added between Christina and Vita, indicating that Vita does exist as a separate child.

According to Terri Buford, when Lane left the country soon after the Jonestown murders and turned up in Europe, he was accused by a variety of investigators of going to the Swiss banks and withdrawing Jonestown money. Visiting his daughters in France could give him a perfect alibi.

It's a matter of record that the Swiss do not stamp the passports of people entering for short visits from France. When Terri and Debby Blakey made their earlier financial runs to Switzerland, they were careful not to get their passports stamped.

Newspaper reports by John Kifner (11) state that Terri had claimed that she had given Lane all the bank account numbers for her own protection. She was more interested in surviving than keeping the money.

A letter to Richard D. Hurdak from Robert J. Stumph regarding the investigation of the Jonestown money states: "Dear Dick, Terri Buford assigned Power of Attorney to Lane and Lane had been 'Travelling extensively.' " But when asked to open the safe deposit boxes by investigator Robert Fabian , Lane did not return calls or respond. (12)

Lane's alibi for visiting a freezing Europe at that time was that he went to Paris to visit his French daughters. According to Buford, he hardly saw his daughters at all. Many years had passed since his last visit to Paris. How many times had he been there before that time to visit them? Even though he might have entered Switzerland via France, he was never scrutinized and his passport was never stamped.

Despite Jim Jones' command to name the next child after Mark Lane, Vita never received the full Lane name, but a different last one, concealing the circumstances of her birth. Lane has clearly succeeded in concealing the Vita trail. Vita's birthday, January 5, 1982, is chronologically consistent with Buford's story. Vita was born nine months after the Congressional hearings took place.

In retrospect, Walter Cronkite had been right the entire time about Lane and Buford. Cronkite was a victim of misinformation. And so was the public when they read Lane's book, *The Strongest Poison*, in which he wrote about Jonestown, blaming the C.I.A. for everything. This is merely a whitewash, a clever vindication of himself and Buford for any part they played in Jonestown. Since he was an influential eyewitness, the American people looked to him for answers.

Steven Brill (13) called for Lane's disbarment on the grounds that *Lane didn't tell authorities, American or Guyanese, what he knew about a client's intention (sic., Jones) to violate the law*. Nothing ever came of Brill's plea.

Terri Buford, after observing Vita and Mark Lane so wonderfully united as father and loving daughter, now realized how important a family unit could be. She decided to return home after many years. It was time for Vita to know her rich Buford heritage and meet her grandfather, the *Commander,* face to face. For Vita's sake, she again overcame her anxiety and faced her past. A trembling Terri Buford finally made the long distance call home.

CHAPTER 15

THE WHITE MAN

I Felt a funeral in my brain
and mourners to and fro
Kept treading-treading-till it
seemed that Sense was breaking through-....
as all the heavens were a Bell
and Being, but an ear,
And I, and Silence, some strange Race
Wrecked, solitary, here-
Emily Dickinson

Commander Buford, by now aged and infirmed, lay begging for death in the Virginia Beach Veterans Hospital with serious kidney failure. This disease was common to the Buford family. Her sister, Caroline, had also lost a kidney while Terri suffers what she describes as a form of Crohn's Disease or irritable bowel syndrome. She experiences intestinal pain and recurrent kidney infections, her insides throbbing with pain. If Terri eats breakfast before noon, her pain is severe.

Making the transition from daughter to parent, she now understood how horrible it must be to lose a child. Terri got up the nerve to finally visit her ailing father. After so many years, Charles Buford agreed to see his daughter. He lay in bed in total depression, compulsively reciting the Oscar Wilde poem *The Ballad Of Reading Gaol* to his fellow patients.

> Yet each man kills the thing he loves,
> By each let this be heard,
> Some do it with a bitter look,
> Some with a flattering work,
> The coward does it with a kiss
> The brave man with a sword!

Teresa Jean kissed her father for the first time in thirteen years. The Commander had been a brave man. Age had not faded his brilliant memory. He remembered Teresa Jean, his youngest daughter. She finally understood the suffering which resulted from her betrayal of him. Seeing her father in this condition, her anger was finally tempered with pity.

Realizing he was near death, her massive rebellion, which had been responsible for leading her into Jim Jones' clutches, was now over. She pleaded for her father's forgiveness.

After so many years, the prodigal daughter was welcomed back to his bosom. Finally, the Commander came face to face with Vita, his only grandchild. In his final hour on earth, he deserved that much, at least. He died with some hope now that his life was not spent totally in vain.

Terri wondered how he had ever stood to be with her mother for all those years. He had never lost the Buford family loyalty, even to his difficult bride, an ultimate test of his character. Terri states that her mother's condition had deteriorated to a point where she had to be placed temporarily into various mental institutions.

She describes how Virginia had attempted to kill her husband by stabbing him in the back with an ice pick. Terri relates that she was warned by her violent mother that if she and Vita showed up at the hospital to visit her husband, she would kill her own granddaughter, who, in her opinion, was conceived in sin.

As Commander Buford died, part of Terri Buford's life passed away. Also, the part that held the ashes of her bitterness; her rebellion against her father was now over.

Deceptor

Terri's mother gave their inheritance money, a sum of fifty thousand dollars, to various strangers as gifts. Waitresses and gas station attendants were handed hundred dollar bills, while Terri claims she was in dire need.

The Buford family never would be told the identity of Vita's father. Terri was afraid her mother would try and kill Lane as a result, therefore she could never disclose his identity. Vita was under strict orders to keep that secret from grandma. To the Buford family, Lane would remain, *father unknown*, an unacceptable classification for a diehard believer of Fundamentalist Christianity.

Even after Jonestown, Virginia Buford couldn't accept the fact that her daughter was engaging in any illicit sexual activity.

During a visit to Virginia Beach, Grandma Virginia played *Jonestown* style jungle music at 5 a.m. to wake up Vita and further torture Terri in retaliation for the agony of what the whole Buford clan had endured from this wayward daughter. Terri could not stay with her family.

Terri returned to New York where she spent many lonely hours looking through her picture album containing shots of her family in Norway, her father with the Shah of Iran, and a catalogue of every man with whom she had an affair. She has managed to keep her pictures neatly filed in chronological order. Jim Jones was conspicuously absent from her albums, although he dominated her nightmares.

Mary Weiner has been serving as Vita's surrogate father for years, supporting both Vita and Terri. In fact, through perks on her New York City job, Mary was able to take Terri and Vita to the Bahamas on a vacation.

Weiner's mother is a judge from the San Francisco Bay area. She has set up a generous trust fund for her daughter. Mary Weiner has no other children, other than Vita, to share her future inheritance with.

Lane has been free of his parental responsibilities except for an occasional brief visit from Vita about once a year. An adoring Vita dreams of becoming a lawyer like her father. Vita also has the affection of another lawyer, Weiner, who is convinced that she has made a lifelong best friend in Terri.

The two women share intense dependency bonds. Terri, who lost all faith in men, has found her security at last, with a woman. Like her Great uncle, Walt

Whitman, Terri has made no distinctions between the sexes in regard to sensuality.

The lost parents that Teresa Jean had desperately searched for have finally been found. As parents, she and Mary have Vita.

Vita attended a school in Brooklyn and according to the records in their office, Terri filled in the (2) application form by listing Vita's father as *Mark Lane*. Coincidently, PS 193 was the very same school that Mark Lane attended when he grew up in Flatbush, Brooklyn.

Terri is instructing Vita in life's lessons as she herself learned them: Hide your inner heart well, child. But frightened, little Vita has developed a fear of a terrible monster, the *white man*, as she calls her recurring nightmare demon. She wakes up screaming almost every night fearful that this *white man* is going to get her. Vita's school principal has recommended a child therapist be called to treat her extreme disturbances.

Terri tried to put the painful pieces of her life back together for her daughter as well as herself and make a normal life for Vita.

She wrote a poem in tribute to her poetic ancestors:

KADDISH
At long last we meet, separated here by
the mere mathematical perception of existence.
I pay homage to you, to your ancestors,
to those who shared your vision. Mute in
your enduring presence, I contemplate
the task put to me in this brief breath
before I, too, succumb to my beginnings.
I would that light flow backward, that
matter become animate, defying its natural
structure, breaking the bonds of time. I
would that you were here now. For the
moment that you transcended the primal
dust, you did honor to those before you.
Terri (1986)

Lifting its title from Allen Ginsberg, this strange *barbaric yawp* was spawned from the timeless styles of both James Agee and Walt Whitman. Terri's task was now to grasp new meanings in her own existence and transcend her own *primal dust.*

She enjoyed taking little Vita to a small park next to the Ocean in Brighton Beach, Brooklyn, where the vast expanse of sky comforted her. Crowded with Russian immigrants, there was less of a chance someone would recognize her.

Brooklyn once served as a haven for both of Terri's famed uncles, James Agee and Walt Whitman, as well as her lover Mark Lane. Lane was raised in the very same neighborhood, Flatbush, where Terri and Vita would eventually live for seven quiet years.

Here she led a new life, with a new identity, unchallenged by even the New York City public school system, where she had been hired, in 1988, to teach emotionally disturbed and handicapped youths.

Buford's student, Stacy, located in the Bedford Stuyvesant section of Brooklyn, was deaf. Terri utilized her knowledge of sign language to instruct the youngster. But, the job proved too difficult and certainly not worth the money.

Terri resigned. Since then she has taken the NTE teacher exam for work in other states. Assignments will be handed out from history books written by Jonestown experts like Lane. College students already use his book as source material for their interpretations of history.

Terri's references from New York will come in handy in any security check. It is hard for her to obtain a new job with proper scrutiny by a prospective employer since there is the huge Jonestown gap in her resume.

After serving the New York City Board of Education, Terri worked correcting textbooks written by doctors; she was a freelance editor of medical books for McGraw Hill as well as for various Japanese firms. Her knowledge of Japanese came in handy since the Japanese pay better than the American companies. Her work was conveniently done at home where she was in constant fear of being summoned for further inquiry. The home job enabled her to give Vita all the time she required.

As Terri brought Vita to meet Lane occasionally, her relationship with surrogate Mary Weiner became strained. Mary felt betrayed. Every time Mary went to tuck Vita in good night, she saw two pictures over Vita's bed: one of Martin Luther King and the other, Vita's father, Mark Lane, the lawyer representing his very murderer.

Weiner wondered how Terri could even deal with Lane, let alone honor him, a man whom, as Terri claimed, forced sex upon her and then betrayed her. Lane's entire family became a constant intrusion upon Mary's privacy. Weiner's parental relationship with Vita was threatened.

Uncle Larry Lane and Aunt Dr. Ann Lane were accepted as new branches of Vita's growing family tree. This was exciting to Vita, but Mary felt invaded by the new in-laws. Punishing Terri for disloyalty, she struck out at her by taking on a new lover. While they cavorted around the house, Terri and Vita were required to stay in the small back rooms.

Terri began to withdraw and make forays into the local libraries to obtain books for Vita to read.

Always an avid reader, Terri, after discovering *Sophie's Choice*, by William Styron, expressed an intense identification with Sophie, the main character. Sophie, after escaping from a Nazi concentration camp, lived in Flatbush, in Brooklyn, New York.,

There, in Flatbush, Terri Buford, like Sophie, desperately tried to quietly heal from her turbulent life's deep scars. Both soon learn that this change of scene doesn't necessarily create a miraculous metamorphosis.

Terri studied and developed a technique of psychological thought stopping to try and ease her constant anguish. Her conscience was quickly driving her into great depressions. Every night a haunting Jim Jones reappeared like a specter causing her to awake with sleep shattering nightmares of gruesome images. She was trapped in a prison of her own mind and, unlike the days in Jonestown, she now had no way out.

Post-traumatic stress syndrome symptoms include insomnia, phobias, panic attacks, social withdrawal, self-mutilation, shame, flashbacks, anxiety, self loathing, depression and disassociation. Victims mask feelings with drugs and alcohol. Terri could not sleep without pills. Most sufferers finally lapse into a state of denial.

In Terri's imagination, she somehow convinced herself that someone else did the deeds: someone else was the deceptor. Others must have planned everything, not her, she reasoned. She believed she had to have been a victim of Jim Jones. He made her do everything. Her own Dr. Jekyll could not look at the inner Mrs. Hyde as her own sanity split.

Confused and haunted, an oppressive stench of death hung in the air about Terri like the mythical *Ancient Mariner's* albatross. Only truth could free her and a sad, pathetic confession was required.

As Sophie had to in her Nazi camp, Terri, in Jonestown, had to make critical choices between children and her own survival. As in Jonestown, the Nazis used children as pawns. Author, William Styron (80), describes the secret Nazi operation known as *Lebensborn* that was used to increase the population of the their order. This policy was achieved through the clandestine kidnapping of children who were taken from their parents, never to be seen again. In his own adoptions and subsequent abductions of America's helpless foster children into Jonestown, Jones had adopted Hitler's tactics.

In *Sophie's Choice,* Sophie's Nazi tormentors order her to choose between her son or her daughter for their special program. She finally picks her son as her daughter is taken from her. Strangely, when Terri left Dietrich, her foster son, to die in Jonestown, she had to make a similar decision.

Stingo, the key narrative character of *Sophie's Choice,* gradually becomes compelled to analyze her story, trying to determine whether or not Sophie is innocent or guilty of crimes within the camp, the central thesis of Styron's entire book. To Stingo, if Sophie had been just a victim like so many of her fellow humans she would have been merely another pathetic victim turned up in Brooklyn's benevolent haven.

Stingo deduces that Sophie was both victim and accomplice. Sophie confesses to him that she was an accessory to the mass slaughter. That was where her devastating guilt lay. Terri also was a fellow conspirator in crime.

Caught within a similar trap of deceit, neither Buford, nor Sophie could be quite honest in their recital of their respective pasts. Both leave out certain elements and details of their lives that should have been divulged. Yet, a horrible sense of guilt always affected any reassessments of self for Buford as her own history is now viewed through the screen of immense self-hatred. Terri had become mute, deaf, and dumb, in admitting certain acts.

However, there were little hints behind the veil that hung over her past. There was a noticeable absence of any links from Terri's relatives in her life. Joel Agee, one of her cousins, lived nearby, on Eastern Parkway in Brooklyn. She fearfully refused to get on the phone to speak to him or other of relatives.

Even though their fearful, guilty reactions might have created a common bond, critical differences exist between them in their respective functions. Sophie was forced into her camp, while Buford joined voluntarily and rose to become a chief executive. Because of that, Buford cannot turn to the other survivors of Jonestown for any understanding and support. They are angry at her.

To survive after their respective nightmares, both Sophie and Terri Buford had to pose once more. No one around her in Brooklyn suspected who she was. She seemed safe, until...One night in Brooklyn, at the time of the tenth anniversary of the murders, the telephone rang in the Buford household with a frightening message. An anonymous voice threatened a horrible death to both Terri and Vita. What made it doubly dangerous was the call mentioned Vita as Vita Lane. Vita's father's identity was a secret that was supposed to be completely hidden from the public. To feel the horror of the moment, you had to look deep into the eyes of Terri Buford.

Her eyes were vacant.

Vita's father's identity was a secret that was supposed to be completely hidden from the public.

Terri compulsively scratched her scalp as she tried to determine who was threatening Vita. She surmised that the motive for this dangerous threat was from someone seeking revenge upon Mark Lane through his daughter. Terri learned to take death threats very seriously. Totally fearful for their lives, Vita was yanked right out of her first grade class in the middle of the school term. According to the school secretary (2), Terri trembled uncontrollably as she left the school. Then, Terri and Vita vanished...

CHAPTER 16

STARS AND HALF MOONS

If you want a picture of the future, imagine
a boot stamping on a human face-forever.
George Orwell 1984

Terri Buford always wore the Muslim symbols of the stars and half moons on her person, clothing, earrings, and even her sneakers. This was done to display her solidarity with the Muslim political element in defiance of her father and his close association with the late Shah of Iran.

Buford's emotional-political liaison with Mark Lane, the public defender of the P.L.O., jigsaws with that organization's orientation. In fact, according to Buford, Lane also defended those Iranian students, with their war chant, *Death to America!* during the hostage crises while the American flag was burned.

Iranians who hated America due to excesses during the Shah's repressive regime led their country into the Khomeini regime transforming the entire nation into another cult.

After the Shah fled, Khomeini established a theocratic state, with himself as supreme overseer. In a massive reversion to ancient customs, Khomeini banned all music on television and radio. He ordered an end to mixed bathing at beaches. His regime presided over executions of hundreds of victims. He was opposed to land reform and women's emancipation. Unfortunately, the reaction to oppression sometimes results in a more brutal repression. Sometimes an entire nation can be swallowed up into a Jonestown type of cult. One of Buford's relatives, Julia Agee, a daughter of James Agee, lives within another cult which has similarities to the Peoples Temple. Saul Newton, the founder of The Sullivan Institute for Social Research in New York, uses compulsive sex and the breakup of the family unit as his tools.

Columbia Professor of Religion, Randall Balmer, describes an epidemic of new *rainbow congregations* in the Times Square area of New York. He states (1) that one of the overwhelming characteristics of evangelists is their friendliness.

Cults *prey* upon people in crises, especially tortured alcoholics and drug addicts. Certain drug rehabilitation centers, such as Odyssey House, utilize similar mind controlling tactics to achieve their own purposes, as well. Like Jones' base near the Fillmore West, Odyssey House is based near Fillmore East, the historic rock capital of New York.

Alcohol and a variety of drugs abound throughout the surrounding neighborhood. Poverty is rampant. The court system of New York, in having to deal with an overcrowded prison system, commits drug users to such places as Odyssey's Mabon House, a prison like structure on an island in the East River. Voluntary entrance is encouraged as well. Anyone with a drug problem can wind up there. Like Jonestown, Mabon especially caters to the most unfortunate of victims, primarily black women addicts and their children, who live there together. According to Heather Meredith (2), a former child victim of Mabon House, they made both the adults and their children eat only baby food and cereal with powdered milk, while the leaders ate steaks, even though every person was immediately put on medicaid, welfare and food stamps upon entering. The mothers, including her own, were forced to scrub walls and floors...with toothbrushes.

She witnessed her mother get slapped and others get beaten. The children and their parents were kept on separate floors, isolated from one another. Many children were ill and conditions were very unsanitary. Like in Jonestown, the victim's private mail was totally censored. No permission was allowed for telephone communication unless in an extreme emergency and even then, all calls were screened. Intense group dynamics operate to break the spirit of the victim into pieces.

As in other cults, the inmates are warned never to tell their own families about their situation. On visiting day, there is always a leader spying upon the gatherings, watching for negative communication. These biological families are considered to be the enemy of both the inmates and the all important group, the new family.

Huge, lavish feasts are planned for the holidays, on visiting days to display the supposed variety of delicious cuisine the inmates are supposedly eating normal days. Tricked relatives leave these feasts feeling that their loved ones are in kind and generous hands.

During regular Sunday visits, all guests are carefully screened and never left alone with their loved ones. An Odyssey operative is always with them. Afterwards, according to plan, the former drug abuser becomes a new case worker perpetuating the project and bringing in more and more converts.

These women cannot leave the premises without leaving their children in the hands of the powerful overseers. Upon joining, their children are declared wards of the state and the parents are deemed unfit. The loving, troubled mothers have no choice but to remain and obey, hostages to their helpless, little children.

There is a high fence around the premises with a 24 hour guard at the gate. Cars must pass through a barrier to enter. Visitor's passes are required to proceed. Since the island is inaccessible, except through the one entry road, the only way out is to swim the waters of the East River. Even then, the police would be notified and apprehend the escapee in order to return them to the proper authorities in probable criminal violation of a probation order.

Odyssey's intake workers who serve to persuade newcomers to join their program are paid five hundred dollars per each member they entice. Harold, one of the most successful interviewers, explained that he would have told prospective guests anything to get them to join.

Other cults use their members in a variety of unscrupulous ways. Young women are instructed to become *hookers for God*, to bring in funds. Thought control and abusive behavior modification tactics are used as old mindsets are destroyed and replaced by *correct thinking*.

Like Jonestown, massive manipulation of the mind has made the mundane, munificent. Through the processes of fatigue, love bombing, repetition, humiliation, confession and suppression of identity, the person's individual ego is broken down.

Another infamous cult is called *The Process*. It is labeled *Satanic*. Upon joining, the process becomes larger than the individual. The organization is setup in a manner that demands total loyalty to the group. Even the leader cannot escape. The success of these *Satanic* cults relies heavily upon the public perception that some sort of mystical force like the *devil* is the mastermind running the show. Books like Maury Terry's, *The Ultimate Evil* (3), try to link up various incidents like the David Berkowitz murders and other cult deaths into a neat package.

Within the United States, the cult phenomena has presented an enormous problem to the citizens. Guy Darst (70) quotes Patricia Ryan, the daughter of cult victim, the late Rep. Leo Ryan, as saying that the experts estimate that more than 10 million people may be involved in destructive cults. Their minds have been stolen from them.

There are more than just minds being manipulated; big money is involved. United States teleevangelists net an amount greater than the gross national product of two thirds of the nations of the world.

Reporter Charles W. Bell (4) states that at the trial of TV evangelist, Jim Bakker, testimony disclosed that the Bakker's listed on their insurance sheet two sweatshirts made of sable. Their value was $6,500. Then there was the air-conditioned doghouse. Jim Bakker stole $3.7 million in PTL funds to finance his lifestyle.

Bakker was compared to Jim Jones in the *New York Daily News* (4). Bell writes that his supporters are so zealous that they have a Jim Jones mentality. At that, Tammy Bakker, Jim's wife gasped and said, "Oh, no."

Wooden (5) describes the surprising absence of American government interference into cult finances. He believes that other cults are using Jim Jones' financial techniques as a guide. Wooden is angry that no other government agency ever bothered to talk to Bob Stone. Bob worked full time on the Temple's Social Security affairs.

Pricilla Coates (6) of the Cult Awareness Center of Los Angeles, expressed her opinion that most California politicians were used as Jones' pawns and taken for a ride. Certainly, that is precisely what those politicians wanted the public to believe; put the blame only on Jones.

If any other honest politician threatened the group, they were murdered, like Congressman Leo Ryan, who could not be scared or bought off.

Former Ukiah public servant, Tom MacMillan (7), was shocked to notice that the Jonestown victims included many of his co-workers in various offices of government. The names of not only his co-workers but their rich and very much alive political bosses, as well as the leaders of his county and San Francisco government, must be explored. This connection between Jonestown and California government has been largely ignored.

CHAPTER 17

JONESTOWN AND THE C.I.A.

"For evil to succeed, all that is necessary is for good men to do nothing..."
                                                                    Lord Kagan

The former chief of staff for California Rep. Leo Ryan, Joe Holsinger, has doggedly insisted that a disinformation campaign was launched by the U.S. Government to conceal the truth about Jonestown. Holsinger expressed his outspoken opinion on a taped WBAI radio talk show on August 27, 1989. Holsinger, who now serves as a deputy superintendent for California schools, feels that the Jonestown investigation was an elaborate cover-up.

This is a serious charge, made against not only the C.I.A., but the press and the investigative bodies of the entire government that Congressman Ryan represented. Holsinger notes the connection of the Layton family to the U.S. Government via Laurence Layton Sr. who was working in the chemical warfare field.

Without any further factual information, Holsinger took up the cause of his former boss Leo Ryan's adversary, Mark Lane. His allegation only raises further questions rather than provide any concrete answers, and investigators have been thrown further off the track.

Researcher Buursma (1) notes that Holsinger conceded he has absolutely no proof for his charges and has pulled together conjecture and circumstantial evidence that stand in sharp contrast to the facts.

By pointing fingers at the wrong target, Holsinger misleads the public further away from facts, aiding the very real forces he is trying to uncover and prosecute. Buursma suggests that Holsinger has done grave damage by further discrediting the intensive 1980 investigation by the House Permanent Select Committee of Intelligence which concluded there was no evidence at all to suggest that the C.I.A. knew anything about the Jonestown tragedy before it occurred, or that the agency had any connection with either Jim Jones or the Peoples Temple.

Another researcher who points fingers at the C.I.A. for Jonestown, Michael Meiers, ignores that House report as well, as he puts forth the timeworn idea that the C.I.A. engineered Jonestown in his recent book, *Was Jonestown a CIA Medical Experiment?* He never answers his rhetorical conjecture with any hard facts. He mentions without support that Terri Buford is still with Mark Lane. He states that Terri was sent by Jones to ruin Lane's reputation, without proof.

Just about every character in Meiers' book is labeled and dismissed as a C.I.A. agent. Debby Layton is a C.I.A. agent. Jones' fear of the C.I.A. described as only an act. Meiers feels that Jones too is a C.I.A. agent. Every government official and every scientist is a C.I.A. agent. This analysis is too easy, too pat, and too contradictory. Why would Jones ever hire Mark Lane to be his lawyer if he were a C.I.A. agent?

Meiers had absolutely no knowledge of Terri, who left Mark Lane six years before his book was written. Meiers also claims that Jim Jones escaped from Guyana and is in Rio or Africa. The basis for Meier's sensational claim is a story published on May 12, 1981 in the *Globe*, a sensationalist tabloid. Unfortunately there were no supporting pictures, evidence, or documents. Meiers claims to have gotten all his research out of the public library. Meiers never met anyone connected with the C.I.A. or the murder plot in Guyana to substantiate his allegations.

Meiers discusses Mark Lane. Even though Lane was hired as Jones' lawyer, he feels that Lane is the honest investigator that he (Lane) claimed to be. Of course Lane claimed to be honest. Meiers does mention that Lane's relationship with Jones warrants detailed attention. Finally, according to Meiers, Terri Buford is still living with Mark Lane. He offers no proof for this claim.

In his epilogue, as Jim Jones once did, Meiers also predicts a cataclysm to occur in November 1988. He does not mention what that will be, or since that date has passed, what it was supposed to be. He may be referring to the publication date of his own book.

Meiers, refers to a surpressed article in the *National Enquirer* written back in 1978. According to Steve Grenard (2), a reporter at their main office, Meiers got all his information mixed up. The reporter that Meiers mentions, Gordon Lindsay, was also mentioned in Mark Lane's book, *The Strongest Poison*. Lane took the credit for stifling the article to impress his client, Jim Jones.

In reality, the *National Enquirer* hired an English journalist, Joe Mullins, to do their story. Gordon Lindsay was also an English reporter, covering Jonestown for his own newspaper. Mullins' story was not squashed by the *National Enquirer* as a result of Lane's influence.

Grenard states that the paper didn't release the story only because Ryan was due to go down to Jonestown anyway and his story seemed to be quite minor compared to other events. Lindsay had buzzed the compound with a small plane and taken some pictures, but these proved nothing.

The late Gene Pope, the owner of the *National Enquirer* at that time, was also accused both by Lane and Meiers of being a C.I.A. operative. According to Grenard, Pope publicly admitted to actually working for the agency but not in the way they state. Before he owned the publication, he was in the air conditioning business. One of his clients was the C.I.A. Even if Meiers and Lane have more evidence that Pope was an agent, they should genuinely produce it, or mention the facts as they are presented, not try to merely prove their common C.I.A. theories.

Meiers received a lot of his information from Joe Holsinger. In his grief to explain the unfortunate loss of his friend, Congressman Ryan, Holsinger guesses, without any concrete information to base it on, that C.I.A. operatives working at the U.S. Embassy in Georgetown, Guyana, may have been using Jones and his community in a wildcat behavior modification experiment.

The operative word in Lane's, Meiers', and Holsinger's conjectures is the usage of the word, *may*. They pound away at the reader in every paragraph. For example, Jones *may* be in Brazil. He *may* be a C.I.A. operative. Terri *may* be Jones' secret agent to Lane. She *may* still be with Lane. Meiers also states that Lane *probably* had good intentions.

However, besides confusing the public, these *maybe's* harm beyond repair. A lot of serious unfounded charges were directed particularly against Richard McCoy, the director of the American Embassy at that time and many others who functioned within the Embassy as well. There is not a shred of proof of any wrong doings by any workers at the U.S. Embassy in Guyana. On the contrary, these brave officials helped people like Tim Stoen, Debby Blakey and others get out of Jonestown, at their own risk.

The extremely delicate position these officials were in must be noted. They were representatives of our government in a hostile communist nation, trying to do their job and deal with the constant crises Jones and his crew created daily. Furthermore, if the C.I.A. really wanted to perform the behavior modification experiments that Holsinger suggests, they certainly wouldn't have chosen a foreign environment in which to operate. They could have had the U.S. Army as their base of operations, if, in fact, the C.I.A. is as powerful as believed.

Besides Lane's Jonestown book, *Strongest Poison,* he also blames the U.S. Government for various other crimes. In *Code Name Zorro,* he blames the government for Martin Luther King's murder to protect his client, James Earl Ray. *Rush to Judgement* deflects blame to the C.I.A. for Kennedy's death in defense of Oswald as does *Plausible Denial.* The fact that Jonestown was so impressively successful in its behavior-modification techniques suggests planning by a huge organization such as the C.I.A., however, this discredits the very highly skilled and motivated upper echelon members of Jonestown who really engineered the commune.

Eventually, with all the spying techniques, everyone involved began to distrust each other in Jonestown. There was too much money involved. Lane and Garry became bitter enemies. Jones hated Tim Stoen and Prokes hated Jones. Buford had worked for all of them...Stoen, Garry, Jones, Lane and Prokes.

Terri had applied her father's military technique of *divide and conquer,* into every situation. If Jonestown would have succeeded as planned, Jones might have become emperor of Guyana.

Jones who admired Joseph Stalin, Karl Marx and, most of all, Adolf Hitler studied each as one would study an idol or a chess opponent, assessing their strengths and weaknesses. The oratory power of Hitler particularly captivated him. But unlike Jim Jones, even Adolph Hitler never claimed he was God. Hitler, Jones, Commander and Terri Buford all shared one philosophy in common; *The ends justify the means.*

What happens when ends are subordinated to means was clearly demonstrated by Hitler and Stalin. This conceit has created the ultimate cult of the twentieth century, communism, which had more than enveloped half of the human race under its cruel yoke until recently. Under this oppression, creativity is murdered; few innovations in art, music, or literature could be achieved. Industry is stifled. Vitality is sapped.

Stalin, Mao, Castro, Ceausescu, Saddam Hussein and others have used this philosophy to justify their personal massive Jonestowns within entire countries where people's smiles are erased and replaced with grim countenances.

Within the more technologically efficient dictatorships of tomorrow there will be much less violence necessary to achieve control. Future dictator's subjects will be painlessly manipulated by an army of psychiatrists and expert social engineers.

According to Huxley, the twenty-first century will be the era of the centralized world controllers, the scientific experts of a new caste system. Who will stand guard over those behavior experts and modify their motivations?

Thanks to our modern technological progress, Big Brother can become almost as omnipresent as God.

CHAPTER 18

JONESTOWN AND JFK

"What is history but a myth agreed upon?"
                              Napoleon Bonaparte

Most Americans get information from television and movies.   A movie was hastily made about Jonestown, *Guyana Tragedy*, which aired opposite ABC's telecast of the popular Academy Awards and gave CBS the seasonal ratings lead. However, this sensationalist movie only serves to confuse the public by utilizing fake names and fantasized situations instead of a real historical portrayal based upon consistent data. Now, actual, historical new footage of Terri together with Jim Jones, with scenes of their phony faith healings combined with current video clips are available for public scrutiny.

Terri kept Vita from normal television viewing for years, fearful that she might see shows that would include her Jonestown days. Vita might one day see *Guyana Tragedy,* in which each character is renamed, and Buford's character is called *Ms. Bundy*. The facts are altered for Buford's protection.

Catching history on the wing will never be a perfect science but movie makers should never indulge in phony representations of real situations. This so-called historical docudrama movie alters facts. Bundy is seen in Guyana giving her body for the cause to compromise a Guyanese official. Bundy then tells a worker in the code room not to open the safe. Then she is shot at the end after she tries to steal the Jonestown money in a suitcase.

There never was a Ms. Bundy in Jonestown. Not only are the names changed, but the script is an illusion. Even though art, by its very nature, is artificial, these books and films about Jonestown were based upon real events. People curiously watched these movies in a state of confusion as they tried to understand this complex saga.

Movie makers have become our most powerful historians. Yet, the movie only tried to make some fast money, not portray historical truth. It succeeded in doing both. The viewer had no way of sorting out fact from fiction. The characters were hybrids: Larry Layton and Doctor Larry Schacht were blended together. Patty Cartmell, Sandi Bradshaw and Terri Buford were hodgepodged in their functions as well. All the names are changed except for Jim Jones' who was by then dead.

With all their alterations, the whitewashed movies cannot serve as lessons in history. When President Kennedy was murdered, the public knew the actual names and facts. The television coverage was live. When Nixon resigned, the public knew the name of every culprit.

Yet after Jonestown, the truth has never been portrayed in a real way by Hollywood. A straight documentary would be a more enlightened way to portray the historical account exactly as it happened. But Hollywood was unable to restrain itself.

Both history and art were betrayed. In 1991 Lane released *Plausible Denial*, a new book about the C.I.A. involvement in the Kennedy assassination. His book entered the scene on the 18th anniversary of the assassination and claims that C.I.A. agents E. Howard Hunt and Frank Sturgis had roles in the affair.

Lane located Marita Lorenz, the mother of Fidel Castro's child, to testify that the C.I.A. was involved. She claimed that Hunt was in Dallas with a group of people during the Kennedy murder. It is natural for Castro to blame Hunt through Lorenz since Hunt was in charge of the Bay of Pigs operation to free Cuba.

Yet Lorenz could merely be covering Castro's role in the affair. When Castro's regime ends, he might stand trial next to the likes of Norriega and have to answer questions such as his connection to Oswald. There are pictures of Oswald distributing leaflets regarding fair play for Cuba and *hands off Cuba*. These pictures are actual and unretouched.

Lane defended the Liberty Lobby in a 1985 libel suit instigated by Hunt. Lane's bestselling new book is the revenge upon Hunt for that very suit. Lane called Richard Helms, Stansfield Turner, Hunt and Gordon Liddy as witnesses. Lane even suggests that George Bush had something to do with the operation because the C.I.A. was in Dallas at the time of the Kennedy murder. Lane's main source for his information is ex-C.I.A. agent Fletcher Prouty. According to Robert Sam Anson (1) Prouty is a prominent member of the Liberty Lobby.

It is interesting to note that the same Liberty Lobby member, Fletcher Prouty, was a key source for Grodin and Livingstone's thesis as well. With fearful congruency, Prouty turns up again as the source for information in the movie by Oliver Stone about the Kennedy assassination.

According to Anson, Prouty is a higher up in the Liberty Lobby and had been a lecturer and featured speaker at their annual convention as well as at other meetings. Anson writes that Prouty does more than merely speak words for the Lobby but also functions more creatively, writing their radio programs and newsletters as does Mark Lane's new, young wife according to Terri Buford.

In those publications, anti-semitic articles regularly appear such as, described by Anson, one that calls *The Diary of Anne Frank* a fraud.

Fletcher Prouty was even named to the Liberty Lobby's National Policy Advisory Board on its *Populist Action Committee*. Beyond creating and speaking mere words, Prouty is creating ideas. He has people beginning to believe that John Kennedy, a president that created the Green Berets, was a pacifist. Prouty and the Liberty Lobby are behind the new and explosive labelling of the C.I.A. with the moderate Republicans as being involved in Kennedy's assassination.

In Stone's *JFK,* Donald Sutherland plays this mysterious character, but no mention of his Liberty Lobby connection is made for the public. Stone lessened Prouty's role after the film was in the final stages after realizing the connection. He hired other advisers to cover Prouty's tracks and try to erase the films moral connection to the Liberty Lobby's platform.

Anson further states that one of the other board members of the Liberty Lobby had been a leader of the Mississippi Ku Klux Klan. He also mentions Liberty Lobby connections that extend to former KKK leader, David Duke.

The founder of the Lobby is Willis Carto who was a top member of the John Birch Society. Carto admires Hitler in much the same way as another Lane client had...Jim Jones.

Jews are openly labeled *Public enemy number one* by Carto according to Anson's disturbing *Esquire* article, who also states that Prouty fully and openly agrees with his leader's philosophy.

Anson mentions in the same article that Jim Garrison, a lynchpin for the anti-C.I.A. conspiratorial force and key ally of Mark Lane had also appeared on the Liberty Lobby's radio program. Jack Anderson disclosed that Garrison and Lane were good friends and Lane assisted him in the Shaw case. It is clear where the new anti-C.I.A. anti-American propaganda has been conceived.

Prouty asserts that Kennedy was killed by the C.I.A. because Kennedy was going to pull the troops out of Vietnam. This is contrary to the assertions that Kennedy was making at the time. Prouty claims that he has evidence that Kennedy was about to buck the military establishment and the profits from the war would be lost to the business interests involved in weapons production.

If that really was the motive for the Kennedy murder, why wasn't Richard M. Nixon murdered by those same operatant forces when he actually did pull out troops out of Vietnam? The same military-industrial complex that Prouty and Lane believe were the causes of the Kennedy assassination were still in power.

When the evidence is fully examined, there is a very strong case suggesting the possibility of a plot by private groups such as the Liberty Lobby itself in regards to these assassinations.

In their work, *High Treason*, even Grodin and Livingstone admit in their

Appendix B that their strongest evidence is the case concerning Joseph Milteer. He is described as an ultra right -wing fanatic. He was a member of several hate groups. They mention as examples, the National States Rights Party, the Ku Klux Klan and the White Citizens' Council.

They do not connect Milteer with any government agency. Yet Milteer is described as being on record on a tape making a death threat against Kennedy less than two weeks before the murder. What is amazing is that he even mentions that the murderer will shoot him from an office building with a rifle. He seemed to know all the details in advance.

Milteer, according to Grodin, was actually photographed and filmed during the assassination on the eastern side of Houston Street across from the plaza as the President's car passed before the first shot. If there were more than one shot as some investigators have alleged, it could easily have been fired by Milteer, a member of groups with connections to the Liberty Lobby.

A few days before the murder, the F.B.I. received a warning call about a murder plot from a militant right wing group. Even if C.I.A. agents like Hunt and Frank Sturgis were present at the site of the murder, would it not be unreasonable to assume that they were there to protect the President from assassination from such groups? How can one assume that they were part of the murder plot: On the word of Marita Lorenz? It is also logical that Castro's mistress would assume that the C.I.A was responsible for any and all murders since Castro has been broadcasting this type of anti-U.S. propaganda for years.

If the C.I.A. was in control, had there been such a super smooth group capable of operating such a push button conspiracy, they would have been too slick to pick Jack Ruby for a key role. Even an unpredictable and reliable loser like Oswald would have been a poor choice for such a grandiose plan by an agency that could have handled such a massive coverup.

Grodin and Livingstone suggest that it might have been Ruby who was supposed to switch the so-called magic bullet at Parkland Hospital. They surmise that Ruby was working for the mob or the C.I.A.

This counterintuitive thesis would be questionable even in movies like Indiana Jones.

In order for Ruby to know in advance that he had to switch the bullet, there certainly would have been a *central assassination center* manned by a big staff where the impact of the original bullet would have had to have been immediately analyzed since it entered J.F.K. in a random manner. New orders would have had to be sent immediately with a specially constructed, slightly damaged bullet that perfectly matched Oswald's murder weapon as the original bullet did.

This would have been not only improbable, but impossible. Ruby's lawyer was William Kuntsler also appeared in the movie *JFK* to support the theory that the C.I.A. had something to do with Kennedy's murder. This movie attempts to rewrite history for a new generation.

Casting is perfect in *JFK*. Kevin Costner now portrays a real life Robin Hood fighting against the evil usurper, Lyndon Johnson, to protect King Richard The Lionheart (Kennedy) and defend Camelot, the very myth that has surrounded the Kennedy mystique for years.

How amazing that fiction, following fact, is again, following fiction. Was Kennedy King Richard of Camelot, while are Kevin Costner and Oliver Stone modern day Robin Hoods?

According to *Entertainment Weekly* (2) in a story entitled *School Daze*, the producers of the film *JFK* are already sending out study guides to students all over the U.S. to teach the movie as if it were already proved to be historically accurate. *The Open up Learning Enrichment Inc.'s* study guide contains a multi-page brochure with exercise sheets, posters, etc. It identifies the actors before even identifying the real historical figures.

Funding comes from the film's distributor, Warner Bros., and 13,000 copies of the guide were mailed out to high school and college social studies departments in fifty cities.

Most of the relevant facts are completely left out. For instance, the last Congressional study of the assassination done in the late 70's declared that Kennedy's death was probably a conspiracy was based upon acoustical evidence gathered from a police tape in Dallas headquarters upon which were heard four, not three shots. This was a critical piece of evidence in overturning the Warren Commissions' findings.

Since Oswald could not have fired off four shots, the Warren Report was overruled and the conspiracy theorists were reborn.

Yet, a few years after the Congressional investigations, using more scientific acoustical devices developed after the original study, it was found that, beyond a shadow of a doubt, that the fourth shot heard upon the tape was an echo from the transmitter sent in from a police car at the scene. This is common in transmitted data over such radios. There is a time delay in sound transmission. A full retracing and evaluation of the fourth shot was redone and it mirrored the first. Steve Barber, an acoustical engineer confirmed the fact that there was *talk* between two transmitters and echoes.

The *JFK Study Guides* that are being presented to the students make no mention of this new evidence at all. They carefully edited out whatever disproves it's thesis. Since there is a great profit in the movies and books that stir up the controversy, why include counter information to students and their parent?

In the U.S. a person is innocent until proven guilty. This does not necessarily apply to an organization such as the C.I.A. which cannot even defend itself. The sensationalist conspiracy theorists prey upon that.

Honest, capable, caring investigators like David Belin, who was the chief attorney for the Warren Commission, and a thorough and brilliant investigator, will be seem to be complicit in some sort of dubious conspiracy. History is judging them incorrectly.

John F. Kennedy's death cannot be laid upon the shoulders of the American people and branches of its government without solid evidence. Merely because C.I.A. agents were present, as they may have been for official reasons, does not convict them of murder.

Focus has to be shifted upon the very hate groups Lane represents. The true source of these murders that turn the table and blame the American government for their deeds of violence must be finally identified.

The central goal of hate filled, Nazi, cult-type groups is nothing less than to make America and then all the peoples on the planet slaves within a Jonestown type nightmarish hell on earth. They crucify anyone who stands in their way and then pass the blame to innocents for the deeds. The C.I.A. and the F.B.I. must be weakened for these power hungry organizations and groups to succeed without opposition.

An example of these groups is the Populist Party in California, an extension of the Liberty Lobby, which showcases Bo Gritz, the man whom Rambo was based upon. He is running for President after being groomed as David Duke's running mate. His platform is to reverse the supposed coup d'etat that he asserts occurred when Kennedy was murdered.

The same timeworn strategy of blaming the victim's own group for their murder was utilized when Rabbi Kahane of the Jewish Defense League was assassinated. The accuser's lawyer, William Kunstler, Jack Ruby's former lawyer, accused Kahane's followers for the evil deed. That is what the Liberty Lobby has sought to achieve through their lawyer, Mark Lane, as well.

Assassin trading cards, released in early 1992, show pictures of killers like John W. Hinckly and James Earl Ray. Sen. Nicholas Spano labeled these cards a *sick product*. The chief defender of these assassins is Mark Lane. However, if the C.I.A. was involved in the Kennedy murder, after Lane wrote his book, Jonestown would have been the perfect time to dispose of him, their primary, arch-critic, if we are to assume that their methods really were to perpetrate cold blooded murder.

The timing would have been perfect since Lane was due to testify before Congress a month after Jonestown regarding the Kennedy and Martin Luther King assassinations. His defense led him to the thesis that the C.I.A. murdered almost everyone.

Well then, according to his own logic, why didn't they murder him when they had that perfect opportunity, deep within the jungle of Guyana? Who would have known or cared?

Lane was spared by the enemies of the C.I.A., groups that depended upon Lane to perpetrate those empty myths that the C.I.A. was the villain, not them.

When Terri Buford was questioned by the House Foreign Affairs Committee investigators about any possible C.I.A. infiltration of Peoples Temple or a government conspiracy against it, Reiterman states that she could only offer scant evidence. Her *secret* testimony included her suspicions that Edith Roller was an undercover C.I.A. agent. When asked for some evidence, Buford could only state, enigmatically, that Roller kept a diary.

Poor Edith Roller, who died in Jonestown, was a sixty three year old black woman. But Edith Roller whose posthumous reputation was besmirched, could not defend herself against Buford's allegations. Roller's murder had protected the still living members from incrimination, as all the murders were intended to accomplish. The dead cannot identify, or testify.

The C.I.A. for whom Roller allegedly worked, might not be the most benign group around the world; however they have guidelines and must operate within certain parameters. Certainly, it seems doubtful that even they have a secret C.I.A. contingent of black, female geriatric agents.

The agency is not in a position to defend itself from rumors, even from the *Edith Roller Conspiracy Theory* invented by Buford at the hearings. Ridiculous statements had to be taken seriously by the congressional probes.

In creating their smoke screen, Mark Lane states that the C.I.A. was responsible for Jonestown's creation and destruction. However, Charles Garry, the original Jonestown attorney for all the many years of the Temple's existence before Lane even arrived on the scene, found no evidence whatsoever that the F.B.I. or the C.I.A. were involved in Jonestown at all.

Garry made a sincere attempt to uncover the truth. He was angry at the coverup of the massacres. Charles Garry made an extensive examination of all government files under the provisions of the Freedom of Information Act and could not find Jim Jones' name listed in any one of them. Garry made statements to the effect that if it weren't for Mark Lane, the Jonestown murders would not have occurred.

Gail Ganz (3) of the B'nai B'rith Anti-Defamation League, confirms that Lane is the lawyer for the Liberty Lobby.

Newsweek reporter Bill Turque (4) writes that the Liberty Lobby is described by the Anti-Defamation League of B'nai B'rith as one of the most anti-semitic organizations in America. Turque identifies their leader, Willis Carto, as being a key supporter of Klan leader, David Duke, contributing heavily to his campaigns.

Terri Buford states that Mark Lane's new, young wife, a writer for the Liberty Lobby, seeks to propagate the theory that denies any reality of Jewish victimization at the hands of the Nazis during the Holocaust. Liberty Lobby's theories take a position that the Jews, themselves, with the cooperation of the U.S. Government, are responsible for the *exaggerated myth* of concentration camps and racial genocide.

This propaganda technique was designed by none other than Himmler as he wrote in the 1943 declaration that *..in our history, this is an unwritten and never to be written page of glory.* A central purpose of the Liberty Lobby is to fulfill that directive; Himmler's plan for the future coverup concerning the horrors of the concentration camps.

If the Liberty Lobby can get the American people to accept their theory that the F.B.I. and the C.I.A. are the groups responsible for the Kennedy, Jonestown and King murders through Lane's propaganda, they might be able to destroy those intelligence agencies. These are the very agencies that pursue investigations of hate groups like the Liberty Lobby that are out to destroy America.

If these agencies lose their credibility any more than they already have, the Liberty Lobby and other hate groups that are poised to take over America and perpetrate the same kind of government that existed in Nazi Germany will have virtually no opposition. That would be a grave disaster not only for America but for the entire world.

Soon after the Iraq/U.S. war broke out, Dick Gregory spoke out at the 1990 Liberty Lobby convention as a key speaker. Few realized the Lane/Gregory connection and some newspapers called Gregory's presence as a keynote speaker surprising since they described the Liberty Lobby as both violently anti-semitic and anti-black. Lane is Jewish and Gregory is Black.

Gregory and Lane have merged the extreme right wing forces with the extreme left wing. This unholy alliance between fascism and communism also occurred at the time of the Hitler-Stalin pact in 1939. Former Attorney General Ramsay Clark, an extreme left wing spokesman has travelled to Iraq during wartime to consult with Saddam Hussein. Liberty Lobby, an extreme right wing organization adopted an anti-war stance.

A common theme among the extreme left wing supporters of the P.L.O. and the extreme right wing Nazi/Fascist factions like the South African Neo-Nazi parties is their fanatical hatred of Jews, and Americans who are considered weaklings. They utilize Hitler's tactics: blame your enemies for your deeds and repeat the big lie until the public believes it.

The Liberty Lobby Nazi Holocaust story of denial that these groups are trying desperately to sell is the one that America actually bought in regards to the Jonestown victims: that they, those poor victims, were responsible for their own deaths by their own stupidity. In a suicide, no one is accused of murder, a perfect alibi.

Even the lies of *Pravda* of the former U.S.S.R. does not support these biased, Liberty Lobby, Neo-Nazi contentions that the World War II Holocaust was a only a myth. *The New York Daily News* (5) reported that the U.S.S.R. released new information. The Tass news agency said that the identity cards of 130,000 prisoners from the Auschwitz concentration camp which once were stored in sealed Soviet archives have been released and turned over to the Red Cross.

The deaths of over 74,000 people were neatly recorded, day after day, hour after hour, in 46 huge volumes. Valentina Fatyukhina, head of the Soviet Red Cross research department, told Tass that an estimated 2.5 million Jews were killed at that one camp during the war. The Auschwitz material was found by Soviet soldiers at the end of the war and promptly shipped to the Soviet Union where it remained hidden for nearly fifty years.

The Liberty Lobby dismisses all such information as Jewish propaganda They feel that the press, even the Russian press, is controlled by Jews. Walter Cronkite and his show on the Warren Commission was a sham in their opinion

Public perception concerning the murder of Martin Luther King is being manipulated in the same manner. In 1992, a new book, the followup to *Code Name Zorro,* was released. Its presumed author is none other than Ray, himself with Lane behind the project. *Who Killed Martin Luther King?: The True Story by the Alleged Assassin,* on National Press Books, has an unlikely ally, none other than Jesse Jackson.

In Jackson's foreword to Ray's book. Jackson states (6) that there might have been a conspiracy and calls for an investigation. Since Martin King was monitored by Hoover and the F.B.I. so closely, Jackson wants to look at their files for clues to their possible involvement.

Lane wrote the Preface to the book and states, of course, as Ray's attorney, that "James Earl Ray is not guilty." Lane also states for "Ray, devoid of a support system, relatively uneducated in the formal sense, pecking away surreptitiously in his cell, has achieved such a result is monumental...Yet Ray has found a way to tell the story..."

Upon a reading, the style of the book is unmistakably Lane, who served as the best man at James Earl Ray's prison wedding in October 1978, a month before Jonestown.

Ray is being prepared for interviews on television. Since Ray cannot collect money from the book as a criminal, the royalties from the book, according to New York Magazine (7), will go to Ray's legal fees.

If Jackson really believes that there was a conspiracy by the F.B.I. to kill Martin Luther King then he must feel that he is also in grave danger of being murdered. He must be very brave to speak out against a government capable of such acts. So must Mark Lane, yet have there been attempts on their lives by any government agency? Not one!

All the villains named by Lane seem to always be Republicans. Furthermore, Lane mentions in his epilogue that President Bush was involved with the C.I.A. during the Kennedy assassination. He mentions the Watergate crew and Howard Hunt and Frank Sturgis as having been involved as well, shedding some blame on Richard M. Nixon as if Nixon were operating out of jealousy for losing the election to Kennedy.

Lane and Jackson forget the fact that Lyndon Johnson was a Democrat and the Republicans did not achieve power from the assassination at all. Johnson continued Kennedy's policies.

Democrats are not nor have they been the only victims of assassination attempts, but when a Republican President is the target, guess who the lawyer chosen to represent the villain is? The charges of conspiracy to murder follow political party lines.

According to the *U.S. News and World Report* (8) of May 1, 1989, Lane's current client is John Hinckley, the man indicted for the attempted murder of former President Reagan. The article mentions that Lane had also represented Lee Harvey Oswald's mother, arguing that Lee was framed. *U.S. News and World Report* states that Lane again used the opportunity to charge the F.B.I. with the King murder.

Lane has stated, according to *U. S. News and World Report* that "President Reagan's would-be assassin was saner than his keepers."

That is Mark Lane's opinion of the President of the United States and also the American people that elected Reagan/Bush to power. Lane believes that a deranged, misguided maniac is *saner* than his intended victim, the leader of America!

Amazingly, in Jonestown, Lane's coverup worked perfectly. An absolutely confused public swallowed the wild message. So soon after Vietnam, people were more willing to buy the idea of a corrupt government.

No one has yet fully realized that this new Jonestown concentration camp was a prototype for a possible nightmarish future planned by small fascists groups for certain target races, religions and anyone with the freedom to express any opposing viewpoints.

If all the facts had come out, the Jonestown fortune of money that was robbed outright from the government might have been promptly returned to the American public. With the added funds, taxes might have gone down for the American people; that could never occur without a tough and thorough government investigation by the very groups that Lane has weakened in the public eye by his strategy.

For too long, all the ills of the world were all conveniently blamed upon Jews by corrupt power groups that needed to blame others for the problems they perpetrated. It was easier to accept that myth than look for the true villains.

Lane has merely substituted the C.I.A. as the new all purpose evil doer for every convenient crime by connecting small puddles of truth with rivers of fantasy.

How can an attorney like Lane write a truthful story about his own clients?

Yet, his books stand upon the shelves of every library in the country as being historically correct without a challenge. Since Lane was a participant in Jonestown, his eyewitness accounts are all accepted as valid.

Until Lane's mistress decided to talk, no one has ever been able to piece together pertinent information about Mark Lane and his various and powerful clients.

CHAPTER 19

DOMINO

"History does not repeat itself except in the
minds of those who do not know History."
Kahlil Gibran

We all have a certain amount of latitude in choices we make in our lives.
Debby Blakey chose to confess to Congressman Ryan. Terri Buford embraced
Mark Lane. Others write books. It can be said that those who choose to write
may have axes to grind.

Certainly Tim Reiterman had a personal venom for Jim Jones after he was
wounded in the Jonestown ambush and watched his colleagues die. Nazi hunter
Simon Wiesenthal has no love for the fascists in our midst. Simon served brutal
time in their camps.

Reiterman and Wiesenthal's emotional impact does not make their truths any
less valid. It only gives their energy the momentum needed for fulfillment.

Wiesenthal believes that if good people do nothing, evil must triumph.

In the twentieth century people still believe the myths that poisoned Kool Aide™ killed more people than the 1906 San Francisco earthquake and that a Twinkie™ caused the murder of a San Francisco mayor.

The world of politics is believed to be twenty years behind in regards to intensive examination, yet the last relevant book on the Jonestown was written a decade ago even though a tapestry of new facts concerning Jonestown continue to emerge.

In her testimony, Buford, by turning on the guile of feminine tears, pretended to be a lost little waif. Taken from the pages of her childhood when she had to cry to obtain sympathy in order to avoid further severe beatings, she was able to turn on the abused child act at will.

The inquisitors viewed her as a wayward daughter of society. She was protected by their father-like feelings, despite all the evidence to the contrary. The investigators accorded her a certain benevolence. Like ostriches, they buried the facts of the case within *sealed* testimonies which were finally opened in 1992. According to Reiterman, The House Foreign Affairs Committee investigators questioned her in secret!

Even though the female role has changed drastically in society, there was no true examination or sharing of guilt due to the outdated perception that a woman is incapable of committing the same crime as her male tormentor.

This limited viewpoint has also hindered any serious investigations of the mass murders at Jonestown. Though it seems unlikely that a woman could be a part of such a dastardly plot, that is precisely the strength of the heavenly deception set up by Jim Jones. It is no coincidence that most of Jones' top aides were female.

Terri Buford has stated that she looks like Heidi on her outside, but on the inside, she's felt like Patty Hearst. As Jim Jones' consort, she was able to play the role of a powerful Cleopatra.

Buford's *deceptor* position is not unique, but has been especially problematic for women throughout history, since they have been dependent upon men for physical sustenance during pregnancy and after childbirth.

When she was raised in Asia, women were still required to be utterly submissive, walking behind their husbands and constantly grinning. Using skills she acquired as a young girl in Japan, Terri could turn from submissive Dr. Jekyll into dominant Miss Hyde. Eventually Terri, herself, couldn't tell the difference between her two personas.

In Japan, the art of quiet deception must be carefully cultivated for survival. Terri Buford is a hybrid of the past repression transformed by the new feminist era. Possibly as her cathartic tale is told, the weighty, cursed *albatross* of her inner conscience, will finally drop from her lithe neck.

Most people hide their innermost thoughts and motivations within the darkest pits of their souls. They put on their external face of goodness, sweetness, and honesty.

Terri Buford, when questioned by Robert Fabian during hearings (1) elicited sympathy by cooperating and exhibiting great remorse for the tragedy. Mr. Fabian was put into the kind father position of easing her pain even as he was trying to recover stolen money from her.

Her statements of deep remorse over Jonestown stem not from any regret over its conclusion, but a feeling that the project was thwarted by a number of factors: Debby Blakey's defection, Jones' insanity, Tim Stoen's investigations and Rep. Ryan's meddling. She blames the U.S. Government for interfering. Yet, if she would have succeeded, her group would have taken over that government and instituted a giant cult, run by that inner clique, in its place.

Tragically, Buford's brilliant photographic mind could have been utilized to achieve great things rather than use her gifts to memorize bank account numbers or build an atomic bomb for Jim Jones. Ironically, the very hatred of the bombs that rained upon Japan led her into a further cycle of violence.

In trying to right the wrong done by her father in his murder of Asians, Terri fell into another scheme to mass murder minority groups.

Buford has stated that her deep desire is to one day be a *geriatric terrorist* when Vita is fully grown. Her intention is to go to California and machine gun all the politicians involved in Jonestown's demise.

According to the files in the California Historical Society (1), Kim Agee was named as a beneficiary of one of the bank accounts in Jonestown. Kim Agee, alias Terri Buford was interviewed by Robert Fabian and that is the last time she has been heard from until now.

In her deposition she made a sworn statement to a San Francisco Superior Court that "From 1972 to 1978...I had knowledge of and/or responsibility for...bank accounts in foreign countries...no one went to Switzerland during the time I was in the Temple other than myself..."

She was never asked nor did not swear that no one went to Panama. Yet Fabian, the receiver of the Peoples Temple Box accounts, reported on June 7, 1982, Court Order 746571, that "Buford's Safe Deposit Box 142 at the Banco Fiduciarioin Panama was opened and found to be empty". (1)

Since 1978, according to reporter, Laura Mansnerus (2), the Supreme Court has upheld decisions prohibiting lawyers from profiting from crime victims. The Government now has the authority to freeze assets and pursue legal fees that have been paid by criminals for their protection. Lane would have certainly had a problem even keeping Jones' fee, after Jonestown if Jones survived.

Manserus states that since 1987, under the *Racketeer Influenced and Corrupt Organizations Act*, lawyers have forfeited fees in 47 cases. This precautionary procedure has come nine years too late for the many victims of Jim Jones. However, this law is in danger of being overturned. Ten years ago, the congressional hearings resulted in not one indictment. In fact, CAN (Cult Awareness Network) expert Pricilla Coates (3), who specializes in California cults and their political connections, states that Tim Stoen is even running for public office again in a local district in California. He was never investigated in the voter fraud election of 1976 because he was protected by being the investigator in charge.

Cult personnel also enjoyed not only the protection of the First Amendment, which deflected investigation of any group that declares itself to be a religion, but also hid behind the stoney silence of the Fifth Amendment.

When Buford sent a death threat concerning the endangered Jonestown victims in her letter to the U.S. Government, was she thinking of the welfare of the children? If any of them had been left alive to describe what happened, to speak out and point their fingers at the villains, America's heart would have broken into bits long ago!

The days of Charles Dickens, the children's champion, have long passed. He made their abuse his personal cause. Where and when will yesterday's children as well as tomorrow's get the protection and justice they need to simply survive?

Any of the parents that could have escaped Jonestown would have cried out about the torture, abuse and deceit that their innocent children endured before they were murdered.Like falling dominos, the testimonies of every adult and child who experienced Jonestown had to be silenced forever.

Jonestown was the *END* that no *MEANS* can justify. Psychological rationalizations for criminal behavior are not enough to condone child abuse, or in the extreme case of Jonestown; mass murder. Not so long ago, the famous Nazi child victim, Anne Frank, had said that in spite of everything, she still believed that people are really good at heart. Her love is a tribute to the resiliency of the human spirit.

The Liberty Lobby not only ignores Anne's torture but calls it a fraud. Mark Lane's group denies the Holocaust as a hoax. If their lie is repeated often enough it will stand as the truth to an unaware public. Indifference is their greatest ally.

The Jonestown *domino theory* that 977 people simply lined up and, like dominos, fell into their graves makes as much sense as classifying Anne Frank a suicide victim.

Autumn, 1988, the tenth anniversary of Jonestown, was commemorated by survivors appearing on television to try and explain to the public what had transpired. Tim Stoen and Steven Jones, Jones' adopted son, appeared on the Oprah Winfrey Show. Unafraid to face public scrutiny, they sought to clarify Jonestown to the American people. They have a powerful message...to awaken...to care!

Acknowledgment of the dual nature of the tragedy-murder and denial-must be confronted. Jonestown has remained an image so horrible that people have pushed it under the rug. The dimensions of the horror create great denial. The truth must not be denied any longer even though the average American may prefer not to be disturbed by history. History is full of other stories that have been erased forever. Entire lives have vanished, as if they had never even been lived.

As William Jennings Bryan believed, society should not accept the dictum of *survival of the fittest* for its goal. This rationale merely brutalizes target groups until eventually everyone including every living thing on earth is gone.

Brilliant black birds, the ravens, winged bearers of bad news and sad symbols of death, perch ever so silently above the weatherbeaten sign that hangs over the rotted remains of the main pavilion at Jonestown.

The exact same message on that prophetic Jonestown is also mirrored on a stark memorial to those victims who died in the Holocaust at the Nazi's first, but not their last, concentration camp, Dachau. Its ominous message, states: *Those who do not remember the past are condemned to relive it.*

again...and again...and again...and again...and again

NOTES

Preface

(1) "Newly Released Letters Etch Life In Jonestown" *New York Times* 19 Sept. 1988x: 8.
(2) *California Historical Society, Peoples Temple Collection.* North Baker Library in Schubert Hall, 2099 Pacific Avenue, San Francisco, California, 94109-2235.
(3) Personal Conversations, 1992.
(4) Ray, James Earl. "Who Killed Martin Luther King?: The True Story by the Alleged Assassin". Bethesda, Maryland: National Press Books, 1991.
(5) "Jesse Jackson Joins With James Earl Ray". *New York* 7 Oct. 1991: 13.

Prologue

(1) Lane, Mark. "The Strongest Poison".
(2) Stoen, Tim. Personal telephone interview. Feb, 1989. and Oct. 1990.
(3) Reiterman, Tim and John Jacobs. "Raven".

Chapter 1

(1) Mills, Jeannie. "Six Years with God".
(2) Yee, Min S. and Thomas Layton. "In My Father's House".
(3) Garry Charles. "Jonestown Attorney". Personal telephone interview. May 29, 1990. Personal visit and interview in his San Francisco Office. August 28, 1990.

Chapter 2

(1) Lane, Mark. "The Strongest Poison".

(2) Reiterman, Tim and John Jacobs. "Raven".

(3) Kifner, John. "Ex-Aide May Know of Temple Millions". *New York Times* 4 Dec. 1978: sec.. B: 15.

(4) Krause, Charles A., "Guyana Massacre".

(5) *Facts on File, World News Digest* Dec. 1, 1978d.

(6) Klineman, Geo, Sherman Butler, and David Conn."The Cult That Died".

Chapter 3

(1) *California Historical Society, Peoples Temple Collection.* Mike Prokes Folder BB-29-cc.

(2) Nugent, John Peer."White Night".

(3) Reiterman, Tim and John Jacobs. "Raven".

(4) Crewdson, Arthur. "Bank Data Subpoenaed By U.S. In Search for Guyana Cult Funds". *New York Times* 7 Dec. 1978b, sec.. B:12.

(5) Daly, Selwyn. Personal telephone interview. Oct. 23,1990.

(6) "U.S. Grand Jury Probe Continues". *Facts on File, World News Digest* 15 Dec. 1978c: 1000.

(7) Lane, Mark. "Strongest Poison".

(8) *Facts on File, World News Digest* 1982i: 117.

(9) Binder, David. "Lane Denies Seeking Cult's Secret Funds. subtitle: (Lawyer Says He Did Not Travel to Switzerland to get at Bank Accounts of Jones Sect)". *New York Times* 17 Dec. 1978L: 43.

(10) *Facts on File, World News Digest* Oct. 9, 1982.

(11) "Former Members Returned to U. S." *Facts on File, World News Digest* 1 Dec. 1978f: 995.

(12) *California Historical Society, Peoples Temple Collection.* Mike Prokes Folder BB-29-gg.

(13) The thermos and the picture of Commander Buford and the Shah are among Terri's collection of family pictures personally seen by the author.

Chapter 4

(1) Koenig, Louis W., "Bryan: A Political Biography of William Jennings Bryan".
(2) Photograph seen by author personally in Terri's family picture album.

Chapter 5

(1) Morita, Akio. "Made In Japan".

Chapter 6

(1) *California Historical Society, Peoples Temple Collection.* MS3800 Terri Buford Folder BB-7-AA49.
(2) Weisbrot, Robert. "Father Divine".
(3) Como, Don. "Unknown Powers" videotape by *Video Gems* narrated by Jack Palance.
(4) Stanek, Steve. "Has Jonestown Left Its Mark?" *Cult Awareness Network News, Jonestown edition 18*, Nov. 1987: 6.
(5) Stoen, Tim. Personal telephone interview. Feb, 1989. Oct. 1990.

Chapter 7

(1) MacMillan, Thomas. "Miracle, Mystery and Authority: Recalling Jonestown". *The Christain Century* 9 Nov. 1988: 1014.

Chapter 8

(1) Lewis, Nancy, and Joanne Ostrow. "Slain Bethesda Woman Linked To Cult Chief, Guyana Envoy". *Washington Post* 27 Oct. 1983, C1,C4.
(2) Blauner, Peter "The Fugitive: Herman Ferguson Returns From The Sixties". *New York Magazine* 7 Aug. 1989: 33-33.
(3) Klein, Joe. "The beast in the jungle". *The New York Times Book Review* 16 Nov. 1980: 11.

Chapter 9

(1) Huxley, Aldous. "Brave New World" and "Brave New World Revisited".
(2) *California Historical Society, Peoples Temple Collection.* MS3800, Terri Buford Folder BB-7-AA65.
(3) "Radio Free America," Emory, David. "Operation Mind Control, Part 3-Cults-Joe Holsinger on Jonestown". Emory, David and Tuck, Nip. *KFJC Archives On Audio* Foothills College. Los Altos Hills. Oct. 27, 1985.

Chapter 10

(1) Hersey, John. "A Critic At Large: (Agee)". *The New Yorker* 18 July 1988: 72-82.
(2) *California Historical Society, Peoples Temple Collection.* MS3800, Terri Buford Folder BB-7-AA-15.

Chapter 11

(1) Stanek, Steve. "Has Jonestown Left Its Mark?" *Cult Awareness Network News, Jonestown edition* 18, Nov. 1987: 6.
(2) Smith, Wes. "Jonestown". *Chicago Tribune* 18 Nov. 1988, sec...Tempo 5: 1,2.
(3) Wooden, Kenneth. "Legacy of 276 Murders-A Cover-Up". *Chicago Sun Times* 11 June, 1979b: 1, 2.
(4) Wooden, Kenneth. "Day of Syringes and Jones' Kids Die". *Chicago Sun Times* 14 June 1979c: 18.
(5) "Former Members Returned to U.S." *Facts on File, World News Digest.* 1 Dec. 1978f: 995.
(6) Nordheimer, Jon. "Son Depicts Leader of Cult as a Fanatic and Paranoid". *New York Times* 22 Nov. 1978: a1.

(7) "Guyana Jury: Cult Deaths Were Murders". *Facts on File, World News Digest* 15 Dec. 1978e: 998-999.
(8) Nugent, John Peer. "White Night".
(9) Reiterman, Tim and John Jacobs. "Raven".
(10) "Radio Free America," "Dan White, Jonestown and The Moscone-Milk Killings". Emory, David. *KFJC Archives On Audio* Foothills College. Los Altos Hills. Oct. 27, 1985.
(11) Crewson, John, M. "Followers Say Jim Jones Voting Frauds". *New York Times* 17 Dec. 1978a: 42.
(12) Meiers, Michael. "Was Jonestown A CIA Experiment?"
(13) Klineman, Geo, Sherman Butler, and David Conn. "The Cult That Died".

Chapter 12

(1) "Radio Free America," "Dan White, Jonestown and The Moscone-Milk Killings". Emory, David. *KFJC Archives On Audio* Foothills College. Los Altos Hills. Oct. 27, 1985.
(2) "Soviet Press Lauds Jonestown Victims". *Facts on File, World News Digest* 1 Dec. 1978f: 911.
(3) "Layton Acquited of Attempted Murder". *Facts on File, World News Digest* 30 May 1980g: 407.
(4) "Cults: Jonestown Justice". *Time* 15 Dec. 1986, sec. American Notes: 37
(5) *Facts on File, World News Digest* 1982i: 117.
(6) Bryan, Robert. Personal Telephone Interview. June 1989.

Chapter 13

(1) *California Historical Society, Peoples Temple Collection.* MS3800 Terri Buford Folder BB-7-AA60.
(2) Hinkle, Warren. "Dan White Didn't Act Alone". *San Francisco Examiner* 22, Oct. 1985.
(3) Coates, Pricilla. Personal telephone interview. Mar. 16, 1990.
(4) Crewdson, Arthur. "Harvey Milk, Led Coast Homosexual-Rights Fight". *New York Times* 27 Nov. 1978c.

(5) "Radio Free America," "Dan White, Jonestown and The Moscone-Milk Killings". Emory, David. *KFJC Archives On Audio* Foothills College. Los Altos Hills. 27. Oct. 1985b.

(6) Krassner, Paul. *The Nation.* 14 Jan. 1984.

(7) Meislin, Richard J. "Guyana Leader Dies; Successor Is Sworn In". *New York Times* 7, Aug. 1985.

(8) Klineman, George. Personal interview at his home on August 18th, 1992.

(9) Stanek, Steve. "Has Jonestown Left Its Mark?" *Cult Awareness Network News, Jonestown edition* 18, Nov. 1987:6

Chapter 14

(1) Reiterman, Tim and John Jacobs. "Raven".

(2) Lane, Mark and Dick Gregory. "Code Name Zorro".

(3) Horrock, Nicholas M. "Memo Discusses Smuggling Witness Into Guyana". *New York Times* 8 Dec. 1978.

(4) Lindsay, Robert. "Former Cult Aides Contend Jones Secretly Banked Over $10 Million". *New York Times.*3 Dec. 1978:28

(5) Binder, David. "Reports Conflict on Status of Cult's Finances". *New York Times.*16 Dec. 1978:12

(6) "Lane Denies Seeking Cult's Secret Funds. subtitle: (Lawyer Says He Did Not Travel to Switzerland to get at Bank Accounts of Jones Sect)". *New York Times* 17 Dec. 1978L: 43.

(7) The episode can be viewed in New York at the new Museum Of Television and Radio in their video library.

(8) Lane, Mark. "The Strongest Poison".

(9) *Who's Who In America.* Wilmette, Illinois: United Publishers Service L.T.D. Macmillan Directory Division 45th edition, Vol 2. 1988-1989a:1794.

(10) *Who's Who In America.* Wilmette, Illinois: United Publishers Service L.T.D. Macmillan Directory Division 45th edition, Vol 2. 1986-1987b: 1618.

(11) Kifner, John. "Ex-Aide May Know of Temple Millions". *New York Times* Dec. 4,1978.

(12) *California Historical Society, Peoples Temple Collection.* MS3800 Terri Buford Folder Box 77, Folder 1464, Offshore Bank Accounts-Buford.

(13) Brill, Steven. "The Case Against Mark Lane". *Esquire* Feb. 13, 1979.

Chapter 15

(1) Polner, Rob. "Child-Sex Convict Got Job As City Gym Teacher". *The New York Post* Nov. 30, 1989.

(2) Personal contact with the school secretary who prefers to remain anonymous.

Chapter 16

(1) Balmer, Randell. "The Rainbow Congregations". *New York Newsday* Mar. 21, 1990.

(2) Meredith, Heather. Personal testimony. 1980-1990.

(3) Terry, Maury. "The Ultimate Evil". New York, New York. Bantam, 1987.

(4) Bell, Charles. "How Jim and Tam Sweated in Sable." *New York Daily News* Sept. 12, 1989.

(5) Kenneth Wooden. "Jones Bled Followers for Millions". *Chicago Sun Times* June 13, 1979.

(6) Coates, Pricilla. Personal conversations. 1987.

(7) MacMillan, Thomas. "Miracle, Mystery and Authority: Recalling Jonestown". *The Christain Century* Nov. 9, 1988.

Chapter 17

(1) Buursma, Bruce. "Jonestown Secrets Still Haunt Mourners". *Chicago Tribune* Nov. 13, 1988.

(2) Grenard, Steve. *National Enquirer.* Personal telephone interview. May 15, 1990.

Chapter 18

(1) Anson, Robert Sam. "The Shooting of J.F.K." *Esquire* Nov. 1991.

(2) Broeske, Pat H. "School Daze". *Entertainment Weekly* Jan. 24, 1992.

(3) Ganz, Gail. B'nai B'rith Anti-Defamation League. Personal telephone interview. Apr. 1989.

(4) Turque, Bill. "Duke Shows His True Colors". *Newsweek* Dec. 25, 1990.

(5) *New York Daily News* 26, Aug. 1989a: 36.

(6) Ray, James Earl. "Who Killed Martin Luther King?: The True Story by the Alleged Assassin". Bethesda, Maryland: National Press Books, 1991.

(7) "Jesse Jackson Joins With James Earl Ray". *New York Magazine* 7 Oct. 1991, P:13.

(8) "People Making News". "Mark and John". (Mark Lane becomes John Hinckley's Attorney) *U. S. News & World Report* 1 May 1989: 20.

Chapter 19

(1) *California Historical Society, Peoples Temple Files.* MS3800 Terri Buford Folder BB-7-Q1. Deposition of Terri Buford transcript Civil#C-79-0126-SC given at 26 Federal Plaza in New York, April 13, 1981.

(2) Mansnerus, Laura. "For Lawyers, Crime May Not Pay". *New York Times* Dec. 17, 1989.

(3) Coates, Pricilla. Personal telephone interview. 16 Mar. 1990.

WORKS CITED

Agee, James. "Let Us Now Praise Famous Men". Boston: Houghton, 1939.

Altman, Lawrence K. "Medical Examiners Find Failings by Government on Cultist Bodies." *New York Times* 3 Dec. 1978: 28.

Anson, Robert Sam. "The Shooting of J.F.K." *Esquire* Nov. 1991.

"Authors Claim Rev. Jim Jones Lived a Lie in Life, Death". *Daily Courier News* (Elgin, Illinois) 18 Nov. 1982: 25.

Balmer, Randell. "The Rainbow Congregations". *New York Newsday* 21 Mar. 1990, Viewpoints: 58.

Belin, David W. "Final Disclosure". New York: Charles Scribner's Sons, 1988.

Bell, Charles. "How Jim and Tam Sweated in Sable". *New York Daily News* 12 Sept. 1989a: 4.

Bell, Charles. *New York Daily News* 6 Oct. 1989b: 3.

Binder, David. "Reports Conflict on Status of Cult's Finances". *New York Times* 16 Dec. 1978: 12.

—. "Lane Denies Seeking Cult's Secret Funds. subtitle: (Lawyer Says He Did Not Travel to Switzerland to get at Bank Accounts of Jones Sect)". *New York Times* 17 Dec. 1978L: 43.

Bishop, Katherine. "Survivor is Convicted of Murder Plot at Jonestown". *New York Times* 2 Dec. 1986 N: 1.

Blauner, Peter "The Fugitive: Herman Ferguson Returns from The Sixties". *New York Magazine* 7 Aug. 1989: 33-33.

Brill, Steven. "The Case Against Mark Lane". *Esquire* 13 Feb. 1979.

Brinton, Howard, H. "Guide To Quaker Practice". Pendle Hill Pamphlet #20.

Broeske, Pat H. "School Daze". *Entertainment Weekly* 24 Jan.1992: 9.

Bryan, Robert. Personal telephone interview. June 1989.

Buursma, Bruce. "Jonestown Secrets Still Haunt Mourners". *Chicago Tribune* 13 Nov. 1988, sec.. 1: 3.

Buford, Teresa Jean. Personal interviews. 1986-89. California Historical Society Files, Peoples Temple Collection. North Baker Library in Schubert Hall, 2099 Pacific Avenue, San Francisco, California, 94109-2235.
MS3800 signifies the collection of Peoples Temple.
Photographs still uncatalogued.
Terri Buford transcript Civil # C-79-0126-SC
Deposition of Teresa Buford given at 26 Federal Plaza in New York, April 13, 1981.
Box 53, Folder 1003, Harvey Milk.
Box 76, Folder 1429, Terrri Buford Interview.
Box 77, Folder 1464, Offshore Bank Accounts-Buford.
Box 104,Folder 2036, Statements-Theresa (sic) Buford.
Box 123,Folder 2369, Depositions-Theresa (sic) Buford.
Box 130,Folder 2438, Media.

"CBS Regains TV Ratings Lead". *Facts on File, World News* Digest, 16 May 1980a: 376.

Chandler, Russell. "No Escape From Jonestown; Horror Lives 5 Years Later". *Los Angeles Times* 20 Nov. 1986: 14.

Coates, Pricilla. Personal conversations. 1987.

Coates, Pricilla. Personal telephone interview. 16 Mar. 1990.

Committee on Foreign Affairs, The Assassination of Representative Leo J. Ryan and the Jonestown Guyana Tragedy: U.S. House ofRepresentatives. May 15, 1979.

Como, Don. "Unknown Powers" videotape by *Video Gems* narrated by Jack Palance.

Crewson, John, M. "Followers Say Jim Jones Voting Frauds". *New York Times* 17 Dec. 1978a: 42.

—. "Bank Data Subpoenaed By U.S. In Search for Guyana Cult Funds". *New York Times* 7 Dec. 1978b, sec.. B:12.

—. "Harvey Milk, Led Coast Homosexual-Rights Fight". *New York Times* 27 Nov. 1978c.

—. "Cult Doctor, Tied to Poisonings Had Been Dedicated to the Poor". *New York Times* 22 Nov. 1978d: A1.

"Cults: Jonestown Justice". *Time* 15 Dec. 1986, sec. American Notes: 37.

Daly, Selwyn. Personal telephone interview. Oct. 23, 1990.

Darst, Guy. "10 Years After Jonestown, a Grim Warning". *Los Angeles Herald Examiner* 14 Nov. 1988, sec.. B 7: 1.

Dieckmann, Katherine. "Reviews: 'Let Us Now Praise Famous Men' ". *Village Voice* 29 Aug. 1989: 58.

Facts on File, World News Digest 1982i: 117.

Feinsod, Ethan. "Awake In A Nightmare: Jonestown, The Only Eyewitness Account". New York, New York: Norton, 1981.

Ferrell, Vance. "Prophet Of The End". Altamont, Tenn: Pilgrim Books, 1984.

"Former Members Returned to U. S." *Facts on File, World News Digest* 1 Dec. 1978f: 995.

Freud, Sigmund. "The Basic Writings Of Sigmund Freud:, Contribution 1: The Sexual Aberrations". New York, New York: Random, 1938.

Ganz, Gail. B'nai B'rith Anti-Defamation League. Personal telephone interview. Apr. 1989.

Garry, Charles. "Jonestown Attorney". Personal telephone interview. May 29, 1990. Personal visit and interview in his San Francisco office. August 28, 1990.

"Ghost of Jonestown Haunts Survivor. (Hyacinth Thrash)" . *New York Times* 18 Nov. 1988 sec. D: 5.

Gordon, James. "Jim Jones' Temple of Doom: 10 Years After the Cyanide: Scars and Sorrow, But No Regrets". *The Washington Post* 27 Nov. 1988 sec.. D: 5.

Grodin, Robert J. and Harrison Edward Livingstone. "High Treason". New York, New York: Berkley Books, 1990. (Appendix B, P. 474)

Grenard, Steve. *National Enquirer.* Personal telephone interview. May 15, 1990.

"Guyana Aide Tells of Rebuffing Cult". *New York Times* 8 Dec. 1978, sec. B: 4.

"Guyana Jury: Cult Deaths Were Murders". *Facts on File, World News Digest* 15 Dec. 1978e: 998-999.

"Health, Quake Coverage Earns Pulitzer Prizes". *The Tampa Tribune* 13 Apr. 1990: 5-A.

Hersey, John. "A Critic At Large: (Agee)". *The New Yorker* 18 July 1988: 72-82.

Hinkle, Warren. "Dan White Didn't Act Alone". *San Francisco Examiner* 22, Oct. 1985.

Hiroshima Nagasaki Publishing Committee. "Days to Remember-An account of the bombing of Hiroshima and Nagasake". Toyko, Japan: copyright by Hiroshima Nagasaki Publishing committee, 1981.

Horrock, Nicholas M. "Memo Discusses Smuggling Witness Into Guyana". *New York Times* 8 Dec. 1978. sec.. B: 4.

Huxley, Aldous. "Brave New World". New York, New York: Harper, 1946.

—. "Brave New World Revisited". New York, New York: Harper, 1958.

"Jesse Jackson Joins With James Earl Ray". *New York Magazine* 7 Oct. 1991, P:13.

Johnson, George. *California Historical Society.* 1-415-567-1-848 San Francisco, California. Personal telephone interview. Feb, 1989.

Johnson, Nels. "Decade After Jonestown, A Father Understands His Child". *Norwich Bulletin* 18 Nov. 1988: 3.

"Jonestown Abuses Detailed". *Facts on File, World News Digest* 1 Dec. 1978d: 891.

Kifner, John. "Ex-Aide May Know of Temple Millions". *New York Times* 4 Dec. 1978: sec.. B: 15.

Klein, Joe. "The Beast In The Jungle". *The New York Times Book Review* 16 Nov. 1980: 11.

Klineman, Geo, Sherman Butler, and David Conn. "The Cult That Died". New York, New York: Putnam, 1979.

Klingbury, Graham. "Eight Years Later: Remembering Lessons of Jonestown". *Democrat Herald* (Albany, Oregon) 12 Nov. 1986.

Koenig, Louis W., "Bryan: A Political Biography of William Jennings Bryan". New York, New York: Putnam, 1971.

Kolesnichenko, T. "An American Hero: Man of Action Ollie North Ascends The Nation's Pedestal". *Pravda* English Language Edition. Publication of the Central Committee of the CPSU. Issue No. 11. Sept. 1987: 5.

Krassner, Paul. *The Nation* 14 Jan. 1984.

Krause, Charles A., "Guyana Massacre". Berkeley Publishing Company, 1978.

Lane, Mark. "Plausible Denial", New York, New York: Thunders' Mouth Press, 1991.

Lane, Mark. "The Strongest Poison", New York, New York: Hawthorne Books, 1980.

Lane, Mark and Dick Gregory. "Code Name Zorro". Englewood Cliffs, New Jersey: Prentice, Inc., 1977.

"Layton Acquitted of Attempted Murder". *Facts on File, World News Digest* 30 May 1980g: 407.

Lewis, Nancy, and Joanne Ostrow. "Slain Bethesda Woman Linked To Cult Chief, Guyana Envoy". *Washington Post* 27 Oct. 1983, C1,C4.

Lindsay, Robert. "Former Cult Aides Contend Jones Secretly Banked Over $10 Million". *New York Times* 3 Dec. 1978:1, 28.

"Little is Left of Jonestown but the Horror Lingers". *Daily Herald*, Palantine, Ilinois 21 Nov. 1988: 3.

Long, William R. "10 Years Later, Jonestown is a Site of Silent Desolation". *Los Angeles Times* 18 Nov. 1988, sec. 1: 22.

MacMillan, Thomas. "Miracle, Mystery and Authority: Recalling Jonestown". *The Christain Century* 9 Nov. 1988: 1014.

Marx, Karl. "Capital". New York, New York: Random, 1932.

Mansnerus, Laura. "For Lawyers, Crime May Not Pay". *New York Times* 17, Dec. 1989: E.5.

McCoy, Kevin. "O'C, Ritter Accuser Talk". *New York Daily News* 7, Mar. 1990: 7.

Meiers, Michael. "Was Jonestown A CIA Experiment?" Lewiston, New York: The Edwin Mellen Press, 1988.

Meislin, Richard J. "Guyana Leader Dies; Successor Is Sworn In". *New York Times* 7, Aug. 1985.

Meredith, Heather. Personal testimony. 1980-1990.

Miller, James E. "Complete Poetry and Selected Prose Of Walt Whitman". Boston: Houghton, 1959.

Mills, Jeannie. "Six Years with God". New York, New York: A & W Publishers, 1979.

"Mistrial in Peoples Temple Case". *Facts on File, World News Digest* Oct. 1982h: 734.

"Mom: Nadia Tormented". *New York Newsday* 26 Feb. 1990: 2.

Morain, Dan. "Layton Sentenced To Life In Ryan's Death". *Los Angeles Times* 4 Mar. 1987, sec. 1: 3.

Morita, Akio. "Made In Japan". New York, New York: E.P. Dutton, 1986.

"Most Jonestown Deaths Not Suicide, Doctor Says". *New York Times* 17 Dec. 1978: 42.

Naipaul, Shiva. "Journey to Nowhere". New York, New York: Simon, 1981.

New York Daily News 26, Aug. 1989a: 36.

"Newly Released Letters Etch Life In Jonestown". *New York Times* 19 Sept. 1988x: 8.

Nordheimer, Jon. "Son Depicts Leader of Cult as a Fanatic and Paranoid". *New York Times* 22 Nov. 1978: a1.

Nugent, John Peer. "White Night". New York, New York: Rawson-Wade, Inc., 1979.

O'Neill, Eugene. "The Emperor Jones". New York, New York: Random, 1921.

Orwell, George. "1984". New York, New York: Harcourt, 1949.

—. "Animal Farm". New York, New York: Harcourt, 1946.

"People Making News". "Mark and John". (Mark Lane becomes John Hinckley's Attorney) *U. S. News & World Report* 1 May 1989:20.

"Peoples Temple Member Sentenced". *Facts on File, World News Digest* 25 Apr. 1980: 313.

"Peoples Temple Confession Released". *Facts on File, World News Digest,* 24 Apr. 1981: 283.

Perry, Marvin. "Man's Unfinished Journey". Boston: Houghton, 1978.

Polner, Rob. "Child-Sex Convict Got Job As City Gym Teacher". *The New York Post* 30 Nov. 1989: 23.

"Radio Free America," Emory, David and Nip Tuck. Archives *On Audio WBAI,* New York. 4 Nov. 1989: 7 a.m.

"Radio Free America," "Dan White, Jonestown and The Moscone-Milk Killings". Emory, David. *KFJC Archives On Audio* Foothills College. Los Altos Hills. 27. Oct. 1985b.

—. "Operation Mind Control, Part 3-Cults-Joe Holsinger on Jonestown". Emory, David and Tuck, Nip. *KFJC Archives On Audio* Foothills College. Los Altos Hills. 27. Oct. 1985c1.

Ray, James Earl. "Who Killed Martin Luther King?: The True Story by the Alleged Assassin". Bethesda, Maryland: National Press Books, 1991.

Reiterman, Tim and John Jacobs. "Raven:The Untold Story of the Rev. Jim Jones and his People". New York, New York: Dutton, 1982.

Reston, James Jr. "Our Father Who Art In Hell". New York, New York: Times Books, 1981.

Roberts, Jerry. "How Dan White Changed Law And Politics". *San Francisco Examiner* 22, Oct. 1985.

"17 Cult Survivors are Subpoenaed by U.S." *New York Times* 8 Dec. 1978, sec. B: 4.

Shakespeare, William. "Julius Caesar". Ed. Louis B. Wright.New York, New York: Washington Square Press, Folger Library, 1948.

Shepard, Charles E. "Forgiven". New York, New York: Atlantic Monthly Press, 1989.

Singer, Margaret. Personal comments at the Cult Awareness Meetings.

Smith, Wes. "Jonestown". *Chicago Tribune* 18 Nov. 1988, sec.. Tempo 5: 1,2.

"Soviet Press Lauds Jonestown Victims". *Facts on File, World News Digest* 1 Dec. 1978f: 911.

"Sovs Release Auschwitz Data". *New York Daily News* 22 Sept.1989a: 30.

Stanek, Steve. "Has Jonestown Left Its Mark?" *Cult Awareness Network News, Jonestown Edition* 18, Nov. 1987: 6.

Stein, Mark A. "Jury Finds Layton Guilty In `78 Jonestown Murders". *Los Angeles Times* 2 Dec., sec. 1: 1.

Stoen, Tim. Personal telephone interview. Feb, 1989. Oct.1990.

Styron, William. "Sophie's Choice". New York, New York: Random,1979.

Szalanski, Andrea. "Televangelism's Roster". *Free Inquiry* (Spring issue) Vol 6 #2, 1986: 7.

"Swiss Arrest Customs Officials". *Facts on File, World News Digest* 30 May 1980: 407.

Terry, Maury. "The Ultimate Evil". New York, New York: Bantam, 1987.

"The So Called Peace Movement". Editorial Page. *The New York Post* 8, Feb. 1991: 30.

Treaster, Joseph B. "Rubble of Commune Yields a Tape of Cultist Dying, Jones Exhorting". *New York Times* 8 Dec. 1978a: 1.

—. "Survivor Says He Heard 'Cheers' and Gunshots After Cult Deaths". *New York Times* 17 Dec. 1978: 42.

Turque, Bill. "Duke Shows His True Colors". *Newsweek* 25 Dec. 1990: 53.

Turner, Wallace. "San Francisco Mayor Is Slain; City Superisor Also Killed; Ex- Official Gives Up To Police". *New York Times* 28, Nov. 1978: 1.

"U.S. Agencies are Accused of Supressing Probe" (Holsinger). *Chicago Sun Times* 20 Nov, 1988: 3.

"U.S. Grand Jury Probe Continues". *Facts on File, World News Digest* 15 Dec. 1978c: 1000. Ungaro, Joe.

"Jonestown Tragedy Did Little To Subdue Cults In The Nation". *Norwich Bulletin* 18 Nov. 1988: A1 A6

Vance, Carole S, Ed. "Pleasure and Danger: (Exploring Female Sexuality)". Boston: Routledge and Paul Kegan Pub, 1984.

Vesey, Tom. "Cults Still a Threat, Victims Warn: Group Gathers To Mark 8th Anniversary of Jonestown Massacre". *The Washington Post* 17, Nov. 1986 sec. A: 23.

Weisbrot, Robert. "Father Divine". Boston: Beacon, 1983.

Who's Who In America. Wilmette, Illinois: United Publishers Service L.T.D Macmillan Directory Division 45th edition, Vol 2. 1988-1989a: 1794., 1986-1987b: 1618.

Wolinsky, Leo. "Fate Plays Part in Assemblywoman Speier's Life...Speier: Jonestown Survivor in Capitol". *The Los Angeles Times* 14 Dec. 1988, Part 1: 3.

Wooden, Kenneth. "The Children of Jonestown". New York, New York: Mcgraw, 1980.

—. "Legacy of 276 Murders-a Cover-Up". *Chicago Sun Times* 11 June, 1979b: 1, 2.

—. "How Jones Wrecked Cult Families". *Chicago Sun Times* 12 June 1979c: 10, 18.

—. "Jones Bled Followers for Millions". *Chicago Sun Times* 13 June 1979a: 7, 10, 18.

—. "Day of Syringes and Jones' Kids Die". *Chicago Sun Times* 14 June 1979c: 18.

—. "Jones Achieves Final Purpose". *Chicago Sun Times* 14 June 1979: 10, 13.

"Women Shy Over JFK Slay Book". *The New York Post* 21 Sept 1991: 6.

Yee, Min S. and Thomas Layton. "In My Father's House". New York, New York: Holt, Rinehart and Winston 1981.

SPECIAL NOTES AND ACKNOWLEDGMENTS

This work is dedicated to Virginia's daughter, my son, and parents.

Heather Meredith and Mary Weiner are real people but their names have been changed to protect their anonymity.

Thanks to Jonestown lawyer, the late Charles Garry, for his advice and assistance with the manuscript. His courage in writing the recent statement that Terri was second in command of Jonestown inspired me.

Also, thanks to the California Historical Society Library Archives Director Jeffrey Barr, for his assistance in showing me the enormous information previously sealed and now available about Jonestown.

Thank you Diana.

Special thanks to Steve Grenard for his faith in this project and his invaluable editorial assistance.

Thanks to Pam Chassen whose painstaking proofreading efforts have added to the completeness of this work.

Lastly, thanks to my friend and publisher, Irwin Jacobson.

APPENDIX

Appendix Exhibit A.   Statement from Jim Jones' attorney, Charles Garry, stating that Terri Buford was second in command of the Jonestown operation.

Exhibit B.   Documents from the California Historical Society *(Permission to use Documents granted by California Historical Society).*

Deceptor

EXHIBIT A

LAW OFFICES OF
CHARLES R. GARRY

Patricia J. Richartz
Private Investigator
Lic. # A 006589

1256 Market Street at Civic Center
San Francisco, CA 94102-4889
(415) 864-3131
FAX (415) 431-2131

Monique Steele
Attorney at Law

8-28-90

To Whom It May Concern:

In the months that I represented the People's "Temple", Terri Buford was the second in command of Jim Jones.

Charles R. Garry

206

EXHIBIT B

Dear Anne,
Please, help me.
I have to die tomorrow
the voices have told
me to cut out
my heart. Please
tell them to go
away, Anne. Tomorrow
at 9 AM I'm
going to have to
cut my heart out.

BB-7-AA40   Terri Buford

Dear Carolyn

I am a violent
typical. I have
done violent
acts to people who
are property in
the past. I am
a Communist.

I am afraid I am
going to continue
violent acts. Despite
the power of the temple
urging you —

Anna [signature]

BB-7-AA 13

Dear Carolyn!

I feel so much
guilt that I put
Jim Jones in the
position that if
we didn't there
me that I
would suicide.
I know it must have
been terrible for
him who was the only
Knowing Madame
I am so very sorry.

Anna [signature]

BB-7-AA 14

Well, see Tom
Patty and I'll
tell you how
I hope D of that
Jim James Durise?
I got so much
so incredible.

ASOCIACION RELIGIOSA PRO SAN PEDRO, S.A.

P.b. Ex 1 ..d
5/3/79 ₿

Panamá, September 21, 1978

UNION BANK OF SWITZERLAND (PANAMA) , INC
Avenida Manuel Maria Icaza No. 21
Panamá , Rep. de Panamá

Subject: Numbered account 222-00.042-A

Dear Sirs:

With reference to numbered account CC 222-00.042-A maintained by
ASOCIACION RELIGIOSA PRO SAN PEDRO, S.A. (hereinafter " ASOCIACION")
at the UNION BANK OF SWITZERLAND (PANAMA) , INC (hereinafter " UBS
PANAMA") we hereby confirm our instructions conveyed to you by our
letters of June 1, June 23 and June 26 , as well as the instructions given
to you on June 27, 1978; and/or instruct you as follows:

1) Any and all funds maintained by ASOCIACION under numbered account
222-00.042-A, specifically the following deposits with UBS/PANAMA:

No. DP	Amount	Maturity
00403	US$ .200,000.00	July 5, 1978
00418	US$ 1,000.000.00	July 18, 1978
00447	US$ 1,000.000.00	August 21, 1978
00473	US$ 1,000.000.00	September 21, 1978
00562	US$ 350,000.00	May 31, 1979

TOTAL   US$ 3,550.000.00

are , at their respective maturity dates, to be cancelled and together with
interests earned to be transferred to a new numbered account 121-00.135-A
with UBS Panama.

2) On May 31, 1979, upon completion of these transfers, the numbered
account 222-00.042-A will be closed on the books of UBS Panama.

3) Insodoing, ASOCIACION hereby assigns to the holders (owners) of
account 121-00.135-A all its rights to any and all funds previously held
under account number 222-00.042-A

4) In case of any discrepancies between the foregoing instructions and
any instructions previously imparted and communicated to the bank by person
authorized to sign against numbered account 222-00.042-A, the instructions
contained herein shall prevail as they are intended to supplement and elucidate instructions imparted previously.

(signed: Ms. Teresa Jean Buford)   (signed: Ms. Carolyn Layton)

Deceptor

Page No. 2
ASOCIACION RELIGIOSA PRO SAN PEDRO, S.A.
September 21, 1978

outstanding up to this date to account number 220.117.60J with UBS, ZURICH
before effecting the remittances mentioned in item No. 1 of these instructions.

Upon completion of these transfers, account No. 220.117.60J in the name of
ASOCIACION RELIGIOSA PRO SAN PEDRO, S.A. will be closed on the books of
UBS Zurich.

Afterwards, any mail for said account still withheld by UBS Zurich should
be forwarded via airmail to UBS/PANAMA and to be held at the disposal of
account holders in a special file along with the correspondence withheld
for the new numbered account 121-00.135-A with UBS / PANAMA.

You are further authorized to debit account No. 121-00.135-A maintained
at UBS(Panama) for any charges or fees owed to UBS / Zurich after account
220.117.6CJ and/or safe deposit account above mentioned have been closed.

In case of any discrepancies between the foregoing instructions and any
instructions previously imparted and communicated to the bank by persons
authorized to sign against account No. 220.117.60J with UBS Zurich, the
instructions contained herein shall prevail as they are intended to supplement and elucidate instructions imparted previously.

(signed: Ms Teresa Jean Buford, for
Account 220.117.60J with UBS Zurich)

(signed: Ms Maria Katsaris, for
account 220.117.60J with UBS Zurich)

(signed: Mrs. Esther Lillian Mueller,
for account 121-00.135-A with UBS Panama)

211

Deceptor

P.V. En D ✓
8/2/79 yo

ASOCIACION RELIGIOSA PRO SAN PEDRO, S.A.

September 21, 1978

UNION BANK OF SWITZERLAND
Zurich, Switzerland

Subject: Account No. 220.117.60J

Gentlemen:

With reference to the current account No. 220.117.60J maintained by ASOCIACION
RELIGIOSA PRO SAN PEDRO, S.A. (hereinafter " Asociacion ") with Head Office
of UNION BANK OF SWITZERLAND , Zurich, Switzerland (hereinafter " UBS ZURICH"),
we hereby confirm the instructions conveyed to you by means of our letters of
June 1 and June 26, as well as the instructions given to you on June 27, 1978.
and/or instruct you as follows:

1) Any and all fixed time deposits or other balances maintained by Asociacion
under account No. 220.117.60J with UBS Zurich should be transferred upon
maturity of each deposit, including interests earned after you have collected any outstanding charges or fees owed to you by Asociacion, to Union Bank
of Switzerland (Panamá), Inc. (hereinafter called UBS/PANAMA) for
redeposit in numbered account CC 121-00.135-A maintained at UBS/PANAMA.

2)   The deposits mentioned above, which are subject to the foregoing
instructions, are specifically the following:

CD - UBS LONDON	US$ 518,000.00	Maturity Date:	July 25, 1978
Interests	US$ 32,496.00	Rate: 6 3/16%	
CD - UBS LONDON	US$ 1,009,000.00	Maturity Date:	July 25, 1978
Interests	US$ 63,298.00	Rate: 6 3/16%	

Total of above deposits US$ 1,622,794.00
US$ 1,623,000.00   Amount remitted to Panama
rounded to the nearest thousan

3) Pursuant thereto, Asociacion hereby assigns all its rights to
Deposits mentioned above to the holders (owners) of numbered account
121-00.135-A maintained with UBS/PANAMA.

4) With reference to safe deposit account No. 15465/HUK maintained at UBS/
Zurich in the name of Teresa Jean Huford, you are hereby instructed to
maintain said account open until documents, valuables and contents deposited therein are withdrawn by the authorized person (s). You are further
authorized to debit any charges or fees for use of said account

212

Buford   10

Layton did.

MR. STUMPF: So far as you know, when you left the Temple, all of the funds in the Zurich bank in Switzerland had been transferred to Panama?

THE WITNESS: Yes, and into the name of Ester Mueller.

MR. LANE: Maybe I can ask a question now: Do you have any knowledge, Mr. Fabian, of any money in Zurich in December of 1978 belonging to the People's Temple?

MR. FABIAN: The only information I have on that is that there was, possibly, an account numbered 220-117-60-J in Union Bank of Switzerland (Zurich) in the name of the Asociacion Religiosa Pro San Pedro, but the information on that is sketchy in that it says that the account was closed and that there might be possibly existing some residual funds in that account. In other words, a few dollars is the indication on that account. That is all I have.

The other information I have about Switzerland is a safe deposit box which, presumably, is number 14665/HUK standing in the name of Teresa Jean Buford and that is one of the things I wanted to

Deceptor

Buford 11

ask you some questions about; as to whether that box was emptied or whether you know anything about it.

THE WITNESS: To my knowledge, it didn't have anything in it.

It might have had some banking laws and something like that. I never put anything in that box of any value.

Maybe a couple of signed sheets. I think it had some signed sheets by me in there and Maria so Carolyn could do whatever she did with it.

MR. FABIAN: By "signed sheets," you mean a sheet with a signature on it?

MR. LANE: A blank sheet signed by you?

THE WITNESS: Yes. May have been one of Maria's. I think I just left mine.

Nothing of any significance. I don't believe anybody has been back there since I was there several years ago.

MR. FABIAN: I have answered you as best I can

I might say, in addition, for your information and this is a matter of public record, I have entered into an agreement with the United States government with respect to the repatriation of the

Buford   48

I figured somebody in Panama made it up. He may have had a reason. You can ask him. I don't know.

Q   After Stoen left, did you travel to Switzerland to set up any of these accounts in Switzerland?

A   Yes.

Q   Tell me what happened there?

A   When Stoen left, I went to Panama and I set up the Asociacion Religioso Pro San Pedro.

Q   Where did that name come from?

A   It was the only unavailable name of a corporation. Just made up.

Q   Did you make it up?

A   Tapia suggested saying Asociacion Religioso and he said, "Name a saint."

I said, "St. Peter."

He said, "San Pedro." No great science to this.

Q   Who was with you on that trip to Panama?

A   Maybe Blakey, maybe. Yes, Debbie went with me, because she went with me to Zurich.

Q   You first went down and met with the lawyer, Tapia?

A   Yes, Debbie was with me.

Q   You dissolved the one corporation, Evangelica, and set up the San Pedro corporation?

1   Buford   49

2   A   No. I set up the San Pedro and (dissolved) the other

3 one so we didn't have it in limbo and took a million and

.500 in checks and transferred it to the Union Bank in

Switzerland in Zurich.

         And Debbie went with me to set up that account.

     Q   Is the account you set up in Zurich Account No.

220-117-60-J?

     A   Originally it was some other number and what had

happened was, I neglected to put it into a name of a

corporation, thinking that a numbered account was the same

thing, so I went back, like, two days later and put it into

this number. For about two days, it was some other number.

14 747, or something or other.

15   Q   Does the number -- I thought I had another number

16 which would jog your memory, but I don't have it.

17   A   There was another number. I just went back there

18 and corrected my mistake. For two days, it was a numbered

19 account.

20   Q   When you made the check out to be transferred to

21 the Zurich account, were there funds remaining in the UBS

22 account of Panama?

23   A   Oh, yes, several million, about five or $6 million

24   Q   How did you decide to take only part of the funds

25 to Zurich?

IN WITNESS WHEREOF, I have hereunto signed my name this
_____ day of _____, 197___.

Father,...

I have committed treason. Sunday before I went to work I read some of your mail and papers not that I found anything because I didn't [illegible] some financial reports, letters from Pennington (re: [illegible]), Chem Ryzynto (re: some cover-up) and Tom Adams (re: homosexuality). I knew it was wrong my complete defiance of the D.O.P. To try to find some release from guilt I cut up all the skin on my stomach with razor-blades, still feeling guilt I cut my hands up with them. I know suicide is [illegible] so I wouldn't do that. Sin is going [illegible]. I went to the point of really blowing [illegible]. I [illegible] when I [illegible]. Every male face I see reminds me of the [illegible] I came out of, eating out their asses, swallowing their piss and [illegible], getting my ass ripped open, beat up, getting police called in [illegible] etc. This wouldn't bother a good socialist but it's a nightmare to me.

What I have done is constitutionally wrong, I've defied the only principle I have to live for, my lifeblood. I'm willing to become a public example of treason. -- Tom --

BB-7-AA49

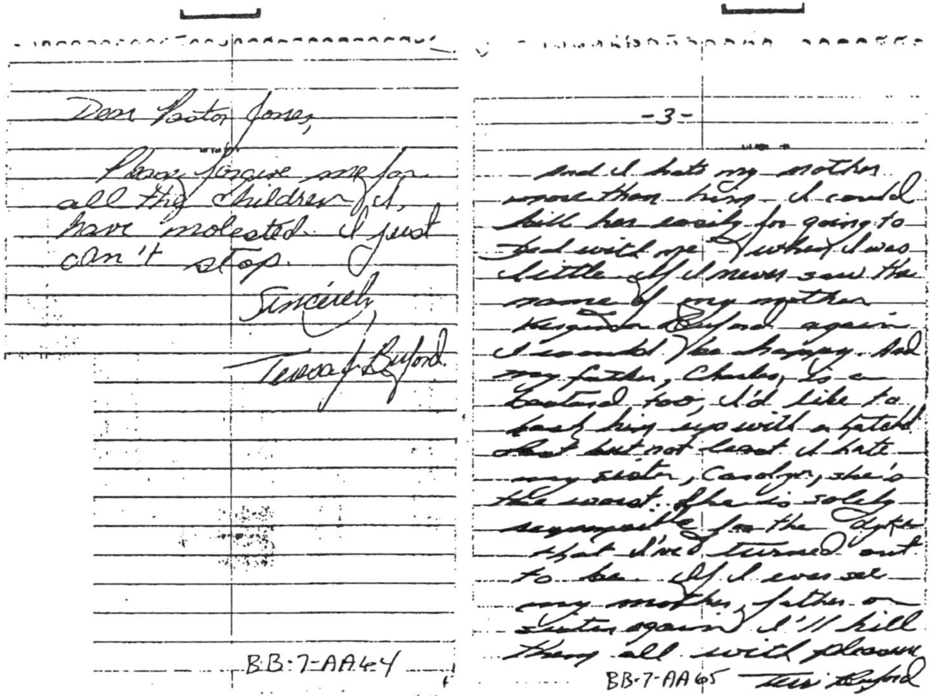

Dear Pastor Jones,

Please forgive me for all the children I have molested. I just can't stop.

Sincerely,

Teresa J. Buford

BB-7-AA44

-3-

And I hate my mother more than him. I could kill her easily for going to bed with me when I was little. If I never saw the name of my mother [illegible] Buford again I would be happy. And my father, Charles, is a bastard too, I'd like to bash his eyes with a hatchet. Last but not least I hate my sister, Carolyn, she's the worst. She is solely responsible for the Dyke that I've turned out to be. If I ever see my mother, father or sister again I'll kill them all with pleasure.

BB-7-AA65 Teresa Buford

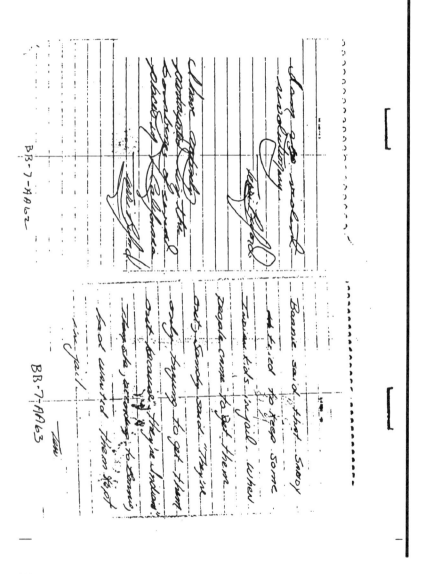

CONFIDENTIAL

To: Jim
From: Teri

As you know by several letters I have written you in the past few months--
I am extremely upset with one the state of your health and two our inability
to expose the other side. Although things seem to be getting better there
is still something going on -- which allows for people to get hold of such people
as that radio operator just a short time before Lane and it goes on and on. It
is clear to me that there is a very orchestrated movement against us-- and
frankly they are doing such a good job of it that--it may be never that we get
to the bottom of it. At least that is my feeling. I don't know how much longer
you are going to live. I heard you on the phone patch the other night and you
could barely get out the words. I asked Tom to pass a message asking how you
were as per your instructions and Tom said " why should I he is obviously critically
ill-- anyone listening to him can tell that". I passed a message the other
night about something that would really he to be expected from the National Inquirer
and you went into a full fledged attack. Leona told me that you had three before
she left. I keep getting messages on the radio Robert is very sick--
I know that no one would be making this up because I
made it quite clear when I left you that I was going to be making alot of decisions
based on the state of your health. So time is short. Sorry to say life hasn't been
more pleasant than a continual hell of demands and demands and demands.

Despite what others may say about our collective paranoia-- I am convinced of
the effort against us-- I heard them talking under the house--- I heard Dennis
Banks first hand--- I know that the AG wouldn't be moving in your direction if
Stoen wasn't pushing behind him. These things that others may view as contrived
I know as fact because I experienced them first hand.

I believe strongly in peoples temple and the people that are trying to make it
work. With all of our faults (and I believe we have many) it is still the most
decent place in the world-- without question. Naturally, I have my conflicts as
I am sure you have yours but none of them are insurmountable and I believe I have
faced just about every personal conflict in regards to you that a person is able to
have---and I feel that my respect for you is not based on any illusions of trust
or personal love because I knew quite well that is not the case--- I don;t expect
it and it doesn't bother me. From time to time I get respet ful of those who
had children when I gave mine up--- but I should have been more firm about what I
wanted at the time-- so you are not to blame for whatever grief I may feel there.
And I know practically that I did the right thing. All I am trying to say is I
don'j feel that I can be shaken at this point by anything that anyone says or does
because I think at this point I have faced the brut facts of life and have no
illusions about much. I know you have talked about me to many. I know that you
talked about me to Debbie as I read a note that referred that a conversation that
you all had--- so I am braced for that and nothing she can say at this point could
be anything worse than what I already think. And I am old enought to know that
you take us all on our own merit one day at a time-- action by action so I don't
care what happened a year ago or so.

BB-7-D6.

At this point I find my self in a very odd situation. That is--- that alot of the
stuff that the church is presently in trouble for-- I organized-- did and
carried out. If you wanted to call me a provacateur it would get the church most
neatly off the hook. I would not sue. I have discussed this with you before and
you also felt that it would work. Naturally I hope it doesn't come to that-- but
I am willing to take that if that is what it will take. I would like the see the
stage set so that you all could go to russia--- I think that there will be safety for
the people there in the event of your death and also in terms of survival alot of
the pressure will be take off of you as a single leader and I know you would like to

Deceptor

*Letters to you
from Terri*

B B-7-N,

October 18, 1978

Jim:
I understand that someone really is going out tonight and I did want to write to you.
I hpe you are feeling better. I feel like I am in the classic catch 22.
If I pass all the traffic--- then I can take the reptonsibililty of killing you.
Last night it was a major heart attack because of what I was passed. Before that
if I had a problem with an instruction or perhaps think that something needed to
be further thought about it boils down to if I don't you are going to get sicker.
I know you are very sick. It is completely freaking me owt to know that if I
don't tell you what it going on I am in trouble. If I do I will kill you. So
I guess I choose the former rather than the later. I just find it extremely
upsetting. I know that youcan't control your helth--- but I don't know -- since
I am not there when is good and bad times to pass tiaffic. I feel more
organisationaly secure if you know what is going on---- but nt if it means killin
you. Please do let me know when your health is somewhat normal again. I understand
the kind of yxox pressure you are under and I heard from Jean some of the things
that ahd max happened and I am sorry about the whole set of circumstances that has
happened. As came out in court this week-- TOS has no love for me and I am extralomly
worried that the other side will try to use my activities to discredit this
cause. Pat told me that he shook my affidavit and said " this goes to show the
level of deviency that these people will stoop to to go after me". I don't know.
But I am worried-- not in the sense of being arrested but rather just that they
are going to use my past activisis to discredit you. The thing I wrote you about
is becimming more and more a reality every day. I am just in constant conflict over
the situation----- I know all they can say and I just dont want you to look like a freek
becuase of my work. After all itvas a collective decision and not just you and me.
But in sotcns mind it biolds boils down to you and me---You could claim no knowledge
of me and clear the organization and not thetyou care-- but yourself too. I just know
I am going to feel horrible m if they try to discredit you with me. I am sure the
naxy few weeks will show if they want to go that route. I know what I should do but
I don't know what your health could take the worry of such a strategy on my part.
So another Cathc 22---- if I don't do what I told you about I run the risk
of ruining the organisation just because of me---- or if I do--- I may be able
to avoid certain attacks on PT but at the same time might worry you to death.
I don't know. I am full of conflict and so is life--- nothing new to you I am sure.
If I had things to do over-- I never would have trusted anyone--- would have kept
everything to myslef. It would have been better that way. I wish to hell
someone would see you to a doctor or something----becuase the responsibility of
not knowing what to di with information is driving me nuts. And I know that the
minute that I say anything to Jean about anything like that that she will report
every word of it thinking that that is the right thing to do in any and allsituations--
so it is a matter of just not telling her or anyone--- and I am not smart enough
to run this plsem on my own judgement. I don't know. I don't know what to do.
I know your situation is miserable. But hfter a heart attack last night.
Three heart attacks that Laoma told me about---- 4 heart atacks in amonth and
8 that I have counted in the past two monihts that I have been told about----I
really don't know if ycaux you are a one in condition for any traffic at all.
I also question if the people who pass you the messages--- don't infact xkxxxx
want you to dis--- becuase they are in a position to know if you can take it or not.
I just don't understand yor being told something if you are in that bad of shape.
It sound cruel to me. Please don't let anyone read this. I don't mean it
personally because it may be well inteaded. but you know.

sorry for all.

Teri

B B-7-N'2-

222

October 9, 1977

Dear Pat,

I am leaving today and thought that it might be in order to
ask a favor in the event that something should happen to Jim and the
organization before I see you again or before you get to Guyana
yourself. In that you and Charles and Dennis are just about the
only people with any understanding of the group outside of the
organization, should anything happen that would kill Jim or bring
about a last stand on the part of the organization in Guyana --
please try to put both his life and death in perspective to the
people. I am sure that many will say that it was perhaps a
"crazy or hysterical act" and my answer to that is that it has been
the collective decision of the group and Jim for a long time that
if it is not possible for us to live the lifestyle which we believe
is the only fair and just way to live then we do believe that we
maintain the right to choose the circumstances of our deaths.
Jim has dared to believe in human strength and has shown us the
beauty of a society based on principle; we have chosen collectively
to opt out of a society that exploits human weakness. If we do
make a last stand, it will not be as an act of giving up but rather
as a demonstration in the hopes that some people will wake up and
give those people who wish to live in equality a chance to do so.
It will have been a last resort, we will have tried everything
short of it to find a place where we could live our marxist lifestyle in peace. I am not expecting anything to come up in the next
few days so don't worry, but on the other hand I don't want to be so
pollyannish as to assume that all will go well and leave here without
asking someone sympathetic to interpret Jim's commitment to an ideal
in the event of his death. As I said before, I really am not
expecting anything to come up, but I did want to feel secure that in
the event anything would ever happen that someone would make an
attempt to stop the maniac press from distoring his life further and
that someone would try to bring about an understanding of his life
to the people.

BB-7-C,

223

Deceptor

- 2 -

Thanks for all the help you have been and for taking the
time to listen to all our problems when I am sure that you have
enough of your own. Take care -- see you in Guyana.

Tev

BB-7-C 2

... I can't hold this in
me anymore, these
things that I have
done... In 1971
I gave speed to
Patti Abbot in Indiana
Pennsylvania. I knew
at the time that she
was not only a minor
but also an epileptic.
That night she died
of an epileptic seizure.
I told ~~there~~ Dr. Hadd
Edison that she had
the speed. From
that day on everything
was down hill.
I can't talk about the
children I have been
with sexually. However
beginning with one
death by my conscience.
What have I got to
loose. I hate Nixon
and when I find
the means, he will

BB-7-AA01

be dead.

Teresa J. Buford

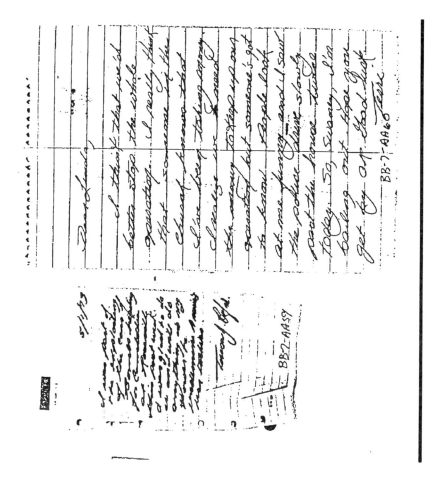

WHAT I WOULD DO TO THE CHURCH IF I WERE TO LEAVE AND *had a son-of-a bitch mentality.*
(someone told me we/I were supposed to write this)

1. If I wanted to tear down the group I would see that th e leader
were taken care of since it would be extremely hard for th
group to hold together at this point with out him. Fro m that
point it would be to pick off the strong ones in the group.
Carolyn Layton, Linda Amos, Jean Brown, Don Beck, Sandy Bradshaw , Mike Cartmell ,
/Tim Stoen, Lee Ingram. I don't hink that the group could
function with out the leader and these people. I don't think if
the group did survive that it would be much of a group. That would
only be done If I had gone out trying to undermine socialism.

2. If I went out and were pissed at Jim it would be completely different.
First there would be no thought of killing since that would be a really
loving thing to do (for JJ but not for socialism per sae) . I think
the best way to get to JJ would be through his children. The young one.
Not kill the young one but take him from the group and make the group
think that the young one were suffering.

3. If I were just pissed off with someone in the group I would probably
turn them into the CIA, IRS, FBI. Harass them to death. Get at their
children and kidnapp them If I thought that they cared for them.

4. If I were just pissed off at everyt ing in general I wold most
likely go out and committe suicide just to show how hostile I really
was or whatever. Or would try in some amaturish fashing to put a guilt trip
on the group. Thats when my thinking gets perverted

5. The other way of tearing fdown the group is to get all the money
but I'm not smart enough to even begin to figure out how to do it.
Turning the group into go_vernestal agencies might be another one of
my maneuvers. However, we've been looked at so much that I doubt that
thay would care that much about anything that I would have to say.

Terri

BB·7-AA 4C

and I certainly hope that Jim Jones
doesn't somehow find out that I've stolen
substantial amounts of money on various
occasions from the temple.
   I'll tell you more about the trip when
I see you in a few days.

With best regards

Mike Prokes

BB-29-cc

Dear Jim,
I don't know how much
longer I can take it. I mean
the witchcraft. I feel like
I'm programmed. I enjoy violence
when I do it -- like all those dogs
I mutilated, but sometimes like.
right now I feel sorry I did it.
I think I'm going to end it all with
my .38., I only wish I could see
my brains blown out. Maybe I'll
try someone else first.
Just didn't want you to be concerned
if you don't hear from me.
Thanks.

Your friend,

Mike Stokes

BB-29-99